THE MISSING MAN

THE MISSING MAN

From the outback to Tarakan, the powerful story of Len Waters, Australia's first Aboriginal fighter pilot

PETER REES

ALLEN&UNWIN
SYDNEY • MELBOURNE • AUCKLAND • LONDON

First published in 2018

Allen & Unwin
83 Alexander Street
Crows Nest NSW 2065
Australia
Phone: (61 2) 8425 0100
Email: info@allenandunwin.com
Web: www.allenandunwin.com

EU Authorised Representative: Easy Access System Europe, Mustamäe tee 50, 10621 Tallinn, Estonia, gpsr.requests@easproject.com

A catalogue record for this book is available from the National Library of Australia

ISBN 978 1 76029 641 4

Internal design by Luke Causby
Index by Puddingburn
Set in 11.5/17.25 pt Sabon by Midland Typesetters, Australia
Printed and bound in Australia by Pegasus Media & Logistics

20 19 18 17 16 15

MIX
Paper | Supporting responsible forestry
FSC® C008194
www.fsc.org

The paper in this book is FSC® certified. FSC® promotes environmentally responsible, socially beneficial and economically viable management of the world's forests.

An estimated 4000 Aborigines and Torres Strait Islanders served in the Australian armed forces in World War II. Len Waters was one of them.

Additional research by Sue Langford

To Cait and Jimmy,
Oliver and Hamish

CONTENTS

Prologue		xi
PART ONE	THE DREAM, YUWAYA NGARRALI	1
1	WORLDS APART	3
2	DEPENDENCY	13
3	DISPOSSESSION	19
4	SKIN	27
5	CHOICE	31
6	STANDING APART	40
PART TWO	SKY HIGH, GUNAGALAGA NGARRIBAA	49
7	DIFFERENT DOORS	51
8	THE ERK	58
9	SOLO	65
10	UTOPIA	78
11	THE THRILL OF IT	89
12	MISADVENTURE IN MOREE	99
13	BAD SHOW	108

14	HERE TODAY, GONE TO MOROTAI	122
15	FIGHTING FIT	132
16	WIND-DOWN	145
17	ONE OF THE BOYS	153
18	COMING OF AGE	163
19	TRUE AUSTRALIAN BLOOD	176
PART THREE	BACK TO EARTH, YANAAWUWLY DHAWUN	189
20	A SUITABLE MARRIAGE	191
21	BLACKFELLA	201
22	FITTING BACK IN	211
23	IN THE RING	220
24	WHEEL OF MISFORTUNE	227
25	STRIKE	234
26	THE LONER	245
27	THE SATURDAY RITUAL	254
28	GRIEF	259
29	BLEAK TIMES	264
30	ICARUS	273
31	FLASH BLACK	284
32	FREE FALL	290
33	ALONE	298
34	TWO WORLDS	304
Epilogue	IF ONLY HE HAD KNOWN	311
Acknowledgements		315
Notes		319
Bibliography		337
Index		342

PROLOGUE

Death generated acclaim for Len Waters. He became a face on a stamp and a name on street signs, parks and a Royal Australian Air Force (RAAF) fighter jet.

Waters was a trailblazer who broke barriers to realise a childhood dream. At a time when Australians feared a Japanese invasion, he enlisted in the air force and passed the stringent tests to join its fighter-pilot elite—the first and only known Indigenous Australian ever to do so.

He flew a Kittyhawk, serendipitously nicknamed *Black Magic*. When he climbed out of it for the last time after 41 strike and attack operations and a further 54 operational flights, he had every reason to be optimistic about the future. In the bustle of post-war reconstruction, anything seemed possible—especially for someone as smart and skilled as Waters.

When Len died, on 24 August 1993, the RAAF knew it had lost a significant figure in its history. A C-130 Hercules transport was detailed to fly old comrades from Waters' former unit,

78 Squadron RAAF, to the town of St George, on the edge of the Queensland Outback. They had laughed, played and shared beers and 'jungle juice' together, knowing their lives were on the line whenever they flew. Some of their mates had never returned. All these old airmen knew that Waters was special. Farewelling him was a sombre event. The St George Anglican church overflowed with mourners, among them his widow, Gladys, his children, members of his family and his friends. An RAAF honour guard escorted the coffin. A wing commander spoke of the 'impact Waters had had on his air force mates', and eulogies were delivered by two of his daughters and his son.

The cortège slowly made its way along the main street to the cemetery. Misty rain fell as mourners approached the grave. A bugler sounded the Last Post, and many voices wailed in grief. As the coffin was lowered, the booming sound of nine supersonic F/A-18 Hornets flying overhead filled the air. Abruptly, one of the combat fighters peeled away in 'missing man formation'—the time-honoured air force farewell salute to one of their own.

Waters was that missing man. He had, in many ways, been missing since 1946.

PART ONE

THE DREAM

YUWAYA NGARRALI

You know you've got to follow your dreams, because if you have enough determination you will get there.

Sally Morgan, Aboriginal author

1

WORLDS APART

When the iron gate at Toomelah clanked shut behind him, seven-year-old Len Waters did not look back. The battered Chevrolet crunched into first gear, and he could only wonder what lay ahead. His parents, Don and Grace, were clearly relieved as they rumbled over the dirt road towards Nindigully, in south-western Queensland, just across the New South Wales border. Their seven children were piled in the back, along with their few possessions.

Disappearing into the distance behind them was the hated Toomelah Aboriginal reserve. Disease and an erratic water supply threatened the health of everyone living there, and within a few years the shanty town of crude shacks would be forced to close. Getting out now was smart—and lucky. It put the Waters family beyond the reach of the reserve authorities, who could remove children from their parents as they saw fit. Granted approval to leave by the Toomelah manager, Don and Grace wasted no time.

Their 100-kilometre drive across the floodplains of north-western New South Wales in late 1931 took the family away from the reserves and missions where they had always lived to a new beginning in a small Queensland village. The Waters family belonged then, as now, to the Kamilaroi people, who help form the wider collection of tribes and extended family groups known as Murris. Once they had roamed 75,000 square kilometres of tribal lands in southern Queensland and north-central and north-western New South Wales. Such freedom no longer existed. Although breaking away from reserves like Toomelah was not easy, Don and Grace were determined to give their children the freedom to *be* children. They also wanted to give them an education and the widened horizons and greater choices that learning brought.

But for now there was the more prosaic matter of making a home for a growing family. At 31, Grace was pregnant again. She and Don had married in 1918, while she was a hotel waitress in Garah, near Moree, and he was a farm labourer. Their first son, George, was born later that year at Euraba reserve.

On New South Wales reserves, the larger one's family, the greater the risk that a child would be removed. The Waters had witnessed the distress that the Board for the Protection of Aborigines had wrought. Under its wide-ranging powers, often applied without warning, Board representatives could simply grab children and drive off with them. Len's younger brother,

Kevin, has stark memories of 'wailing mothers clinging to the sides of trucks as their kids were taken away' from Toomelah.

Although the Board claimed that it removed only orphaned or neglected children or the children of 'immoral parents', Aboriginal people knew that all children were vulnerable to removal—and all families to the distress that caused. Between 1910 and 1970, an estimated one in six or seven Aboriginal children were separated from their families, compared with about one in 300 non-Aboriginal children. The goal was to eradicate the children's Aboriginal identity, to make them 'think white, look white, act white'.

The dread of having a child removed was the overriding reason for the Waters' move to Nindigully. Grace and Don did not want to lose their daughter, Florence, to the Aboriginal Girls' Training Home at Cootamundra or see her 'apprenticed' to a distant property where her well-being would depend on the kindness of her employers; nor did they want to lose any of their sons—George, Jim, Len, Fred, Kevin and Ranald—to the Kinchela Boys' Home, near Kempsey, or the Bomaderry Aboriginal Children's Home on the New South Wales south coast.

Violence at these homes was ever-present. In 1933, the manager at Kinchela had been warned not to use a stock whip on the boys, tie them up, or send them out as labourers. These institutions were feared by the Kamilaroi and all other Aboriginal people. Once children had been removed, they were seldom reunited with their families—often only after they had suffered physical and psychological damage.

At Nindigully, the Waters family became part of a community of around 50 people. Life was simple, and there were few luxuries. By the banks of the Moonie River, Don built a large shed with saplings and corrugated iron. Ill-fitting awning windows provided basic protection from the elements. There were three rooms, lined with hessian sacking with newspaper pasted either side, and a kitchen out the back. The floor was rammed earth. 'We poured water over it and drew a brush broom over it. It came up hard as anything,' Kevin remembers. The Moonie River doubled as a playground and bathroom.

The Waters' shed has long disappeared, and Nindigully's population has dwindled to a handful of people. Just as it was when the Waters lived there, the centrepiece of the village is the rambling old Nindigully pub, whose liquor licence dates back to 1864. On the road into Nindigully there is now a sign pointing to the pub and another reading, 'Free beer yesterday'.

Don Waters would have appreciated the humour, for precious few things were free during the Great Depression. But hard as it was to eke out a living then, nothing could stop someone with Don's skills. He was proficient in shearing, mustering and droving, ringbarking and fencing. He was also an expert hunter who could live off the land when times were tough, a self-trained bush mechanic, a plumber and a carpenter. He soon had a team of men working for him. They travelled from property to property and would often be away for weeks at a time. Kevin later described his father as 'the most talented man I ever saw in the bush'.

It was this practical ability that Len Mitchell had long recognised. He was the station manager at Boonall West, near

Toomelah, and he and Don formed a close working association. Don respected Mitchell so much that he named his son, Len, after him. When Len Mitchell had moved to Nindigully to manage Balagna station, it was only natural that he would encourage Don to join him. That offer of work had provided the Waters with their pathway out of Toomelah.

Next to the Nindigully pub stood Jack Sternes' general store. It too has gone, but in the 1920s and '30s it serviced not just the village but surrounding properties. 'We stock everything from needles to crowbars,' was Jack's proud boast, emblazoned on the Nindigully store and its sister store at St George, 40 kilometres away. 'Everything' also included newspapers and magazines, and young Len Waters could often be found in the store scanning the latest aviation magazines.

Len had always been fascinated by flight. He loved watching boomerangs arcing back to the elders at Toomelah, or wedgetail eagles hovering high overhead in the thermals and soaring over the brigalow scrub. He badly wanted to understand the mystery of flight. Kevin recalls how his brother's imagination was fired by the exploits of his aviation heroes. Len's sister, Florence, said: 'His enthusiasm was infectious. We derived great pleasure in sitting back and watching him simulate flight.'

Len later commented: 'I was obsessed with the pioneering era and the early fliers. I grew up in the era when the skies were being explored. There was Amy Johnson, [Charles] Kingsford Smith, Bert Hinkler, [Charles] Lindbergh, and Jean Batten in New Zealand.' With the exception of the North Atlantic, Australians had been the first to cross all of the world's major oceans. Charles Kingsford Smith and Charles Ulm had tamed the Pacific in 1928 before crossing the Tasman Sea the same year. In 1931, Bert Hinkler was the first man to fly solo across the South Atlantic Ocean. 'I was always thrilled when I heard their news,' Len said.

Besides accounts of the record-breaking exploits of such aviators, each month Len would read magazine stories and comic strips about the mythical pilots Biggles, Flash Gordon and Buck Rogers. The Australian-published monthly *Aircraft* and its British counterpart, *Popular Flying*, were among his favourites. In 1932, such publications cost sixpence an issue.

In the depths of the Depression, there wasn't much to do in Nindigully but dream. This was a time when aircraft, almost invariably made from wooden frames covered with canvas and held together with wire bracing, were opening up the skies through government-subsidised air routes. One of *Aircraft*'s aims was to make Australians 'air-minded'—to encourage them to support aviation. As Qantas, itself not long established, presciently summed it up: 'The future is in the air.' Popular media, whether films or newsreels, on-the-spot radio broadcasts from air displays and races, or interviews with famous pilots, built awareness of aviation, which it was hoped would link the Outback to the city.

Len was inspired. He began to make model aircraft, likely based on what he saw in his aviation magazines. He used the thin rough pine of grocery packing boxes, almost balsa-light, that he had scrounged from the back of Sternes' store. 'When I was about eight or nine years of age, when other kids were playing with ordinary toys, I'd be making model planes and flying kites,' he later recalled. Soon, on the sandy banks of the Moonie River, Len could be seen running, model plane held high, arm arched back ready to catapult it into the heavens. With an almighty throw, the plane would soar skywards, then level out before nose-diving into the scrub. Len watched it closely, noting whether more of a bow in the wings would help it stay aloft a little longer, just like a boomerang. The family helped him make the models, whittling propellers that, nailed to the nose, would whir and whirl as he ran.

In mid-1932, one of Len's heroes came to St George. The town's weekly paper, *The Balonne Beacon,* announced that the newly knighted Sir Charles Kingsford Smith would be landing his famed *Southern Cross* monoplane at St George racecourse on Saturday, 2 July. Smithy was on a six-week tour of Queensland, and he would offer 40-kilometre joy flights throughout the day. For adults the cost was a steep 20 shillings, halved for children. Arrangements for the visit were handled by Jack Sternes, the local agent for Vacuum Oil, the aviator's backer. Smithy might have been close to ruin after the collapse of his company, Australian National Airlines, and in need of any money he could earn from these barnstorming flights in the bush, but he had a soft spot for St George: some years earlier, his father had been manager of the local branch of the Bank of New South Wales.

That Saturday morning, according to long-time St George resident Vida Hardy, the town rippled with anticipation. She remembers Smithy's arrival creating a 'huge fuss—it was very exciting to hear a plane coming into St George'. Another town resident, Ian Coutts, remembers his mother taking her first flight ever with Smithy. It was not unusual for pilots such as Smithy to carry up to a hundred passengers a day and provide entertainment for hundreds more watching from the ground.

A few days later, *The Balonne Beacon* reported there had been a 'great reception from the public, who were present at the racecourse in large numbers'. Even if Len Waters had made it into town that Saturday, the high cost makes it unlikely that he would have flown with Smith. However, he would have been aware of the historic visit of such a hero, so close to home and at a time when Smithy was drawing large crowds in country towns and even larger ones in the cities.

While many Australians were fascinated, there were others who were initially suspicious. In desert country west of Papunya, Central Australia, in 1930 a group of Pintupi nomads was startled by a loud noise. Some thought it was thunder, yet it was quite different. When they finally caught sight of the aircraft a cry went up that it was Walawurru—the feared giant eagle-hawk. Men fitted spears to their woomeras as the aircraft came in fast, circled high and then swooped down. The sound of the shimmering plane, its great size and threatening shadow was terrifying. Spears rained on it as it landed, before the attackers ran off in fear. However, there were others far enough away not to be frightened; rather, they were cautiously interested in this flying machine and wanted to know more about it. Change was coming.

One Kamilaroi elder later described the impact aircraft had on his people. In corroborees held when he was a small boy, he said, 'They acted out the first time they saw an aeroplane—called it *ganinala malga malga*—they'd make up the song as they go along and dance it.' They mimicked the motions of a plane in flight while stamping their feet as in a traditional dance.

A British *Pathetone Weekly* newsreel captured one such performance in 1933, under the title 'Air-Minded Aboriginals'. The clip showed Aborigines dancing to the beat of clapsticks and using their arms to imitate aircraft wings. Others danced with hand-crafted rotating propellers, painted with traditional motifs. 'You can tell by the accessories that passing planes are making them "air-minded",' the commentary observed.

Such propellers were not unlike those of Len's own handmade planes. He would recall of his boyhood that his 'head was in the clouds'. However, when he looked to the sky he saw not only the realm of his flying heroes but a different world that belonged to his people. Looking at the night sky, Kamilaroi people see Kaputhin the Eagle, a totem associated with such spiritual concepts as soaring over obstacles and celebration of the blue skies. Warrambal, the Milky Way, is a sky atlas that indicates camp sites, tribal domains and ancestral places on earth.

Through songs, Len learned how his ancestors had used the stars to navigate to distant destinations. The former Kamilaroi lands contained many such routes, or songlines, and these were put to good use by early colonial explorers who drew upon the knowledge of local Aborigines. As Dr Robert Fuller, an expert on Aboriginal cultural astronomy, has noted: 'In a sense, the Aboriginal people of Australia had a big part in the layout of the modern Australian road network. And in some cases, such as the Kamilaroi Highway running from the Hunter Valley to Bourke in New South Wales, this has been recognised in the name.'

The stars contain a universal calendar of the seasons and animal breeding patterns, and tell stories of such creatures as Dhinawan the Emu, who crosses the horizon over a period of months each year. For millennia, this lore explained the way the world worked. It continues to be passed down from generation to generation, as it was to a young Len. Having been born on the plains where the emu roamed, his totem, like that of his brothers and sisters, was Dhinawan.

For aeons, the Dreaming had underpinned the life of the Kamilaroi in their role as traditional custodians of lands extending from present-day Singleton, in the New South Wales Hunter Valley, to the Warrumbungle Mountains in the west, north through Quirindi, Gunnedah, Tamworth, Narrabri, Walgett, Moree, Lightning Ridge and Mungindi, and over the Queensland border to Nindigully.

Grace and Don were determined that the stories that had shaped Kamilaroi culture and history would not be lost to their children. They would learn the stories of the sky while learning about modern aviation and the many changes western civilisation was bringing—not all of them beneficial to Aboriginal people. For them, the challenge was to balance the parallel worlds in which they found themselves and help their children cope with the inevitable collisions between them.

2

DEPENDENCY

Len Waters loved to tinker with his father's old Model T Ford, a car that had so revolutionised travel in the bush that it became known as the 'Squatter's Joy'. He could quickly detect the causes of a rough idle. 'I was always mechanically minded. We used to work on the old cars that Dad had. We'd do all our own maintenance work,' Len remembered. Kevin recalled how he and his brothers would strip the engine to replace the rings and bearings as their father looked on. Being able to turn his hand to anything that needed doing, Don was a good teacher.

And Len was a quick learner. He had begun school at Toomelah and, because he had been taught to read by his mother, was able to skip a year and go straight into Grade 1. Facilities at the mission's Aboriginal school were in no way designed to benefit the brighter students. There was just one teacher for the 150 or so children crowded into one large room. The building and equipment were of poor quality, and the teacher was generally untrained. This was in keeping with the fact that the education of Aborigines was set at a lower standard than for public schools. If the family had remained at Toomelah, policy would have prevented Len from going beyond Grade 5, the highest grade offered to Aboriginal students in New South Wales.

By 1920, a separate education system was operating in the state's 35 Aboriginal schools. The syllabus included some reading, writing and arithmetic, but the main emphasis was on training for manual or domestic work. A high school education was viewed as unnecessary. This entrenched discrimination saw Aboriginal children excluded from rural public schools in New South Wales—and from any public school where white parents objected to their presence.

Even being a returned soldier brought no remission from this colour bar—as Kamilaroi man and World War I veteran Mick Flick discovered in Collarenebri. Despite his persistent protests, his six children were refused entry to the town's public school or to any other in the district. Increasing his bitterness, the Protection Board repeatedly threatened to forcibly remove his children from the family *because* they were not being educated adequately. Flick carried this grievance for the rest of his life.

Reports of district inspectors for the Aboriginal schools asserted that satisfactory results were being obtained, 'the children receiving an education appropriate to their mental capabilities, and fitting them to later take their places in the white community.' The Protection Board claimed that the 'average Aboriginal child appears to show an aptitude for manual work, and some excellent displays of raffia, basketry, carpentry, and sewing' were to be found in these schools, perhaps reflecting the abilities of the teachers rather than the potential of the students. Given such attitudes, it is not surprising that Don and Grace Waters wanted to avoid the school at Toomelah.

They had experienced first-hand how such schooling limited Aboriginal children's opportunities. Grace was born in 1900 in the border town of Mungindi. Her father, George Bennett, was a Kamilaroi man and a noted horseman who worked as a stockman; her mother, Mary, was the daughter of a white man, Fred Moody, and a Gunditjmara woman from Victoria's Wimmera, Maria Taylor. As a girl, Grace was a voracious reader. She pored over the Bible and had a tendency to quote from it throughout her life.

It is unclear just how much schooling she had—she may have been tutored by the wife of a station owner who took a liking to her, or been put in touch with a tutor by an Aboriginal family, the Nobles, who had links to a mission in the Lake Macquarie area. Years later, Grace would tell her youngest daughter, Beatrice, 'I never went to school but met the girls who did, on the corner coming home.' Still, she was not just smart and well-read but fluent in both English and the Kamilaroi tongue. Despite her diminutive stature, Grace commanded respect from an early age.

So did Don Waters. Born in 1898, he lived at Whalan Station, a declared reserve near Toomelah that aimed to help

Aborigines assimilate by teaching them Christian ways. His mother, Florence Wightman-Dennison, was a member of the Awabakal clan from the Hunter Valley. In an arrangement that was not uncommon at the time, Florence had worked for the family of Fred McWaters, a Moree businessman who had migrated from Great Britain. A big man with red hair and a beard, he later dropped the 'Mc' from his surname—possibly to avoid interest from the police.

While Aboriginal boys and men worked on properties as labourers, girls were often employed as nursemaids or domestics. Many did so at the whim of their white masters. Pregnancies abounded, and there was little concern for the consequences for either mother or child. This was Florence's experience. Finding herself pregnant, she returned to her family on Whalan Station to give birth to Don—a light-skinned, fair-haired boy. After Fred left her, Florence began a relationship with a Scotsman, William McIntosh, with whom she had another son, Ronald, in 1902. Both boys had limited educational opportunities at Whalan, learning basic reading and writing and not much more.

In 1911, Florence and her sons, together with the other nineteen adults and 32 children at Whalan Station, moved to the newly established Euraba Aborigines' Reserve nearby. Families moved into roughly built huts. As the population quickly grew, more huts were built, along with a schoolhouse and a residence for a manager who was appointed to teach the children and regulate life on the reserve. Reflecting the discriminatory attitudes of the day, the *Sydney Mail*, in a feature article on the reserve, commented:

> *A mistaken idea is prevalent amongst us that those children are dense and very slow to learn. Such is by no means the case, and quite a number of the boys and girls . . . possess intelligence above the ordinary. This is especially the case with the pure-blooded children, who are, almost in every way superior to the half-castes, and who display an aptitude that would gladden the heart of the most exacting of teachers. There are, of course, some exceptions . . .*

The paper commented that the majority of Euraba's residents were 'half-castes', mixed-race people who, in its view, belonged neither to the Aborigines nor the whites.

Such condescension underlined just how complete was white Australia's dismissal of Aboriginal people in those years. In books, newspapers and the speeches of politicians and public figures, they were portrayed as Stone-Age people who had been left behind while other races developed and progressed. As a missionary at the Bomaderry Aboriginal Children's Home put it in 1917, the Aborigines were 'looked upon as a race the white people cared little for, and for whom God cared just as little'. At the time of the *Sydney Mail*'s article, few Australians thought about Aborigines in terms other than 'protection' and 'segregation'.

Aborigines had been made a dependent people, and their children were 'generally despised'. At Euraba, the level of dependency was clear to see. Each Monday a week's ration was given out to every man, woman and child, consisting of flour, tea, sugar, baking powder and meat. In the fertile black soil, they cultivated their own vegetable crops in subsistence gardens to supplement the rations. Residents were sometimes allowed out to attend travelling shows when they set up at nearby Boomi. Otherwise, they were on a tight rein. The effort needed to break free from a virtual police state could shatter the spirit of many—but not the Waters family.

3

DISPOSSESSION

Len Waters' maternal grandfather, George Bennett, was a nuggety tracker at Moree when he enlisted to fight in the Great War. Aged 35, he travelled to Armidale on 26 April 1916, a day after the first anniversary of the Gallipoli landing. The Defence Act allocated to medical officers the responsibility for determining race. In George's case, a request on the recruitment form for details of 'marks indicating congenital or previous disease' brought a note from a medical officer that he was 'very strongly aboriginal in type'.

His application was accepted, his Aboriginality neatly sidestepped by the description 'natural born', even though the recruiters noted his complexion as dark, his eyes brown and hair black. One of his relatives, Charlie Turner Bird, had a slightly different experience. A 21-year-old Awabakal shearer from Goondiwindi, he enlisted in Sydney not long after George and was listed simply as 'Abakwal born' [*sic*].

The two men joined the Australian Imperial Force (AIF) even before the Commonwealth government, in the face of declining enlistment and a rising death toll in Europe, was forced to relax the Defence Act's ban on men not substantially of European heritage from serving their country. George never explained why he joined up, but perhaps he and Charlie saw military service as a way to escape the racial discrimination Aborigines suffered. Or they might have decided that if Australia was at war, so were they. Australia was their country too.

Unable to write, George signed with an 'X' to become a Digger, one of more than 1000 Aborigines to do so at a time when the estimated Aboriginal population was 93,000. In 1917, George fought on the Western Front at Bullecourt, Ypres and Passchendaele with the 29th Battalion AIF. Then, in August–September 1918, he took part in the advance that followed the battle of Amiens. Both he and Charlie were gassed as the Germans fought desperately to hold their positions near Mont Saint-Quentin. Released from hospital at the end of the war, George was admonished for being drunk in London. He was not alone. White or black, all soldiers had suffered dreadfully, and there were few more egalitarian ways to blur the pain than getting on the drink.

In August 1919, George returned to Euraba reserve, where he and Charlie were honoured with a Welcome Home ceremony. For a community still struggling with the effects of the flu pandemic—which killed around 15,000 people in

Australia—their presence lifted spirits. The stories George told that day were 'listened to with breathless attention', according to a local newspaper. It did not matter that he and Charlie had fought a white man's war. They had survived, and the people of Euraba felt proud of them.

Being George's elder daughter, Grace Waters played a central role in the day's events, which opened with what was described as an old-time tribal feast, before moving on to a program of step-dancing and singing in both Kamilaroi and English. King Bungo, a tribal leader from the region, sang 'The Kangaroo Hunt', while a young man named Jacob earned applause for his song, '*Weeum, billee ngunatha ngunn, noorhah bidduginnan*'—'a young man makes a clean sweep of his camp before bringing his new-found bride there to reside'. Not long married to Don, Grace probably would have coyly appreciated Jacob's song.

And then it was her turn. Her sweet voice ringing out along the banks of the Whalan Creek, Grace was said to have sung 'a very nice patriotic song'. The day concluded with 'For He's a Jolly Good Soldier' and 'God Save the King'. George's and Charlie's names were engraved on an honour board to ensure their courage was remembered. In time, George would become a hero and role model for his grandsons.

When George was discharged, he had agreed with the army medical officer that he was 'not suffering from any disability due to or aggravated by war service'. In fact, he would suffer for years from respiratory problems caused by mustard gas. For him and most other Aboriginal soldiers, demobilisation meant a harsh return to pre-war reality. They returned to Australia to find their reserves being carved up to provide blocks of land for white veterans under soldier settlement schemes while they received nothing. Others had sent money home from the Front only to discover that venal protectors had stolen it. This often meant that their families, unable to support themselves in their absence, had been broken up and the children taken to orphanages. Most were not paid their post-war entitlements, and those who had been wounded were denied the repatriation health services that were available to white veterans.

While George fell into this category, the fact that he returned alive was at least something to celebrate. In 1919 there was not much else for the people at Euraba to be cheerful about. Conditions were deteriorating and the social fabric was fraying. The situation continued to worsen, and by 1925 the reserve was described as 'the worst site it was possible to choose for an aboriginal home, being nothing better than a black swamp'. It flooded in wet weather, and water had to be carted there in summer.

Grace and Don's first five children were born at Euraba before the Protection Board finally closed what had become a blighted shanty town. Len Waters was a two-year-old when his father helped dismantle the ramshackle buildings at Euraba so they could be moved to Toomelah, 20 kilometres away, on a reserve covering more than 200 hectares of virgin scrub. A boundary fence restricted movement in and out. In Kamilaroi, Toomelah means 'lifted and shifted', but in effect the Euraba residents were again hastily dumped on unsatisfactory land.

This was a time when reserve managers were expected to impress upon children that the practices of the elders and even their parents were primitive and barbaric. In nightly prayer services, the people at Euraba and then Toomelah were encouraged to seek forgiveness—for being born 'black'. Because the practice of traditional culture was actively discouraged, the Kamilaroi language was rarely used. Instead, families were pressured to speak 'good English'. Kamilaroi was spoken almost surreptitiously, at funerals, cultural gatherings and behind closed doors. Kevin Waters recalls that when he was a child, people interspersed English conversations with common Kamilaroi words in their determination to keep the language alive. But this had to be done discreetly to avoid raising the ire of the manager.

The lawyer and modern day land-rights activist Noel Pearson has described the protection laws that governed the lives of Aboriginal people on missions and reserves in this period as 'notoriously discriminatory'. He noted that 'the bureaucratic apparatus controlling the reserves maintained vigil over the smallest details concerning its charges . . . Superintendents held vast powers and a cold and capricious bureaucracy presided over this system for too long in the 20th century.' To one member of the extended Waters family, Madeline McGrady, the white managers at Toomelah made it seem as if 'the edges of the mission were the edges of the world'. Residents felt 'owned by the government': they needed written permission to leave even to go shopping.

While the system sheltered residents from the hostility of society beyond the reserve, in practice 'protection and segregation' was akin to the apartheid policies later introduced in South Africa. It also happened to benefit the pastoralists who had gained their power by occupying lands that had been the communal territory of the Waters family's ancestors for tens of thousands of years. The principle of *terra nullius*—an empty land belonging to nobody—provided the foundation in British law for the appropriation of the entire continent of Australia. After the arrival of the First Fleet in 1788, it allowed the Crown to sell land taken from Indigenous peoples against their will. In their own country, they were soon considered as the enemy.

When the various colonial and state governments came to issuing pastoral leases, they did so knowing that the lands in question were still home to Aboriginal people living and hunting in traditional ways. Histories of the relentless expansion of squatters' properties describe opposition from 'numerous and warlike' blacks 'who sometimes waged all the war they were capable of against both the invading white man and the strange animals with which he was flooding the country'. At Balagna, the disturbing history of the station remained unspoken. On the property was a reminder of the violent past: a thick slab hut—long since dismantled—with holes in the walls for rifles to be used against hostile Aborigines. Because Australia had not been conquered by an army, the police became integral to the dispossession of Aborigines, their forced relocation, and their subjugation. By 1859, after years of land seizures and frontier bloodshed, the squatters were entrenched and sheep and cattle were the cornerstones of the colonial economy. In 1861, the Brisbane *Courier* observed: 'Upon the successful working of the princely properties on which this produce is raised depends . . . the growth and stability of the wealth of the country.' Aboriginal workers were often regarded as more skilled than whites, but in Queensland regulations introduced in 1919 between government and pastoralists set Aboriginal pay at 66 per cent of the white rate for the next 50 years. Only token 'pocket money' was given to workers out of their earnings. The remaining money was paid into trust accounts, which were difficult to access. Many Aboriginal workers had their earnings stolen or taken by fraud.

As more and more of their lands were taken for farms and towns, Aboriginal people were forcibly resettled on the reserves and missions. In the process, families from different groups were often thrown together, eroding the traditional system of marriage and kinship. Law and governance were thrown into confusion. People were no longer sure about their roles, rights and responsibilities to either the land or other people. This breakdown struck directly at the moieties, the two halves into which the Aboriginal world divides the universe. Children inherit their moiety from either their mother or their father; those of the same moiety must treat each other as siblings. Moiety, totem or clan, and skin group together determine interactions with other people, animals, plants, the land and waterways, dictating whom one can marry, where they live, and their daily responsibilities.

Traditional practice was for brothers from one family to marry sisters from an appropriately matched family. Thus, when Don Waters' half-brother, Ron McIntosh, married Grace's sister, Ruby, in 1921, the families managed to avoid the kind of kinship breakdown that was always a risk on the missions and reserves. This was a crucial factor in allowing the wider family into which the Waters and McIntosh children were born to maintain a robust sense of traditional cultural identity in a rapidly changing world.

4

SKIN

Don and Grace Waters were realists. They knew traditional ways would never return and that their children would need to fit in to the new world as well as the old one. During the early years at Toomelah, Grace began the children's education through correspondence lessons. This decision, rare among Aboriginal families at the time, meant that before Len entered the crowded Toomelah school, his formal, western education had begun.

At the same time, Grace was determined that her children would stay in touch with traditional culture. She and her mother, Mary Moody, began teaching Len his first language, Kamilaroi. His uncles and community elders taught him Kamilaroi practices and ceremonies, land resource management and the finer skills of hunting, fire-making and woodcraft, including the carving of emu eggs, nulla nullas and boomerangs.

Learning folklore often involved trips 'on country'. A frequent destination was Boobera Lagoon, about 40 kilometres away, which had particular cultural and spiritual significance for Kamilaroi and Bigambul people. In the mythology of the Dreamtime, the lagoon is said to be the resting place of Garriya, the local Rainbow Serpent, the protector of the land and the people. This spirit being is the source of all life, but if it is not properly respected, it can be a destructive force.

Len recalled how he, his brothers and cousins accompanied uncle Walter Binge to the lagoon on a fishing trip. Walter told them about a giant snake that lived there. One night, three whitefellas had gone fishing on the lagoon and slept in their boat. As the story went, it was a still night, the moon was full and the lake was calm. Before dawn, the huge snake came out of nowhere and overturned the boat. The three men were never seen again. The story was scary enough to make Len and the other boys avoid the lagoon at night. But it also cleverly extended the power of the Rainbow Serpent to whitefellas, suggesting that everybody who lived on the land was subject to its law.

Looking back, Len recalled how important it had been for him to spend his first seven years embedded in his culture. This had given him a pride in being Kamilaroi that brought with it a sense of belonging and a sense of identity. He was fortunate, too, that his parents retained their own strong sense of identity and culture and quietly passed this on. That confidence, Len said, enabled the whole family to act 'in a way that was accepted by the mission managers and the wider community, even though they knew full well who they were and where they came from'.

Don unwittingly found himself in the middle of an emerging debate. During the 1930s there was a growing realisation among government agencies, anthropologists and church leaders alike, that 'protection' and 'segregation', however well-intentioned, was simply not working; nor did it reflect the international conscience as espoused by the League of Nations. Protection from abuse and exploitation was one thing, but segregation from white communities had clearly failed. The emerging new policy of assimilation envisioned 'natives of aboriginal origin, but not of the full blood', would ultimately be absorbed into the general community 'on an equal footing with the whites'.

Don was seen as someone who would assimilate. He had joined the Australian Workers' Union in 1918 and renewed his ticket every year. He was a strong Labor supporter and his children remember that he always voted. Surprisingly, he owned racehorses, racing them on tracks at Boomi and Toomelah. Son Kevin remembers his father helping to build the track fence and grandstand at the reserve. 'One of his horses was a big old chestnut sprinter called Breeze and he won some races.'

With his light-coloured skin and strong work ethic, the Toomelah manager saw Don as a half-caste who would fit into white society. He was so light-skinned Len would later describe his father as 'almost a white man, and you would never have taken him for an Aboriginal'. His brother Kevin said, 'the English genes were pretty evident'. As his granddaughter, Julia Waters, put it, 'Because Pop was so white, he could take his family away from Toomelah even though Nana was much darker.' Don was no longer classified as Aboriginal, and this also applied to his wife and his children, none of whom was as light-skinned as their father.

Don's half-brother, Ronald McIntosh, had a different experience. Because his skin was quite dark, he had to stay at Toomelah. He and the other families on the reserve remained subject to extensive surveillance by police, who could harass and arrest at will, and by the manager, who could enter private premises whenever he liked. Madeline McGrady recalled waking at night at Toomelah 'with torch light on our faces. We were terrified but we knew it was no use to complain. The only person we could complain to was the manager, and he usually was the one who had called the police out in the first place.'

Ruby Waters, who married Len's brother, Jim, said:

> *We didn't have any rights because we had the white man standing above us all the time, telling us what to do. When I think back, the part I find the most distressing is when my sister was taken away. We were told she was being taken to Goondiwindi to see a dentist . . . It was really terrible. We all suffered the heartache of her being taken away. The pain is still in my heart. We finally met again after 31 years. Those other people were her family now.*

5

CHOICE

When Len Waters walked into class at the Nindigully Public School on the first school day of 1932, a new world opened up for him. Including the Waters children, there were about eighteen students—rather fewer than at the crowded mission school at Toomelah. Len, his older brothers George and Jim, younger brother Fred and sister Florence boosted dwindling student numbers, ensuring that the one-teacher school would not have to close.

Right from the start, Len was an assiduous pupil, bright, inquisitive and hungry for knowledge. He was not only proficient at reading but also had well-developed numeracy skills.

Four years later, aged twelve and entering Grade 7, he was nearing the end of the educational line. Grade 8 was the highest available at Nindigully—or in most rural schools. Then, at the beginning of 1936, Jim Wolfe, a young education graduate from Brisbane, was appointed the school's new teacher. He was struck by how well dressed the Waters children were—'not flashily dressed but always cleanly, neatly dressed.' They further impressed him with their regular attendance and punctuality. All were smart, but Wolfe quickly realised that Len was 'singularly bright'. Florence later recalled that he 'had tremendous confidence' in her brother. As Wolfe put it, Len was 'brilliant at mathematics and geography'; he and Betty Walker, a bright white girl the same age whose father was the manager of Sternes' store, made for a 'wonderful class'. What astonished Wolfe was that Len already understood mathematical concepts not taught in primary school, including calculus.

Althea Wolfe remembers her father not just as an old-fashioned gentleman who valued education but as a man with a social conscience. Jim Wolfe was expected to lock the tap on the school water tank each night before returning to the Nindigully pub, where he boarded. He never did so because he thought local Aborigines camped in the district might need the water. If the inspector of schools had discovered this, it would not have boded well for Wolfe. Such thoughtful acts won the respect of all in the small community. Known as 'Schoolie', Wolfe soon became the go-to person for advice or as an unofficial mediator of disputes.

It was a water tank that first alerted Wolfe to Len's problem-solving talents. The tank was to be erected on a stand set on tall timber poles. To raise it high required ingenuity and calculated risk taking. The differential between the pivot points for the near and far posts had to be considered, along with the lift angle and the force required for the lift. As the posts were swung into the vertical position, care had to be taken not to dislodge them from their footings. Jim was impressed as Len, with an intuitive understanding of the physics involved, confidently proposed a solution. The tank was duly swung into place atop the tower.

In Nindigully, the Waters family witnessed something that to many might have been painful and difficult: the melding of two cultures. The social environment in the town was one of acceptance and respect. The family's Aboriginality was not an issue. At the time, an exemption certificate system operated in the state, but card index records show that neither Don nor any of his family were ever on the list.

By the mid-to-late 1930s, Australia had begun slowly emerging from the Depression. In nearby St George the shops reflected signs of tentative recovery. The local newspaper, *The Balonne Beacon*, ran advertisements for new Studebakers and Dodges, silk hosiery, and 'day and evening frocks', but this was not so evident at Nindigully.

The Waters family's corrugated-iron shed was built on land at Nindigully owned by store owner Jack Sternes. It was cramped for such a large family, and the boys slept two to a bed. There was no electricity, and the family relied on large kerosene lamps for light. They cooked on a wood stove out the back, and once a month or so Don would bring in a 'killer' (a sheep to be slaughtered) that augmented the family's meals. As Kevin recalled, lamb or mutton was a luxury. 'We used to play in the sand hills trapping rabbits. That was most [of our] meat in those days. They were good healthy days.'

Occasionally, Don would hunt emus. Normally he would shoot one with his .22 rifle, but once, when he ran out of ammunition, Kevin recalled him chasing two or three down a fence. Separating one, Don stunned it with a stone from his slingshot before killing it. 'We all had [slingshots] sticking out of our back pockets,' Kevin said; they even took them to school in case they spied a bird on the way home to add to dinner.

With Don often away for several weeks at a time, the boys would take over the role of providing food. They would both fish and hunt with their father's .22 rifle. As Kevin recalled, 'I remember Len used to sit at the kitchen window and shoot rabbits in the warren that was only about thirty or forty yards from the house.' The boys would also hunt wild pigs, delighting in grabbing a piglet in the scrub which they would fatten in a back paddock until it was ready for the table. These were hard learned lessons in survival.

Don's approach to discipline was clear cut and firm. On one occasion that stayed in Kevin's memory, Len was slow to obey his father's order to get up from the dinner table and wash the dishes. Don would not tolerate slackness. 'I saw him give Len a belting. He was bloody strict.' Much of the rearing of the family fell to Grace. She 'ruled the roost' and had no qualms about giving her kids a 'whack' if they were tardy with household chores. 'She was very strict. You were not allowed to wear a Jackie Howe [shearer's] singlet to dinner. You had to have a shirt on, wash your hands, and Mum insisted on table manners.'

Kevin believed this was most likely because of her work for station owners in homesteads before she married. Equally,

Grace delighted in sitting around a fire after dinner and reading the Bible out loud to the family. Don was not religious, but his children saw him as a 'law and order man'. This was a household steeped not just in love but in solid values.

There were always boxing gloves lying around. Sparring among the boys became second nature, sometimes breaking into fights as tears led to redoubled determination and heavier punches. 'We would spar together when we were kids, and he used to go a bit easy on me, I think,' Ranald, two years younger than Len, would recall. At night, sitting around the table under the soft glow of the kerosene lamps, they often played cards or Bobs, a home version of billiards. A bridge-like structure with nine arches was set at one end of the table, and players stood at the opposite end and used a wooden cue to send balls through the arches. Scores were based on the numbers printed above each arch. Don, who loved the game, carved the cues from local Ringed Gidgee, and as he grew older Len took up the craft, soon mastering it. The boys played rugby league and cricket—Len, already noted for his quick reflexes, became wicket-keeper for Nindigully. And they loved swimming in the Moonie River or running through the sandhills—in Len's case, holding a model plane aloft.

Len revelled in the opportunities that Nindigully opened up. His best mate was Len Mitchell's son Wal, two years younger and a fellow pupil at the school. In the holidays they would chase pigs and play tennis together.

While Don and his family developed close connections with the Mitchells and Balagna station, they did not forget their extended family at Toomelah. They went back to visit them every Christmas and during most school holidays. If Don was away working, then George or Jim would drive the family to Toomelah. There they joined in corroborees and dances held at an area known as the claypan.

Kevin recalls that before each event the ground would be swept and hosed down to minimise the dust, and 'there would be a big old corroboree and sing-song. Clapsticks and a few boomerangs clapping together—and young and old men doing the dancing. Good old Kamilaroi songs. They'd tell a story through their dancing.' Also accompanied by accordions and mouth organs, the dances would go on for hours. They would finish with livelier music and more modern dances, including the waltz and the two-step. Their grandmother, Mary, who was now known as Grannie Craigie, would lead the singing at corroborees. These were important occasions when Kamilaroi culture was passed on by the old people to the children. 'They told us the old stories and Granny Craigie would sing for hours. She was the leader in passing down the language.'

Through these visits the Waters family nurtured their roots and helped maintain their connections to the Murri clans. But after they said goodbye and returned to Nindigully, their relatives at Toomelah were left struggling with heavy-handed paternalism. At nearby Moree, the council had banned 'persons appearing to have aboriginie [*sic*] blood' from the town's artesian baths. A common view was that Aboriginal men had 'strong sexual urges and a strong desire to impregnate white women and that should a young virile Aboriginal man masturbate in the baths he could impregnate a lot of women'.

In 1932, lobbying by rural whites resulted in Moree police removing all Aboriginal people, including those in local employment, to the banks of the Mehi River, where there was no potable water or toilet facilities. This act, justified on the grounds of town residents' health, earned the local constabulary great praise from the Chief Protector of Aborigines.

In September 1932, the Toomelah manager permitted the residents to join a corroboree at Moree in aid of the local candidate for the Hospital Queen competition (held around Australia to raise money for hospitals). *The Sydney Morning Herald* reported that 'the aborigines proved good entertainers, particularly as step-dancers and singers. A gum-leaf band was a big attraction. The corroboree itself caused much amusement.' A story in the *North Western Courier* headed 'Abos to the Rescue' displayed, intentionally or not, the racism typical of the time:

> *The dusky inhabitants of the Toomelah Mission Station, near Boomi, have disproved the oft-told story that the Australian aborigines are, more or less, a drug on the civic market. They have given a lead to many local organisations in public matters and their latest idea is to help the Moree District Ambulance, which serves their area. Being without an accordeon [*sic*], that indispensable instrument in a darkies' orchestra, the Toomelah people ran a dance and raised sufficient funds to get a brand-new accordeon. The orchestra plays very good dance music, especially old-time stuff, and the aborigines are now arranging for a dance at Boomi in aid of the ambulance.*

Back in Nindigully, Len was approaching Grade 8. Jim Wolfe believed he deserved opportunities that the village could not provide. Len was, he said, the brightest pupil he had ever had. So highly did Wolfe rate his ability that he went to the Waters home twice a week to give Len private tuition. But it wasn't just Len's intelligence that stood out. With the straight-backed rectitude he had inherited from his parents, he had a presence that commanded respect. He was also 'very loyal, very well composed, very courteous, the type of fellow who would just have to succeed.'

However, in early 1938, with the country not yet free of the Depression, there was talk of Len leaving school even before he finished Grade 8. Concerned, Wolfe asked Grace to consider letting him stay on. As Len recalled, 'Jim begged my mother, "Don't let this fella leave school, he's a bright kid. You never can tell, he could even be a Rhodes Scholar."' Wolfe suggested that he could organise a bursary that would allow him to attend secondary school as a boarder at the Brisbane Church of England Grammar School. On the one hand, he feared that Len would encounter racism: 'There would be always boys who, when an Aborigine would go past, would say in a falsetto voice, just loud enough for the coloured person to hear, "There goes a black cloud."' On the other hand, Jim thought Len would be well accepted 'because of his whole attitude to people and to teachers in particular'.

Don and Grace faced a choice: send him to Brisbane on a pathway into the privileged world of white Australia, or insist that he join his father and elder brothers, George and Jim, and work to support the family. Grace was against him leaving school—she appreciated what Wolfe wanted to offer her son. But these were still tough times, and Don Waters argued that Len needed to contribute to the family's well-being.

Len sensed his mother was right, but he also understood his father's position. As he put it later, he felt he had 'to give Mum and Dad a hand to rear the rest of the family. Dad liked to keep the family unit going, and he was doing contract work, bush work, and I decided I would do my bit to help.'

6

STANDING APART

His shoulders had not filled out, nor had he reached his full height, but just before his fourteenth birthday Len Waters began a man's job. To Jim Wolfe's regret, Len walked away from Nindigully school and the chance of furthering his education in Brisbane. He had not completed Grade 8. This meant he had not sat for the Queensland scholarship exam. 'But there was no worry that I would have if I had continued,' Len reflected later.

Until he left school, his eldest brother, George, was the family's immediate breadwinner when their father was away from Nindigully on contract work. Jim, the second eldest, had left his father's team to work for the Mitchells on Balagna station as a general labourer. Their sister Florence also worked at the Balagna homestead as a domestic, a job she would hold for seven years. The family found Len Mitchell a 'straight cockie', a good employer and someone they trusted.

When Len joined his father's ringbarking and fencing team in April 1938, he found himself among twelve to fifteen men whose toughness was a challenge to his own. As he later recalled:

> *We worked from daylight until dark and coming into winter there used to be heavy dew on the timber every morning and we'd all be in a line, ready to start work as soon as it was light enough to see the timber we had to work on. We'd just have little twig fires, sitting around warming our hands and sharpening our axes and ready to start work. And with the pace-makers, we had to really work—you almost ran from tree to tree.*
>
> *It was [ten bob or, the equivalent of $1] a week and out of that I used to pay five bob for board. And [work] was seven days a week. For six days everyone worked daylight to dark. Then on Sundays, no one went to town, the other workers were all sharpening their tools for ringbarking, and me being the educated one, Dad and I would have to go and measure up the amount of work that was done through the week. I used to have to make up their wages. So I worked seven days a week for my 10 bob.*

This was far less than the basic wage for 1938 of 81 shillings ($8.10) for an adult male. At the time, it was common for Aboriginal workers to have a significant part of their earnings withheld and passed to the government, ostensibly for the support of destitute Aboriginal people. Under the Queensland regulations introduced in 1919, male Aboriginal workers under the age of eighteen had 80 per cent of their wages withheld. But because the Waters family was not registered as Aboriginal, Len was able to keep his wage, such as it was.

Working in the team brought him into close contact with George. He soon realised that his older brother could hold men spellbound with his yarns: 'He could have bought and sold Henry Lawson and Banjo Paterson. He was one of the most natural comedians one could wish to meet.' George had a dry wit and made good use of hyperbole. One of Len's favourite stories was George's yarn about ringbarking in almost impenetrable scrub. When he shot a kangaroo, George claimed, 'I had to drag the carcass out onto a watercourse because the scrub was so thick I couldn't even open my pocketknife.'

Working in the ringbarking teams introduced the brothers to old bushies, men who had scrimped and scraped to make a living. One of them was an old-timer who had spent time tent boxing on the show circuit and lived on a station on the Moonie River between Nindigully and St George. Kevin Waters recalls his brothers talking of how this whitefella began training them when they had some time to spare. He showed them how to use their feet and where to aim their punches: pound the kidney area and immobilise the opponent by connecting with his sciatic nerve.

If big, eighteen-ounce gloves were being used, as was common in tent boxing, then the aim was to pepper the opponent's biceps. The heavy gloves soon felt like bricks and, with the blood draining from his arms, the opponent would drop them, quick hands and opening him up to a full-frontal attack.

Len soon had 'pretty good skills', including a knowledge of where to focus his attack. His toughness and fitness were also improving as a result of the labouring work.

*

After two years, Len started working in the shearing sheds for what he regarded as good money—£2/6/8 a week, or just over half the then award wage for an adult male. 'I was always pretty thrifty, got myself a good wardrobe, I didn't drink—a couple of my brothers did, but I didn't drink or smoke,' he said. These were values learned from his parents. Don continued working hard and Grace, who was regarded as the brains of the family, did the accounting.

In 1939 the Waters moved from the tin shed into a three-bedroom weatherboard house, closer to Nindigully village. Don built an annexe to provide shade in summer, and also pulled the old shed down and rebuilt it closer to the house. When Don's half-brother, Ronald McIntosh, moved to Nindigully, he and his family took up residence in the shed, their children joining the younger Waters children at the local school.

With the Depression all but over, Don's savings began to grow. Just after Christmas 1940, he and Grace made the decision to move to St George, then a dusty little bush town with dirt roads and a population of around 900. After renting a house for some months, Don was offered the chance to buy two acres of land on St George's Terrace, overlooking the Balonne River, for £360. He quickly snapped up the property, which included an old Queenslander-style weatherboard house with a high and wide verandah, and two other buildings. These he rented out to help pay the mortgage.

Vida Hardy was sixteen and lived next door to the property with her parents when the Waters family moved in. 'Florrie and I used to chat over the fence, and they would come to our place and we would go to theirs,' she later said. 'The house was always spotless. Don Waters was a very proud man, and the family was very well respected in town.' Vida added that there were Aboriginal fringe dwellers camped on the other side of the river, but the Waters were different. They 'were not into drinking', as happened in the camp. 'And they all worked.'

Although most people in St George treated the Waters family like any other residents, 'Kids would still call us blackfellas, which probably came from their parents,' Kevin said. 'If they got close enough, we'd dong 'em.'

The Waters were at the forefront of an emerging group of Indigenous people moving away from government settlements to town to find work and escape the welfare trap. Don had avoided the fate of many unemployed Aborigines, whom the police often forced back onto reserves. He and Grace believed it was their right to live in a more open society. They were contributing to the regional economy and were now part of the community. As private citizens, not state dependents, they were able to keep the money they earned.

For Len and his brothers and sisters, their parents' values were pressed home daily. Don and Grace left no room for slackness or failure to pull one's weight. Contributing to the family's financial well-being was a priority. Perseverance and resilience were reinforced. But in leaving the reserve, they had also to a large extent left the traditional society of clan and skin group. Without necessarily realising it, Don and Grace were creating an environment that influenced the way their children interacted with the outside world. In such a large family, learning to get along with others and to take responsibility developed in parallel.

This was the fertile ground in which Len's character developed. The author Stan Grant might have been referring to the Waters when he described the more progressive Aborigines from his grandfather's generation, just before and after World War II, as people 'with a straight-backed dignity, resolute in the demand for their rights'. Len and his family were among those who 'saw an open door and marched through it'. They were committed, determined, and alive to the possibilities of life in a changing Australia.

*

It was a short walk from the Waters home in St George to the shire hall, where films were screened on Tuesday, Thursday and Saturday nights. Starting in September 1939, the newsreels that preceded the main feature focused on the war in Europe.

Len had wanted to join up from the start, even though he was only fifteen. 'When the war broke out in '39, I couldn't get into it quick enough. As a matter of fact, I tried to enlist . . . in ground staff.' In June 1941, Len—just seventeen—and his brother Jim, who was two years older, hitched a ride to Dirranbandi to meet up with the mobile recruiting van. Because Len was under age, he was rejected. Jim, who decided not to enlist if his brother couldn't, commiserated with Len, telling him, 'We'll wait a year, brother, until you're eighteen, and we'll come back.'

While Len was determined to enlist in the air force and Jim in the army, being Aboriginal meant they potentially faced the hurdle of institutional discrimination. At the outbreak of war, Aboriginal men were still specifically excluded from military service. In May 1940, a Military Board memorandum was issued to military commands stating that enlisting people of non-European origin was 'neither necessary nor desirable'.

While the army and navy implemented the order, the Royal Australian Air Force (RAAF) took a different approach. The record of military aviators in World War I, together with the development of civil aviation in the 1920s and 1930s, made it clear that air power would play an important role in modern warfare. In December 1939, Britain and the Dominions—particularly Australia, New Zealand and Canada—entered into an agreement for air crews to be trained for service with the Royal Air Force (RAF).

Under this plan, known as the Empire Air Training Scheme, Prime Minister Robert Menzies agreed to provide 28,000 personnel over three years, all of whom would do at least their initial training in Australia. In October 1939, Menzies proudly asserted that 'it is no wonder that at this hour of suspense, or real peril, and of supreme effort, Great Britain should have turned to her children, the Dominions, and to us perhaps not least of all.'

In September 1939 there were 3489 officers and airmen in uniform, manning twelve flying squadrons with a total of 246 aircraft. Of the planes, 164 were operational, though many were obsolescent. To meet the numbers Menzies had committed Australia to supplying, the RAAF understood it would have to cast its net wide and ignore the limitations of the Military Board's memorandum. Accordingly, it began to enlist Aborigines and Torres Strait Islanders.

On 7 and 8 December 1941, Japan invaded Malaya and almost simultaneously attacked Pearl Harbor, bringing the United States into the war. Although *The Balonne Beacon* had been reporting the efforts of Australian airmen fighting with the Royal Air Force in Europe, and the efforts of Australian soldiers in the Middle East, these moves brought the conflict closer to home.

Before Christmas 1941, the paper reminded readers that all Australian men who attained the age of eighteen years on or after 1 July 1941, were 'required to enrol within 30 days of the publication of this notice or within 30 days of attaining the age of 18 years'. Len and Jim were eager to enlist, but first they had to wait for the recruitment train.

PART TWO

SKY HIGH

GUNAGALAGA NGARRIBAA

I had this inner drive to succeed . . . I don't honestly know where this came from, but it was always there—striving, striving, and striving to better myself . . .

—Michael O'Loughlin, Sydney Swans Indigenous legend, author, *Micky O: Determination. Hard Work. And a Little Bit of Magic*

7

DIFFERENT DOORS

When the train finally chugged into the wool and wheat village of Thallon in early August 1942, Len and Jim Waters were not the only members of the family who were keen to meet it. Their father, Don, joined them on the 80-kilometre trip from St George. He might have been 44, but as a gun shearer, he easily made it through the medical examination. As Len remembered, 'He was passed as fit as we were.' Don qualified to join the part-time militia force.

There were two recruitment trains in Queensland, each with three coaches. One coach contained compartments for the recruiting sergeant and clerical staff, and a room for trade tests. The second coach was devoted to the medical officer accompanying the unit, with a waiting room, examination couches, and eye-testing facilities. The third coach was an administrative office. One Queensland paper noted that recruitment had been boosted by new aptitude intelligence tests, which assessed candidates on abilities such as the capacity to absorb instruction.

After they applied, Jim told his brother, 'We'll go away together just in case they don't take you in the air force and we can serve together.' But within a week, Len got the news he was waiting for. 'I got my call from the RAAF, so I enlisted straight off.' Jim was accepted for the militia. Since his two sons were now going to serve, Don Waters decided not to enlist.

In the previous year, while he waited for his eighteenth birthday, Len had developed physical strength and endurance. He had begun shearing but was not sorry now to leave the back-breaking work behind. Now, the idea that he might become a pilot seemed less improbable, even if remote.

The day before he and Jim were due to leave, they were in the backyard singing and mucking around with Grace's seven-year-old godson, Bill Saunders, when she suddenly called them to the back door. Don was about to head off shearing, and it was time to say their goodbyes. Bill watched as they embraced and began crying. Someone told him they were going off to war. 'Next morning, Mum woke us up to wave them goodbye as they climbed through the fence with swags on their backs to hitch a ride to Thallon to meet the troop train. They were my heroes.'

Over the next nineteen hours the steam locomotive passed through more than 20 stations on the South Western line, picking up new recruits at each stop. By the time it had wound through Toobeah, Goondiwindi and Cobba-Da-Mana, more than 200 young men toting swags were crowded into the carriages.

From Brisbane's Roma Street Station, the new recruits were bussed to No. 3 Recruiting Centre at the Exhibition Ground. Here they found doors to the three services—army, navy and air force. As Len recalled, 'I went in one door here [to the RAAF] and [Jim] went into another door there [to the militia].' It was the last time they would see each other for nearly three years.

That day, 24 August 1942, Len joined the RAAF ground staff as an aircraftman (AC). His enlistment papers show that to the question of whether he was a British subject, Len answered yes. To the question whether he was of 'pure European Descent', he also answered yes. He listed both his parents as 'Australian' and said his trade was 'shearer'. He added that he could 'make minor running repairs and can drive car'. Despite his ambitions, he could hardly be accused of pushing himself forward.

Jim, meanwhile, enlisted in the militia. At the time, members of the militia were confined to the defence of Australia and the territories of Papua and New Guinea. However, six months later, in February 1943, the federal government redefined 'Australia' as including New Guinea and adjacent islands. This compelled soldiers in the newly defined Citizen Military Forces (CMF) to serve with the regular army, the Australian Imperial Force (AIF), in the South West Pacific Area. Jim would officially become a private in the AIF on 24 April 1943.

When the two brothers enlisted, the Pacific War was on Australia's doorstep. Singapore had fallen, and on 19 February 1942 the port of Darwin had been bombed by Japanese planes, which left 252 Allied service personnel and civilians dead. On 3 March, Broome was strafed. In the months that followed, many towns in northern Australia, including Wyndham, Port Hedland, Derby, Darwin, Katherine, Townsville and Mossman, and Horn Island in Torres Strait, came under Japanese air attack. During 1942, Japanese forces also invaded the Philippines, Burma, Sumatra and the Dutch East Indies (Indonesia), then Rabaul, Lae and Salamaua in New Guinea.

With every reason to believe that Australia would be next, the armed forces had to change tack urgently. Until mid-1942, aircrew were still being trained under the Empire Air Training Scheme to be sent to Europe, leaving few to man Australian home defence squadrons. In March 1942, Prime Minister John Curtin asserted Australian independence from Britain and appealed to the United States for help in the 'struggle to save mankind'. In a speech that stirred the nation, he said Australia was 'committed, heart and soul, to total warfare', and noted that 'Our air force are in the Kingsford-Smith tradition'.

The previous month, the War Cabinet had reassessed the Empire Air Training Scheme and decided to continue it but retain enough aircrew in Australia to man home and Pacific-based squadrons; some experienced airmen would also be recalled from Europe. Soon Australian and American personnel were pouring into Queensland as plans for the defence of Australia and the conduct of the war in the Pacific were rapidly implemented. In the event of invasion, the government was prepared to give away Western Australia, the Northern Territory, nearly all of Queensland and South Australia, and some of New South Wales. Accordingly, nearly all RAAF training bases were established in the flat country of south-eastern South Australia, Victoria and central–southern New South Wales. Even the flying boat base was in Lake Boga, Victoria, behind the so-called Brisbane Line.

Unexpectedly, the Japanese attacks caused a backlash against Aborigines, with a widespread belief that they were likely to side with any Japanese invasion force. Many Aborigines were relocated to 'control camps', and restrictions were placed on their movements, especially those of women. Word spread that there were orders to shoot Aborigines should an invasion take place. Yet Arnhem Land Aborigines formed a special reconnaissance unit in defence against the Japanese.

Having already suffered the loss of their lands through white invasion over the previous century, Indigenous Australians reacted with alarm to the potential loss of a country that had been solely theirs for more than 60,000 years. In World War I, about 1000 Indigenous Australians had signed up. This number increased sharply in World War II, with about 4000 Aborigines and Torres Strait Islanders enlisting. For all of them, war service meant the chance of new horizons. For some, enlisting meant the chance of equal pay and escape from entrenched discrimination. Serving in the armed forces was a statement of citizenship, a political statement that they belonged to Australia and indeed, that Australia belonged more to them than to any white man.

The Waters family would have seen the alarm reported in newspapers. Just a month before the brothers turned up at the recruitment train, the Minister for the Army, Frank Forde, spoke of how Queensland had assumed the 'greatest importance' in the nation's war strategy because the Japanese southward advance had approached closer to that state than to any other part of Australia. The Japanese bases in New Guinea and at Rabaul were at Queensland's doorstep, and all eyes in Australia were turned there. Forde went on to say:

> *We cannot allow ourselves a moment of self-satisfaction until the Japanese are driven from these and other northern bases they have conquered. In all our war preparation we must adopt an offensive and aggressive attitude. We must be prepared not only to defend Australia but to drive the Japanese back. We must be prepared for several years of war, because undoubtedly great struggles are still ahead for the Pacific theatre as well as in other zones.*

Two months earlier, the Darling Downs newspaper *The Pittsworth Sentinel* succinctly outlined the danger and the needed response from Queensland men:

> *Every available fit man, between the ages of 18 and 50, is required, if Queensland is to fulfil its obligation in meeting the RAAF drive for ground staff under the air force expansion plan. Thousands of men are required in order that our pilots in their Kittyhawks will be kept in the sky, to keep out the Japanese invader. Not since the introduction of the air training scheme has the demand for ground staff been so great or so urgent, and no man outside of the forces at the present time can afford to fail to respond to the call.*

Len Waters' motivations were undoubtedly many. A lack of education would likely see him destined to work as a farm labourer or shearer, with little prospect of breaking out of the mould that determined the lives of Aborigines at the time. The war offered a way out. While Waters was a self-described 'flag-waver', he did not enlist in the RAAF 'for the glamour or the glory of it'.

On his enlistment documents, he undertook to serve in the RAAF unconditionally, 'at home or abroad for the duration of the war'. He accepted that should he fail the necessary tests for mechanic, he was 'prepared to accept any musterings for which I am considered suitable'. His fervent hope was that, given this chance, he just might get to fly. This was his dream, but for now he was just service number 78144.

8

THE ERK

Two days after he enlisted, Waters sat for an aptitude test for RAAF ground staff. He needed to show his mettle, but he'd have been happy just to sweep the tarmac. He need not have worried: a score of 64 out of 100 deemed him suitable for aircraft maintenance training. Unknown to him, that same day the RAAF recruitment office contacted the Queensland police in Brisbane, seeking a background check on Waters. The Special Branch replied next day that he had 'no record'. Cleared of any criminal record, Waters had to pass through initial induction and drilling at the Queensland coastal city of Maryborough.

Between April 1942 and June 1945, the depot provided basic training to about 4000 recruits. For two weeks, Waters was one of these, rising early each day to adjust to military routines and discipline: marching, saluting, drills, parades, physical training and unarmed combat. If some rookies took a while to acclimatise to uncomfortable quarters and food a far cry from their mother's, Waters was not among them. Life in the bush had prepared him well to deal with rough conditions.

Next, he appeared before a Categorisation Board. With his experience working on his father's cars and trucks, Waters had no hesitation in deciding what he would apply for. 'I was always mechanically minded. We used to do all our own maintenance work. I put in for flight mechanic. I thought that would be something, thinking ahead again, for the future.' He was sent to Sydney to undergo a tech course at No. 3 School of Technical Training, in the inner-city suburb of Ultimo. Arriving in September 1942, Waters spent the next two months studying the technical detail of how engines worked.

Waters was billeted in the Oceanic Hotel, fronting Coogee beach. Special trams ran between the beach and Broadway to take the trainees to and from the school six days a week. For a boy from outback Queensland, the swift change in his fortunes was dramatic. 'If there hadn't been a war on, you couldn't get a better holiday, in the Oceanic Hotel, right on Coogee beach,' he remembered.

But if he found the tech course easy and staying in Sydney a revelation, there were nonetheless challenges he had not counted on. Foremost among these was the RAAF's daily fitness regime, run by a trainer, Warrant Officer McDowell. Waters thought him 'a physical fitness idiot'. At 5 a.m. each day, McDowell ordered the recruits to run up and down the beach in the still chilly mornings of early spring. 'Then you had to swim out to the shark net and back. It was pretty cold in Sydney. Just before we left, one morning we went down and it was low tide, we looked out at the shark net at what was left of it, there were holes that white pointers could have swum through, and we had to swim out there in the morning!'

Finishing the course, in mid-November 1942 Waters transferred to No. 1 Engineering School, which had been hurriedly established at the Melbourne Showgrounds in Ascot Vale. There, he began learning what the work of a flight mechanic involved. He thrived on the hands-on experience. 'It came pretty easy to me, the flight mechanics course.' The final test involved dismantling and reassembling a Tiger Moth engine, blindfolded. There was no room for mishaps, but the challenge did not faze Waters. 'When you dismantled it, it was all systematic, spread out on the bench, you just had to put it together in the right order. It wouldn't go—no nuts were tightened. It was a pretty fair sort a test. Pity some of the mechanics today don't have to do it.'

In his final examination, Waters achieved 74 per cent and graduated from the course as a flight mechanic in January 1943. From there he was sent to No. 2 Operational Training Unit, Mildura, arriving in late February. He found an inland town utterly different from St George, one that was planned and beautifully laid out. It had a wealth of shops, high standard of housing, broad avenues, and an up-to-date Workers' Club, the social centre for the district.

The RAAF base was situated about six kilometres out of town, growing out of a small regional aerodrome. By RAAF standards, the base was impressive. While barracks accommodation was basic but adequate, maintenance and repair facilities were extensive, and the recreation facilities were better than most. This was at a time when the base was operating at peak capacity as a conversion unit for graduating pilots, and Waters' training meant the chance to work on aircraft ranging from the American Curtiss P-40 Kittyhawk fighter to the American Vultee Vengeance dive bomber, the British Avro Anson light bomber, the Australian designed and built Boomerang fighter, the legendary British Supermarine Spitfire fighter and the British Airspeed Oxford utility monoplane.

At the same time, the Japanese grip on the war was being slowly loosened. By March 1943, a renewed Japanese attempt to strengthen their hold in New Guinea by seizing Wau had failed. With Papua and Guadalcanal secure, the Allies' chief concern was now Rabaul, the Japanese bastion in New Britain. Although the Allied air forces had begun to dominate the air, the Japanese army and navy air forces were yet to be mastered. The air force remained the key to victory but the American General Douglas MacArthur, the Supreme Commander of the South West Pacific Area, considered that: 'The air force as now constituted is not sufficient to support the offensive which is contemplated.' It was clear the war would not be over any time soon.

Not long after arriving at Mildura, Waters became aware of 'a rumour going around' that there were going to be re-musters from ground staff to aircrew and 'anyone who was interested could apply to transfer. All the fellas born with a silver spoon in their mouths, the upper crust, they were getting scarce.' It could not be said that Waters was one of these. Looking back, Waters conjectured that airmen mostly came from country areas. About 75 per cent were either farmers and horsemen or bank clerks. He thought the farmers most likely became the bomber pilots. Possibly because of a calmer temperament, the clerks were the fighter pilots.

But the call for re-mustering to aircrew meant he now had the chance he had long dreamed of. He had spent months mastering skills and knowledge necessary to keep the RAAF's fighters in the air, but circumstances were conspiring in his favour to go one step further. The boy who had run along the banks of the Moonie River could finally envisage himself sitting in the cockpit of a fighter aircraft. This was his opportunity and he had to grab it with both hands.

Unknown to Waters was a change of policy brought about by the heavy demand the war placed on Australia's ability to supply aircrew. A relaxation in educational standards was introduced for entry into the Empire Air Training Scheme. In 1939 there were 670,000 Australian men aged between eighteen and 28, of whom only 16.4 per cent had a state intermediate certificate or better. Calculations showed Australia could only produce 6000 men annually with the intermediate certificate who were fit to hold aircrew certificates. Alarmed, Prime Minister Menzies argued that 'to obtain numbers, rigid educational qualifications will have to be abandoned and selection made in the first instance on personal characteristics.'

While the scheme was initially established to train Australian recruits to fly with the Royal Air Force in the war in Europe and the Middle East, the war in the Pacific dramatically widened the crisis and the need for trained aircrews to defend Australia against Japanese attacks. Thus official RAAF policy focused less on well-educated young men from wealthy backgrounds; instead, it became possible for a stockman or shearer without the intermediate certificate, but who was clearly bright and displayed potential, to join aircrew. Under intense pressure to meet the demand for aircrew, the RAAF's image as the elite of the three services became more socially representative of Australia. For many, it was a matter of right time, right place.

Waters sensed that if he applied himself to night study he might make it into aircrew. It was just as well he didn't drink, as it meant he was not tempted to join his mates when they went to the pub in Mildura after work. Instead, apart from home leave, he swatted 'just about every night'. He knew it was the only way because, while entry standards had been lowered, leaving school before he reached the age of fourteen still left him at a disadvantage. 'I educated myself when I joined up in the ground staff. I became a flight mechanic, and I studied all the time. Lots of times when the other fellows were out on leave, I'd be over in the library, studying.'

His determination and application were paying dividends. He graduated as a Flight Mechanic, Aircraftman Class 2 (AC2), and was promoted to Leading Aircraftman (LAC) in April 1943. He was now, as ground staff were affectionately known, an 'erk' (from Cockney 'erkraft'). But he was not content to pore over engines; he wanted to fly the planes they powered.

In June, he applied for re-muster. This meant that he had to again answer questions about his 'nationality' and race.

Again he wrote 'yes' to both being a British subject and of European descent. He described both his parents as 'Australian'. He did not see the world through a narrow lens of race. And nor did the RAAF.

His aptitude test results for re-muster showed mixed results, reflecting his minimal education. What stood out was, not surprisingly, a mechanical aptitude. Above this, however, was an exceptional capacity for planning and designing, as the test results suggest Waters had an above-average spatial awareness—a necessary attribute for a pilot. To fly an aircraft requires a capacity to deal with multiple sources of incoming information—the more so for a pilot.

At his re-mustering interview, Waters' lack of schooling was noted, and his presentation was described as 'satisfactory' by one member of the panel, and 'a bit rough' by another. However, both found him to be keen and determined, one seeing him already as a pilot. 'Should make grade,' was the assessment on his interview form. The lowering of the educational standard, as foreshadowed by Menzies in 1939, gave Waters his chance. He grabbed it. He might not have to sweep tarmacs after all.

9

SOLO

Back to school again—and for the first time in his life Waters knew it was in his hands to make a dream a reality. It was up to him—an Aboriginal boy from the Queensland bush training to be a RAAF pilot. The odds were against him.

Without knowing it, Waters was charting a course that was unique. Becoming a pilot had a momentum all of its own; what it symbolically represented for Indigenous Australians was beyond his thinking. In a time of war, his choice was not a political act; rather, it was driven by the strongest of influences: motivation to achieve a goal that coalesced with the defence of his country. And he needed to prove himself.

While the story of Indigenous Australians for the previous century had been one of dispossession, subjugation and demoralisation, the Waters family had been determined to break through.

Don and Grace knew well that Aboriginal families were regarded as second-class citizens, but they were determined not to be kept back by this. While they were careful about their position in the community, they did not see themselves as second class, and this pride and self-confidence they instilled in their children. Excellence was a byword. Waters' parents had given him the platform on which to build self-belief. From childhood, he had shown confidence and determination; Jim Wolfe had recognised it at Nindigully and so, too, had the RAAF.

An overnight train journey from Mildura to Melbourne and a waiting transport took Waters to 1 Initial Training School (1 ITS) Somers, on the Mornington Peninsula, overlooking Westernport Bay and Phillip Island. High above tidal mud flats and mangroves, Somers had been established in 1940 to provide ground training for potential aircrew, which included not just pilots but also navigators, engineers, wireless air gunners and bomb aimers for the multi-engined bombers in the war in Europe. By now, the Empire Air Training Scheme was a well-oiled production line churning out increasing numbers of aircrew to man aircraft being manufactured for the war effort.

When Waters marched into Somers on 2 August 1943, that same production line seemed rather basic. It was mid-winter, and with the wind blowing in from Bass Strait, it was bitterly cold. A canvas tent housing three trainees was to be his home for the next three months. For a bed, he had a fold-up stretcher and a straw palliasse as a mattress. The local newsagent did a healthy trade, as a thick layer of newspapers spread on the bed under the palliasse helped prevent some of the cold seeping up from the floor in the dormitory huts. There was no privacy in the ablution huts, but whatever scruples the trainees had soon disappeared. Waters, who had spent many nights sleeping under the stars, took it in his stride. He was used to hardship and, as a country boy, felt some advantage.

At Somers, Waters' LAC rank was automatically downgraded to the student rank of AC2. This again placed him at the bottom of the RAAF hierarchy and meant his pay was cut to six shillings a day. The serious business of learning to fly began firmly on the ground. In the classroom, the trainees began instruction in the physics of flight and the familiarisation of aviation in general. They were issued with the RAAF's 359-page aircrew conversion handbook for Initial Training Schools, which had been prepared by the Royal Air Force. This was an intensive and highly technical book that covered every aspect of flight, from such subjects as electrical circuits to meteorology and the principles of flight. There was considerable detail to absorb and problems to solve with advanced mathematics and an understanding of the physics of flying. There were lectures and more lectures covering meteorology, navigation, Morse Code and law and administration.

As part of their aviation familiarisation, trainees also were introduced to the Link trainer—a flight simulator which trained pilots in instrument flying. This was all good practice for flying blind. While the Link was quite primitive, it was regarded as an extremely useful adjunct. From the outside, it looked like a big box, completely enclosing the user. It could be made to perform like a plane that the user had to control by simply using the instruments in front of him. This provided a safe environment for practice and more practice.

Topping this off was relentless physical training and instruction on armaments, gas defence, first aid and hygiene, followed by long, tough route marches and more saluting, drills and parades to ensure individuality morphed into a state of corporate unity. Drill sergeants did their best to make the rookies feel they were the lowest form of life. As one trainee recalled, 'It was from some drill sergeants that many of us learned new expletives and new obscenities. They had acquired a reputation for roughness and crudity, and most of them did their best to live up to it.' In their spare time, trainees could play in sporting competitions for rugby union, tennis and cricket, all of which Waters enjoyed. In many ways he was a model student; he was too serious about what lay ahead to break rules.

After two months of initial flight training, and examinations on ground subjects, Waters faced the Categorisation Board, whose task it was to select the category of aircrew in which he would continue training. The exam results no doubt played a significant part in category selection. 'I knew that I was holding my own with the majority of fellas who had transferred to aircrew and that when I went before the Board, I was keen to prove myself in every part of the course.' One of those was Morse Code. 'The required standard was eighteen words a minute—32 words a minute on key and eighteen words a minute on visual with the Aldis lamp. I reached the required standard after two weeks and of course I was doing other subjects while the other blokes were still practising.'

Waters prayed he would be chosen as a pilot; being a navigator or wireless air gunner held no attraction. 'And of course everyone wanted to be a pilot. You might be the brightest student on the course but you could quite easily finish up a tail gunner, a WAG, because everything that you do while you're there is taken note of.'

The night before he was to appear at the Categorisation Board, a boxing tournament was scheduled, and Waters had entered. He was down to fight a flight-sergeant drill instructor when he received a timely warning from one of his mates, Wally McKenzie, who had re-mustered with him from Mildura. 'He was a fantastic mate of mine, and he was in my corner that night,' Waters said. McKenzie told him to be careful of his opponent.

> *He had a few tickets on himself, and apparently he wasn't a bad pug and I had to fight him this night. He was a middleweight, the same weight as me, but I thought it was only an exhibition bout, like most of the bouts were. They were mostly four-round bouts. Wally McKenzie said to me, 'You think this is going to be an exhibition match only, don't you?'*
>
> *I said I'd been led to believe it was.*
>
> *[McKenzie replied:] 'This flight sergeant got his mates to put money on him. Just watch him'.*
>
> *I said, 'Well, what have you done?' And he said, 'I've had fifteen quid on you.'*
>
> *Fifteen quid in those days was quite a bit of money. His mother owned a few properties around the Riverina area, so he wasn't short of a quid.*

Any rate, we went out and this fellow tried to put me away in the first two or three punches and as it so happened he finished up on the sick parade the next morning.

That same morning the triumphant Waters waited his turn before the Categorisation Board. Because his name began with 'w', he was one of the last. As he waited, three of his mates said to him, 'You'll be one of the first to be picked as a pilot.' He replied that he couldn't see it, 'because I wasn't born with a silver spoon in my mouth.' When he was called before the Board, the commanding officer asked him, 'Now, Waters, I see here that you mastered Morse Code in half the time. Is there any reason for that? Are you keen on becoming a wireless [operator/air] gunner?' Waters felt a growing alarm and replied, 'No, Sir, I just wanted to prove myself in every category, every subject.'

He feared his proficiency at Morse Code could ironically bring him undone because it would naturally point him in the direction of wireless air gunner. News of the fate of so many men who had joined RAF Bomber Command had filtered back from the air war in Europe, and he had no desire to be 'chopped to pieces' by enemy fighters nor have his remains hosed out of a shredded bomber turret. The CO continued:

'Have you ever considered yourself a wireless air gunner?'

I said, 'No.' He said, 'Just close your eyes and just sit there and imagine yourself sitting in the tail of a Halifax or a Lancaster [bomber] with four .303s in front of you.'

> *'Well,' he said, 'how do you look?' I said, 'I've got a very disappointed look on my face, sir!'*

Waters left the interview worried. His desire to be a pilot was overarching. There was a widely held view, noted by a British RAF officer posted to Australia in 1943, that 'the pilot is considered the "King Pin" and the rest of the crew stooges. Therefore, all aircrew trainees are obsessed with the idea of becoming a pilot or nothing.' Waters wanted to be his own 'King Pin'.

There was great trepidation at Somers next day when the Station Standing Orders were put up on the notice board. Wagers had been placed about who would be categorised as pilot. Waters was pessimistic and bet against himself, with three £5 wagers on the outcome. 'A bloke from Canada said to me, "You'll be right, you'll be one of the first pilots picked." I said, "I don't know. I've got no confidence." He said, "I'll bet you. I'll bet you a fiver!" and a couple of others did too. I lost fifteen quid over it, but I was the third one picked.' At least he was now on track to the higher pay that would come with graduation.

Water's coordination test may well have been a deciding factor, as he was naturally agile and did well at any type of sport. Boxing in particular would have been instrumental in developing speed in eye–hand coordination, and this would have been a significant help in the flight simulator. His spatial perception had been honed by living a life largely outdoors. His Kamilaroi culture gave him an appreciation of the connection between the sky, the stars and the country, thereby sharpening his situational awareness.

These were attributes tailor-made for flying. His examination results underlined his mastery of key aviation subjects, in which he scored well above average. In signals as well as aircraft recognition he scored 100 per cent, while in meteorology he scored 88 per cent. However, in maths and science he scored a bare minimum 50 per cent and 54 per cent, undoubtedly reflecting his lack of secondary schooling.

While the majority of the navigators and wireless air gunners departed Somers for further training in Canada en route to Britain and Bomber and Coastal Commands, the remaining trainees stayed for the third and final month, having been marked for pilot training. Waters was ecstatic. 'I dreamed about it. It was something I never thought was possible. Considering where I'd come from, my background, I just didn't think it was possible for me to become a pilot.'

Indeed, his instructors were giving him the benefit of the doubt. He knew he lacked confidence, and this was reflected in his report at the end of eight weeks that found his ability, 'average minus' and that he 'lacked smartness'. He was also seen as a collaborator rather than a leader, but in this report, as in all others, 'keen and hard working'. The one score on which he recorded above average was 'persistence'. This would be a consistent trait in his RAAF career.

Instructors were encouraged to rate each trait using the principle of a 'normal distribution'—that is, most of the grades were expected to cluster around the average, with fewer at each extreme. Within the select group that represented aircrew trainees, a finding of 'average' would likely be well above average in the general population. The Board had no doubt of Waters' potential as a pilot.

On 10 November 1943, Waters walked through the gates of 8 Elementary Flying Training School (8 EFTS). He had travelled north to the old town of Narrandera, on the Murrumbidgee River in the Riverina, where, three years earlier, a RAAF air school had been established on the site of the present airport. He was part of Course 44. Narrandera was part of a network of RAAF training bases on the vast flat plain during the war, along with flying training schools at Wagga Wagga, Uranquinty, Temora and Deniliquin. It was here he would step into an aeroplane and take the controls for the first time, and here he would go solo.

Narrandera provided a twelve-week introductory flying course. Fundamental to it was preparation for the stress of warfare; the training would instil the type of situational dilemma that a pilot might face. Human error could be fatal. Skills needed to be practised and honed relentlessly. At the same time, psychological, physical and cognitive abilities would be assessed at heightened levels to increase survivability in moments of crisis. Trainees were pushed to the point where their endurance and mental toughness were tested daily.

Waters was introduced to flying training in two stages: the first comprised four weeks of instruction, which included ten hours of flying with an instructor to assess pilot suitability. He knew he had to pass this grading process if he was to undergo a further eight weeks of training. This would include 65 hours of flying in the de Havilland Tiger Moth DH82—with a top speed of just 175 kilometres per hour. On these reliable and forgiving

1930s biplanes he learned the basics of flying. The first step was to become familiar on the ground with the cockpit, controls and taxiing. Then it was taking to the air.

On 16 December, Waters flew for the first time. An instructor, Flight Sergeant Teddy Williams, showed him how the aircraft was controlled and manoeuvred. Communication between him and the instructor was basic, with a tube between the two cockpits linking them. Words spoken into the tube at one end fed into earpieces fitted inside the other's flying helmet, the results being surprisingly clear for such a simple and rudimentary system. For Waters, the experience was a revelation as he learned take-off and landing, straight and level flying, climbing, gliding and stalling, and turns, all in preparation for going solo.

If finally being airborne was the consummation of his childhood dreams, having to deal with Williams was another issue altogether. As was his duty and responsibility, Williams was a no-nonsense instructor, drumming correct procedure into his trainees. Mistakes could not be tolerated; there was no room for error when flying. Waters, who did not yet fully understand this, thought Williams abrasive. 'He was the greatest ear-basher of all time and at times, when we got out of the plane, he'd get out of one side of the cockpit and I'd get out the other side because he'd ear-bash me that much I wasn't game to walk [with him], because I felt like attacking him because he attacked me with words up in the air.' If only through gritted teeth, Williams clearly had his attention.

After less than nine hours with Williams, Waters prepared for his first solo flight on 29 December. He could have asked for no better Christmas present. Just how he would have approached the occasion can perhaps be gauged by the experience of his future squadron leader, Perth-born Dick Sudlow, who described his own first flight at 1 EFTS Parafield, in South Australia:

Taxi to the downwind end of the airfield.

Set the elevator trim and turn into the wind.

Open the throttle slowly but steadily with a little forward pressure on the control column until the tail wheel was off the ground.

When flying speed reached, stick back slowly until airborne and climb away at climbing speed.

Turn left and reduce throttle to cruising speed.

Turn left again and fly downwind, not too far from the boundary fence.

When past the downwind fence, turn left and then left again, facing into the wind.

Approach the airfield gently, slowly reducing speed and height.

Ease off the throttle as you go over the boundary fence.

Stick back gently until you reach what you hope is the right height off the ground.

Close the throttle and stick right back.

Pray.

Waters could hardly wait to go solo. On the day, however, he had to cool his heels while another of the three trainees under Williams' command went before him. 'It was a toss-up which one of us would go first, and young Carter, he beat me. All you do in your first solo was a few circuit bumps—and he beat me by about 10 minutes.' Having two older brothers had honed Waters' competitiveness.

During the three months of summer, the trainees spent as much time in the classroom as they did at the airfield. They completed the course with a flying test and examinations on all their ground subjects. Generally, they flew over the Riverina plain in the triangle between Narrandera, Temora and Wagga Wagga. And they soon came to understand that flying biplanes in the height of summer in inland Australia presented its own challenges. A hot tarmac brought with it rising heat as the temperature rose over the day. For the Tiger Moth, this meant that its large wing surface area was subject to thermals, making it tricky to land. Flying training thus had to be conducted in the early morning.

Having made it to Narrandera did not guarantee further pilot training. The scrub rate at elementary training schools was around 50 per cent. Of those who did not make it, most were given the opportunity to train as navigators or wireless air gunners. Those who remained continued to have aspects of flying drilled into them, part dual, part solo. They did forced-landing practice as a priority, and then, after 20 hours' flying experience, they undertook their first cross-country flight with an instructor.

As the course neared completion, Waters sat for ground examinations. Among the results, he scored 89 per cent for airmanship, 86 per cent for his engine knowledge, 61 per cent for theory of flight, and just 45 per cent for navigation. Overall, his flying aptitude was average, with instrument flying above average. His qualities found to be above average were persistence, endurance, enterprise and distribution of attention. What this meant was that he kept on trying, he consistently performed under conditions of stress, would try things on his own and was able to do more than one thing at a time. This was an improvement on his Somers' report. As previously noted in the RAAF reports, he was seen as a collaborator rather than a leader. As such, the report did not see him as a potential flying instructor—not that he wanted to be.

One examiner observed: 'This pupil started the course very under confident but has since worked very hard and has improved his flying considerably. Attained the required standard.' Another commented: 'This pupil is of a very quiet manner and is very determined to fly. At no time did he display signs of over-confidence, completing his course through sheer determination and hard work. He was slow to absorb instruction at first, although no sequence proved too difficult for him. His behaviour has been very satisfactory during the course.'

In his final report, there was one ticked box that stood out above all else for Waters: after three months and 41 solo flights at Narrandera, newly promoted Leading Aircraftman (LAC) Waters was recommended for further pilot training.

10

UTOPIA

When Waters arrived at 5 Service Flying Training School at Uranquinty on 13 February 1944, the summer sun was baking the Riverina plain and the lure of the Murrumbidgee River at nearby Wagga Wagga was hard to pass up. There were always RAAF trucks available to take the trainees to the river, where they could spend the full day swimming and generally relaxing on the broad, sandy beach.

As one of Waters' contemporaries at Uranquinty, Leigh Hindley, recalled, the kitchen staff would supply them with steak and sausages for a barbecue. 'On return to the base, most of the trainees would spend two or three hours studying the ground subjects in which we had to be proficient and capable of success in the final examinations.'

The trainees were generally in their late teens or early twenties on arrival at Uranquinty, which boasted a railway station and siding, a local bush pub and one store. It was wheat and sheep country, and in summer the days were hot, dry and dusty, with fearsome dust storms turning day into night. Nearby Wagga Wagga, the largest town in the area, provided numerous attractions, from the cinema to dances and pubs. It drew the boys not just from Uranquinty but also from the RAAF base at Forest Hill.

There were some 2000 personnel at Uranquinty, including around 100 WAAFs (Women's Auxiliary Air Force) learning trades and working in administration or as nurses in the hospital. Base romances naturally occurred. All RAAF aircrew trainees had a white flash on the front of their forage caps, indicating that they were 'fliers in the making'. Ground crew staff strongly objected to this, probably because local girls, as well as those on the base, tended to favour the flying boys. Their response was to spread the story that the white flash meant the wearer had VD, so keep clear! The ground staff had their ways.

With Somers and Narrandera behind him and sporting a white flash on his cap, Waters was by now growing in confidence. He knew Uranquinty was about just one thing: to train pilots for single-engine service aircraft. He believed he had won respect 'to a certain extent' and had not struck any hostility because of his Aboriginal heritage. 'Never, never once. I'm not blowing my bags out, but I was always up with the top,' he would recall. He was within grasp of being presented with his pilot wings to become a fully qualified pilot.

The days were long, starting at 7.30 a.m. and finishing at 5 p.m. Waters had to make the adjustment to the new training aircraft, the Wirraway—a very different beast from the much gentler Tiger Moth. Wirraway, fittingly an Aboriginal word for 'challenge', was the first aircraft off the blocks for the new, privately owned Commonwealth Aircraft Corporation (CAC), and was a licence-built derivative of the American NA-16 trainer.

Fitted with a 600-horsepower Pratt & Whitney nine-cylinder air-cooled radial engine, it was a monoplane with a top speed of 354 kilometres per hour—twice as fast as the Tiger Moth. It had vices that the Tiger Moth did not, which had to be taken into account with the unsealed runways. As Dick Sudlow saw it, the Wirraway was a 'truly excellent advanced aircraft', being reasonably straightforward to fly. 'But if you were careless or heavy-handed it could react nastily. I believe if you could fly a Wirraway well, you could fly any other single-engined aeroplane of the time.'

By April 1944, there were 128 Wirraways available for training at Uranquinty, and Waters flew virtually every day, dividing his time between the airfield and lessons on the ground. Not all of his new instructors were immediately impressed with his flying skills. When he was tested nine days into the course, an instructor found that he 'lets aircraft swing in take-off' and that he 'doesn't seem to understand use of trim'. He showed 'poor judgement' by forgetting 'vital actions before landing'. A day later, he had 'improved slightly', but the next day, when he made his first solo test, the instructor was blunt: 'Needs a good kick in the pants to help him along. Appears to have the ability, but not the will to get along.' Nonetheless, it was a 'fair effort' for his first solo in a Wirraway. As for all trainee pilots, instructors did not mince words; the outcome was too critical.

It was at Uranquinty that Waters got to know Sergeant Frank Smith, who was also on Course 44. They would become friends as their training progressed. Another of his mates from Uranquinty was future Squadron Leader Ron Guthrie, who, likewise, had to overcome a lack of formal school education. A year younger than Waters, Guthrie had been 'a trouser salesman with Gowing Brothers in Sydney' before joining the air force. He was on Course 45, a month behind Waters.

Many years later, Guthrie remembered Waters as someone who stood out. 'He was Aboriginal and a bloody nice bloke, a striking sort of bloke, well-built and very popular. He did his job well, and was renowned as a nice fellow to get along with. He and I were mates for the short time I knew him while on the same base. There was no discrimination between him and the rest of the fellows.' After learning the basics of flying, Guthrie also thought that while Wirraways were quite advanced compared with Tiger Moths, they would 'flick on command' and this could easily lead to trouble:

> *If you were a bit harsh on the controls and on landing, if you pulled the stick back a bit too hard you would drop a wing and a lot of people had accidents in that regard. Particularly at night, the tendency was to hang the aircraft up at about ten feet, keep pulling the stick back, and down would go one wing. A co-pupil of mine did that, the port wing dropped and he cartwheeled down the flare-path. You couldn't trim a Wirraway to fly hands-off—there was no aileron trim—it only*

had elevator and rudder trims, and the ailerons had to be set just right by the mechanic on the ground. If they weren't they'd start to roll and of course you had to hand fly it all the time.

The Murrumbidgee River was a natural navigation aid, as was an isolated hill at The Rock, a village close to Uranquinty. These were useful visual markers for rookie fliers. Even so, Waters found it difficult to establish his bearings for the first few weeks. By mid-April he had clocked up 28 solo flights. His struggle to master the Wirraway and develop his knowledge of the local environment through map reading was a challenge. As his examiner, with an irreverent turn of phrase, concluded:

Didn't set an accurate course to begin with and didn't see some very outstanding pinpoints. Doesn't seem to have much idea of what he's doing and trusts in J.C. [Jesus Christ] to get to destination . . . had to be saved from pruning pine trees . . . Mistook Culcairn for Henty for no apparent reason but woke up later on seeing rail and another a/c on course. Coming in to land lowered flaps in any old place and then turned in behind another a/c then bounced after overshooting . . . No dash, doesn't show any interest, slovenly and careless. Below average.

This was clearly an off day. Perhaps the proximity to pine trees shook Waters out of his lethargy. Over the next fortnight, his gradings came back to average or above. At the end of April, as the course concluded, Waters faced general assessment and a training report.

The RAAF was interested not only in his flying performance and aviation knowledge but also his character and potential. As foreshadowed in Menzies' 1939 letter, which referred to the need for selection of aircrew to be focused more on 'personal characteristics' than education, the Directorate of Training at RAAF Headquarters, Melbourne, developed a 'Personal Characteristics Assessments Rating Scale'.

While somewhat simplistic by today's standards, the internal RAAF pamphlet noted that the rating scale was 'now used widely in large scale commercial and industrial undertakings as one of the essential tools in personnel management.' The RAAF instructor would use the scale to rate aircrew trainees. Outlining the qualities that were considered necessary, the pamphlet laid out a means to rate their personal qualities. This consisted of several small scales each rating one quality or trait. The pamphlet continued:

> *Appearance and Bearing, Mental Alertness, Self Confidence, Initiative, Emotional Stability, Energy, Dependability, Leadership and Punctuality.*
>
> *Having decided on the traits each must be carefully described and defined so that it will mean the same to everybody using the scale. Giving the description in the form of a question sometimes avoids ambiguity.*

After aircrew selection had been narrowed to trainee pilot, the RAAF developed a more refined set of ten personality criteria against which each trainee would be measured.

These focused more on personality traits and in combination reflected characteristics that were thought essential for combat pilots. Behind the ordinariness of these traits lay the difference between a fighter or bomber pilot and the man in the street. Because Waters and other trainees were being compared with each other, being found average in any of these criteria was in fact far from average. These qualities were:

Persistence—Does he keep on trying or is he easily discouraged?
Sense of Responsibility—Has he common sense or is he over-confident?
Endurance—Does he put up a consistently satisfactory performance under conditions of strain?
Leadership—Has he taken the lead in any activities? Would he make a good captain of aircraft or flight leader?
Method—Does he work systematically to a plan?
Deliberation—Does he act decisively for reasons or on impulse?
Enterprise—Does he want to try things on his own?
Dash—Is he quick and decisive in action?
Distribution of Attention—Does he find it difficult to do more than one thing at a time?
Self-Control—Does he get flustered?

Overall, Waters' flying aptitude was rated average. On 'distinctive qualities', he was again rated average, although on two of these criteria measures he stood out as above average, for his sense of responsibility and self-control. Having attained the required standard, he was then suitable for advanced pilot training.

For the next two months he was posted to the Advanced Training Squadron at the same base. The serious practice of preparing for combat then began for the trainees, with the focus on instrument flying, night flying, formation flying, dive-bombing, strafing, low-level flying, dogfighting, aerial photography and aerobatics. This took its toll, as several trainees who struggled were cut from the course. The RAAF had laid down a set of criteria by which it made this judgement. If a rookie was deemed a 'failure to learn to fly', this was because he had been judged against what was coined 'flying faults'. These were assessed as: 'afraid of flying, easily flustered, lacks confidence, lacks enthusiasm or tightens up.' Waters came up favourably on these criteria.

At the conclusion of the second part of the course, Waters finished with an average flying aptitude on seven of the RAAF's nine criteria. He had stood out as above average on instrument flying and night flying. On his 'distinctive qualities', he was now rated as above average for persistence and endurance. His ability as a service pilot was rated at 423 out of 700. As his leadership ability was rated average, he was 'not at present recommended for a commission'.

Reflecting on his time at Uranquinty, Waters noted that he failed the first test on meteorology and astral navigation, but explained that all his 'other marks were so high and my flying skill was so good that they gave me an extra five days to study to bring it up.' Through this, he had passed on the second attempt. On the practical service training side, he had always been among the top students in subjects such as air frames and engines—subjects he had covered earlier in his flight mechanic days.

His good friend Wally McKenzie was a different case entirely. He had re-mustered with Waters at Mildura and travelled with him to Somers, Narrandera and then Uranquinty. A year older than Waters, McKenzie had been educated at Xavier College in Melbourne. He had failed three subjects, likely owing to some lifestyle choices. He needed a chance to repeat the exams. 'We used to call him "Shagger Flynn", being a double for Errol Flynn,' Waters recalled. 'Didn't he get the girls in! That's how he was. He was one of the boys who was out every night, he used to sneak out. But they knew that he knew the subjects and he waltzed it in.' McKenzie's war would lead him to 86 Squadron RAAF, flying Kittyhawks.

After four months, the summary of Waters' flying and assessment for Advanced Training School showed that, in classic military understatement, he had 'reached the required standard'. Of the 76 men on Course 44, 38 were 'scrubbed'—a 50 per cent failure rate—but Waters was among those who passed the standard for the coveted wings, a third of whom were re-musterings like himself. They were to be promoted to either the commissioned rank of pilot officer or the NCO rank of sergeant. The usual outcome was that 5 per cent would receive the commissioned rank and 95 per cent the NCO rank.

On a cold 4 July 1944, a day marked by thunderstorms and showers, Waters was promoted to the rank of sergeant. The graduation parade was an impressive ceremony, and Waters saluted proudly as he became a qualified RAAF pilot, presented with his wings by Group Captain Tom Curnow. He was not yet twenty. It was a rare moment, and not just in his life—he also understood its importance for his people. It did not escape him that graduating as a RAAF pilot was a far cry from where he had come from.

> *I was terribly keen to prove myself in the elite, which it is. There is no doubt about that. The flying part of the air force was the elite. Well, I was the coloured boy in it and I might add that they cut us down a bit. The end result when we got our wings there were only three blokes in front of me on my average. So, from my humble beginnings I was pretty proud of what I accomplished.*

That day's edition of the Wagga Wagga *Daily Advertiser* gave a foretaste of what he would soon face with a report from General MacArthur's headquarters of heavy air attacks on Japanese strongholds in the Dutch East Indies. The paper's editorial that day also carried a sharp reminder of how colour still mattered. 'There can be no doubt that the overwhelming mass of Australian sentiment is behind the idea of preserving this country as far as possible for people of British stock, or, as a secondary consideration, selected Europeans. That has been the objective since the earliest colonisation days, and it has been strengthened by the lesson of the United States with its negro and other minority problems.' Aborigines were outsiders—and were to remain so.

Two months later, Ron Guthrie also graduated from Uranquinty. 'To get through the final wings test, man, that was everything, that was utopia,' he recalled later. Waters felt the same elation; he had not only proven himself against the best and brightest but he had also succeeded in graduating as a pilot and being selected for training in a fighter. He had never wanted to be part of a crew, or to pilot a bomber.

> *As far as flying goes, it really did appeal to me to get into fighter aircraft because there was a point to be proven there. Whereas with the couriers and the bombers and the transports and all that, they were a crew. Right from Initial Training, everyone wanted to be a single-seated fighter pilot. It was always regarded as something special.*

A popular theory of 1940 was that, 'If you had large front teeth like "Smithy" and could ride a horse and bicycle, you were pilot material.' Large teeth and bicycles aside, the reality was that to make the grade as a fighter pilot a recruit had to show particular qualities: they had to be confident, assertive and competitive. Key traits were a love of aviation and flying from an early age and a love of driving vehicles of all kinds. This was aided by a capacity for rapid cognitive functioning, allowing for simultaneous inputs to be processed, prioritised and then acted on. While his confidence and assertiveness were there, but muted, Waters had demonstrated these traits. He possessed that quiet steel.

11

THE THRILL OF IT

Clive Caldwell was a swashbuckler. Not without reason, he had earned the nickname 'Killer'—a moniker he disliked. In the Middle East he had shot down 20 enemy aircraft, with a 21st shared with a fellow pilot. Awarded the Distinguished Flying Cross and Bar, he commanded No. 112 Squadron Royal Air Force (RAF) and was the outstanding ace of the Desert War. By the time the Pacific War was over, his tally would rise to a confirmed 27, with three shared. Of these, 22 were in a Kittyhawk, an aircraft he considered without vices and which was serviceable in harsh conditions and a variety of climates. It was not just his lethal prowess in the air that made Caldwell stand out: he was a fighter pilot fully equipped with all the cocky confidence, aggressive spirit, dash and skill of the traditional fighter ace. His modus operandi was 'Think fast—shoot first!'

In August 1943 he became chief flying instructor at 2 Operational Training Unit (OTU), Mildura. He was joined there by another Middle East RAAF air ace, Bobby Gibbes, who had been credited with ten air victories, and two shared, against enemy aircraft. After Gibbes arrived in January 1944, he and Caldwell were troubled by the failure rate of trainee fighter pilots at Mildura while undertaking a conversion course to Curtiss P-40 Kittyhawks, the front-line fighter flown by RAAF squadrons in the south-west Pacific.

The Kittyhawks were the only effective RAAF fighters throughout the fighting at Port Moresby and Milne Bay in 1942, the critical period when the Japanese Pacific advance was stopped, and were continuing to play a major role. The conversion course was thus critical in mastering the considerable firepower from its six .5-inch Browning machine guns fitted in the wings and its sizeable bomb load capacity. The Kittyhawk was capable of accurate dive-bombing and could absorb considerable battle damage and still keep on flying.

It became clear to instructors that several of the newly arrived pilots from RAAF service flying training schools were neither enthusiastic about being a fighter pilot nor being in a war zone. With this in mind, Caldwell and Gibbes began visiting the nearby service flying training schools to talk about the life of a combat fighter pilot. Their approach had an underlying purpose: to weed out the reluctant and identify the most promising. In effect, they were 'pre-selecting' those who would go on to 2 OTU. As a 'better class' of pilot began to come through, the failure rate dropped noticeably. This, again, was consistent with Menzies' 1939 edict that pilot selection be primarily based on personality ahead of other qualifications.

With his background, Caldwell knew that as Chief Instructor he was in a strong position to influence the new generation of fighter pilots. One trainee later recalled he had been in a classroom when Caldwell walked in unannounced, telling the lecturer that he would just sit at the back of the class and listen. In time, Caldwell asked to say a few words. He told the pilots they should listen closely to instructors, whose tactical experience had been gained the hard way—in combat. He stressed that they were never to forget that 'Rule number one for a fighter pilot is—stay alive! It costs a lot of money to train you, so you are valuable, and we can't afford to lose you. Don't try to be a bloody hero—stay alive!'

Caldwell believed in practising what he preached, and in early 1944 he was given command of No. 80 Fighter Wing, equipped with Spitfires, in Darwin. Essential though preparing new pilots for combat was, Caldwell had felt hobbled by not being in the front line. His departure meant that from March 1944, Bobby Gibbes took over as Chief Instructor at Mildura. So it was Gibbes who oversaw the final training that would make Waters combat ready. It is reasonable to assume that Waters was a beneficiary of the weeding-out approach that Caldwell and Gibbes adopted in the months before his arrival at Mildura.

But first, after gaining his wings, Waters was posted to the High Altitude Course at RAAF Station Bradfield, Sydney, to learn the effect of oxygen starvation at altitude. He passed the four-day course. He also spent three weeks at 8 OTU at Narromine, in western New South Wales, learning skip bombing and strafing in Wirraways. His marks varied. He was awarded 51 per cent for airmanship, but 98 per cent for intelligence and 94 per cent for meteorology and navigation. He was given a bare pass for operations and tactics, while on the question of character and leadership, he was awarded 52 per cent. 'This pilot though he appears keen enough is very dull. His flying is average and with more experience he should make a satisfactory pilot in a squadron,' wrote the acerbic OTU commanding officer. Again, Waters' determination shone through—along with his attitude of not pushing himself forward in dealing with officialdom.

Three days later, on 17 August 1944, Waters arrived at Mildura for the final step in his training: conversion to Kittyhawks. The first month of the course was again in Wirraways, with an instructor in the rear seat—not dissimilar from the last month at Uranquinty and the weeks at Narromine. The instructor explained tactics, encouraged and corrected Waters' performance, and provided continual instruction to hone aerial skills.

The initial training focused on dive-bombing, strafing, aerobatics and dogfighting. This involved two aircraft approaching each other head-on and, once passing, each would attempt to get on the other's tail in the 'kill' position. The rawness of the pilots' skills meant this was a potentially lethal experience, but in wartime it was probably unavoidable—it was their task to try to 'kill' each other every time they engaged in a practice dogfight.

Away from the skies, half-day lectures in the classroom concentrated on subjects such as meteorology, aerodynamics, navigation, gun sights and deflection shooting, which involved mastering gunfire during high-speed combat. For rookie pilots, there was nothing better than the thrill of working out trajectory and distance for shooting while actually airborne. It was a practice that Clive Caldwell had not only accidentally discovered while flying in North Africa, but had championed as an important training tool to increase the accuracy of aerial shooting. It was therefore part of the syllabus at Mildura.

Shadow shooting was practised over nearby Lake Victoria, a shallow natural freshwater lake in the Murray–Darling Basin. The process involved one aeroplane flying low over the lake, casting its shadow on the water. The attacking aircraft then used the shadow as a target and fired at it using deflection. The exercise allowed the pilot to see the splashes where the bullets hit the water, showing how far astray his judgement had been. However, there were mishaps, and in an attempt to reduce the training accidents at 2 OTU, pilots training over Lake Victoria were banned from going below 500 feet. Accidents continued to occur, and shadow shooting was scrapped.

The first month behind him, Waters was ready for the final step in the long preparation to become a fighter pilot: mastering the Kittyhawk. It was a single-cockpit aircraft and thus had no room for a co-pilot instructor. He was totally on his own. He had been well prepared on the ground, and clearance was only given when he was able to touch every control and instrument while blindfolded. As his ears filled with the roar of propellers after starting the engine and taxiing down the runway, what immediately struck him was the restricted forward vision owing to the Kittyhawk P-40E's long, in-line engine. There had been giant leaps from Tiger Moths and Wirraways, and now to going it alone in a Kittyhawk.

> *The top speed of a Tiger Moth is about 80 miles an hour, and you landed at 48 or 50 miles an hour. A Wirraway had a top speed of about 180 and you landed at about 80 miles an hour, which was your landing speed. But a Kittyhawk had a top speed of anything up to 300 . . . and you landed between 90 and 100, and the power of the motors, that first take off! I tell you what, you feel the surge of power when you open the throttle, but the thrill of it . . . for the first time. It's a fantastic lift! After the initial take-off, you find out they are not the monsters that you first think they are. After the first take-off everything seemed to be a piece of cake.*

In this euphoria, overconfidence was the hidden enemy. The instructors knew it, and warned the Kittyhawk rookies to take care. Waters heard the message.

> *They said, 'After four hours, you get overconfident and careless.' And they said it is a well-established fact that that's when the accidents happen. And it is amazing. Between four and six hours we had eight prangs even though we'd been warned. I was one of the lucky ones that didn't.*

On 7 September, Waters was at the Mildura strip when one of his fellow rookies, Norman Powell, took to the air in a Kittyhawk. As he prepared to land, the engine began to misfire. In preparing for a second landing, the aircraft spun into the ground. Powell died instantly, and the aircraft was totally destroyed. Waters recalled the tragedy:

> *He came in to land and realised that he'd overshot the field. But instead of doing the correct thing and going right around in a circuit, he thought he'd do a quick bank and turn and she just flicked over and went straight in. He wasn't high enough to get out. Around Mildura, with all those sand dunes, there wasn't five foot of the tail sticking out. It went straight into the sand. That shook us up a little bit. He was a popular boy.*

The P-40E in which Powell died was typical of the Kittyhawks used for training. It had seen combat and suffered damage before being sent to 2 OTU. These aircraft were inevitably subject to further damage during training mishaps. As Dick Sudlow saw it during his time as an instructor at Mildura, training was 'a regular exercise in risk' and this meant that the accident rate was 'possibly higher than at most other types of training units'.

Waters knew this first-hand when he 'almost bought it' in battle practice over Mildura. In squadron formation, he and other rookie pilots did a battle climb to 18,000 feet before pairing off and practising dogfighting with cameras. He paired off with a good mate, Joe Smith:

> *We were having a whale of time. He got onto my tail right away, and I flipped around and got onto his tail and gave him a couple of bursts.*

He was trying to get inside me because you have to lay off flexion when you're trying to shoot at anything. He was trying to get his nose in front of me and I kept keeping inside.

He got on my tail and I was trying to shake him off. I got into as tight a turn as I could, right over on my side, the wings vertical to the ground. It was such a perfect turn that I kept entering my slipstream as he was trying to get inside of me.

All of a sudden it flipped over and I brought it back around again and I looked in the rear vision mirror and he was back on my tail, so I whipped inside him and I thought, well, I'll do it the other way. So I did a reverse turn and I went around and he kept on my tail . . . he came around onto me and got inside me again and all of a sudden, my aircraft did something that I wouldn't like to go through again—it was one of the most hair-raising things that ever happened to me.

Waters found himself in an inverted spin after hitting his own slipstream during a tight turn with the altimeter showing 18,000 feet. He intuitively felt there was something wrong with the aircraft frame, as it wasn't as manoeuvrable as some of the others he had flown. The aircraft kept getting tighter and tighter into the spin and, spinning upside down, stalled completely. He knew he was in danger, heading rapidly towards a local vineyard where thousands of stumps protruded from the ground.

I thought, 'This is going to be nice, going in here with all these stumps, we'll have to try and manoeuvre to get in between them'. I tried everything to try and recover—all the recommended methods. I just started pumping the throttle and the joystick at the same time.

All of a sudden, it just flipped over, the right way up, and I looked at the altimeter and thought I saw 12,000 feet—I thought that's not too bad. I looked around to see where Joe was and looked at the altimeter again, it was 1200 feet.

I started to get the shakes. In the meantime, as well, I tried to bail out. Seeing that I was upside down, all my weight was on the canopy and I couldn't open the canopy and that's when I really did panic. When it flipped over and came out all right, I looked over the left wing and I spotted the airfield there and so I side-slipped over slowly and I just dropped it straight down and taxied back to the tarmac.

I thought, 'Oh God, lucky I was that far up.' I was shaking that much I couldn't even sign the logbook. As I got out of my cockpit and getting the parachute out, Joe pulled up alongside of me and he said to me, 'Where in the fucking hell did you get that bloody manoeuvre from? I've never seen one like that before. I was flying around in circles watching what you were doing, I wasn't going to try to emulate you.'

The chief flying officer who had witnessed the saga walked over to Waters. He barked at him to get back in the air. 'What are you doing back here? You should be up there with the others. Get back in that aircraft and get up there.' Waters understood why—'If you lose your nerve, you've had it.' His hands were shaking so much he was unable to sign the aircraft off. He would later learn that although the Kittyhawk had been pranged before, its frame had not been properly repaired and lined up at the aircraft depot. An aircraft with its frame out of alignment was potentially lethal. Two courses later, the same aircraft was involved in an accident, killing the pilot. Ruefully, but with a touch of pragmatism, Waters later commented, 'He wasn't as lucky as I was.'

Waters' confidential training report for his Kittyhawk conversion showed that luck played no part. In the four weeks' duration of the course he was assessed on both a ground examination and flying tests. On ground subjects, he emerged with a score of 56.5 per cent, while on flying tests he scored 52.2 per cent. On qualities of character and leadership, he was rated at 54 per cent. More tellingly, the wing commander of 2 OTU commented, 'This pilot is very keen and dependable. Has proved sound and capable at all times. Good type for a squadron.'

Another 'elite' pilot was Flying Officer Bob Crawford, with whom Waters would soon be flying in the south-west Pacific. Crawford pithily summed it up: 'You were the master of the machine. And you weren't an earthling, you were an airman.'

Against the odds, Waters was now an airman.

12

MISADVENTURE IN MOREE

When Waters stepped off the train from Sydney in Moree one morning in late September 1944, he found no welcome mat. He wanted to catch up with his brother George before hitching a ride on a truck later that evening to take him to St George, just a few hours away across the Queensland border. The only way to St George from Sydney was the overnight train to Moree, and then by road to his home town. He was now a 'Blue Orchid', the cream of the air force. But he was also a Kamilaroi Aborigine, and in Moree, that could so easily spell trouble.

Waters knew Moree's reputation as a racist town—one of the worst across the north-west of New South Wales. He had witnessed first-hand the town's colour bar not long after he started working with his father. Along with his brothers George and Jimmy, they had driven in the family truck to Moree. That night, he and his father were allowed to stay in one of the town's hotels, but his brothers weren't—the publican barred them because they looked too Aboriginal. They had to sleep in the back of the truck. Waters would recall that his father was always regarded as the 'whitest Aborigine'—a 'compliment' Don didn't appreciate.

For the town's Aborigines, Moree's discrimination meant they were banned from the town hall, library and public toilets, while the few clothing shops that allowed them entry did not allow clothes to be tried on. If they needed medical attention, they were relegated to a special ward at the back of the town's hospital. The colour bar carried through to death, as many Aboriginal people were buried in what was recorded as the 'Dark People's Portion' and 'Aboriginal Section' of the Moree Cemetery.

Waters was on pre-embarkation leave when he arrived in the town. He had been posted to No. 1 Reserve Personnel Pool (1RPP) RAAF at Townsville, from where he would join a squadron in the south-west Pacific. He had not seen his family for two years and had exciting news for them: he knew they would be proud of what he had achieved. That evening in Moree he planned to have a beer with George, who now lived in the town after marrying Ida Stacey. George was a bush worker and was respected in the area. They had not seen each other for four years, and he was looking forward to enjoying his elder brother's wry humour over a few beers. Waters arrived at a time when a de facto curfew was in place in Moree, and Aborigines who were on the streets after 5.30 p.m. risked arrest.

The town's white community wanted them out of sight and out of the pubs, and the council pressured the police to enforce this unofficial ban by whatever means it took. Once police were called, no Aborigine was safe from arrest. They could be thrown in the back of a paddy wagon on the pretext of being drunk and disorderly, and even non-drinkers were not safe. For good measure, there was also the option of being picked up for offensive language or for resisting arrest.

So heavy-handed and efficient were the police in enforcing the curfew that the Aboriginal community believed it was law. Generations of children were warned that they had to be off the streets and at home by this hour, otherwise they would be locked up if the police saw them.

The black community knew that to fall foul of the police meant the real risk of another, much more terrifying consequence: the forcible removal of children. It was best to stay invisible—don't risk antagonising police. The consequence was deep mistrust and hatred of the police, whose role was crucial in the subjugation of Aborigines, on or off reserves and missions. In towns like Moree, the psychology of expectations became more powerful than the reality of law. Through the police, the town had succeeded in having local Aborigines fear a locally imposed curfew that had no basis in state law. From the curfew to the roped-off section at the local picture theatre set aside for Aborigines to the ban on Aborigines using the artesian swimming pool, Moree had become a segregated town.

And then there was the exemption certificate. Known among Aborigines as the 'dog tag', the certificate had been introduced in New South Wales in 1943 by the Labor government. The move was in response to a push by Aboriginal leaders for full citizenship rights, which the government was not prepared to meet. However, as a token gesture it did amend the Aboriginal Protection Act. This change meant that any Aborigine 'who in the opinion of the Board, ought no longer be subject to the provisions of the Act . . . could apply to the Board for an exemption certificate.'

This certificate would free the holder from all special controls and, the Board argued, would help speed assimilation by allowing Aboriginal people to enjoy the rights and privileges of white society so they could eventually blend in. This included the right to leave the state and receive the old-age pension, something denied to people who lived on reserves. Importantly, the certificate also allowed them to drink alcohol. Some Aboriginal people sought exemption certificates as a way of shielding their children from removal by welfare authorities, but they were in the minority.

However, a certificate could be withdrawn on the whim of a Board official. A holder was not allowed to enter or stay on Aboriginal reserves, even to visit relatives. Certificates could be withdrawn for misdemeanours, intoxication or even arguing with a Board representative. The need to show dog tags to police officers was a source of humiliation. The clear message was that their citizenship rights were, by law, less than those enjoyed by whites—even though at this stage of the war hundreds of Indigenous Australians were already overseas fighting for the very rights they were being denied at home. Country Party politician Joe Lawson was to tell the New South Wales Legislative Assembly:

> *Aborigines home on military leave or home from the Middle East wearing the King's uniform are not allowed to visit an hotel to have a drink. At the same time unnaturalised Italians may drink as they please and enjoy full citizens' rights. That is a rotten state of affairs.*

The sting in the tail was that at the time, Australia was at war with Italy.

That night, when George and Len Waters walked into a Moree pub and ordered a beer, they were unprepared for the turn of events that followed. The publican asked George, who was considerably darker than his brother, for his exemption certificate. Len interjected that he and George were full brothers who had left the mission when he was seven years old, but the publican was adamant. Len had with him his RAAF ID card, travel warrant, a posting order and leave papers. However, as neither man was able to produce dog tags, the publican phoned the police.

Len's RAAF pass meant nothing to the police when they arrived—he was just another black in a pub without a dog tag. Len's protestations that he was a RAAF fighter pilot were dismissed as a likely story. That he was about to be posted to a war zone to fight for the very freedoms they were now enjoying was ignored. The two brothers were arrested and unceremoniously thrown into the lock-up overnight. Feeling anything but 'elite', they were hard hit by the reality and injustice of the incident. Len had enjoyed two years of no discrimination. There is no record of charges having been laid against either him or George, but the incident became a bitterly told story within the family.

Their arrests fitted a familiar pattern, as the curfew reflected a situation where laws for Indigenous Australians were implemented on an ad-hoc basis, changing from one area to another. The result was community-wide fear and a sense of powerlessness at a time in New South Wales when Aborigines could not vote, obtain alcohol without a dog tag, receive a pension if their Aboriginal blood was dominant, or obtain cash payments for family allowance. Legally, they were powerless and at the mercy of police.

Through this, social control was all-pervasive and administrative. In Queensland, police had been instructed not to make notes of the orders issued for the removal of Aboriginal people, as those orders might be called upon to be presented in court. This was institutional racism at its worst. Racial profiling—the discriminatory practice by law-enforcement officials of targeting individuals for suspicion of crime based on the individual's race, ethnicity, religion or national origin—meant blacks were inevitably police targets.

The heavy-handed police enforcement of these practices bred a sense of hopelessness in Moree and other bush towns throughout Australia. The police played a fundamental role in the Protection Board's bureaucratic structure as well as its day-to-day activities. Police had absolute power, with protection legislation taking care of any protest. With little scrutiny by the courts, there was no redress available to the likes of the Waters brothers. George did not have an exemption certificate. The end result was a galling experience—a misadventure in Moree and humiliation for both brothers.

Released from his overnight stay in the lock-up, Len finally bade farewell to his brother and managed to hop a truck to St George and the sanctity of the family home overlooking the Balonne River. He brought news that he was not just on pre-embarkation leave but that he had made it—he was a fighter pilot. Indeed, he came home with wings on his chest.

To mark the achievement, he brought a gift for his mother: a hand-coloured studio portrait taken of him after he had been presented with his wings at his graduation parade. The hand colouring gave no indication of his Aboriginality. His facial skin tone was white, not dark. On the back, Waters wrote a moving tribute to his mother, the words of a son going off to war. He thanked her for 'first of all bringing me into this world. For teaching me right from wrong . . . For trying to stop me from leaving school when I did. For washing and cleaning all my dirty clothes when I started work. For . . . worrying herself sick while I was away. For forgiving me for all the nasty things I said and done . . . But most of all, for simply being my Mother, for I am still your most loving son, Len.'

And there was another piece of news—he had a girlfriend by the name of Margaret, or Margie, as he called her. Details are sketchy, but it is thought that Waters met Margie during his time at either Uranquinty or Mildura. She was in the WAAF, probably working in the mess. Their friendship developed quickly, as relationships tended to in the heightened mood of war. For the handsome young fighter pilot about to go to the front line, having a sweetheart at home meant exquisite anticipation of letters and a homecoming. Until now, Waters' only experience of women had been of his mother and sisters, and stories he had probably heard around the campfire while ringbarking and rouseabouting. Margie was new territory. But war waited for no one and, with a feeling of urgency, they quickly embraced romance.

There was, however, one looming problem—Margie was white. Waters had spent the previous two years in the RAAF experiencing no racism that he could discern. He believed he was treated the same as every other trainee—yelled at the same, applauded the same. It was his combat skills as a fighter pilot that mattered, not his colour. While this was much less of an issue for Waters and Margie, it was one of monumental proportions for Grace and Don, who could see the hardships the young couple would inevitably face in 1940s Australia. Grace was alarmed.

All the family were there, except for George and, of course, Jim. No one knew at the time that he had just completed jungle warfare training at Canungra in preparation for service in the south-west Pacific, nor that he had been involved in a top-secret clinical trial to test the efficacy of various drugs in treating malaria. The drug Atebrin (mepacrine) was found to be effective, thus helping to reduce the incidence of the disease among Allied servicemen in the tropics. This was a significant breakthrough, and Jim was among volunteers who were commended by AIF Commander-in-Chief General Sir Thomas Blamey 'for distinguished services in the South West Pacific Area'. The trial over, Jim was posted to the 2nd/23rd Infantry Battalion AIF in preparation for action in the Pacific.

There was no place for exemption certificates on the front line of war.

13

BAD SHOW

The twin engines of the Douglas C-47 transport thrummed as Noemfoor Island loomed into view, just 100 kilometres south of the equator. From his passenger seat, Len Waters looked down on a coral speck lying off the coast of present-day Irian Jaya, a 335-square-kilometre jewel that sits, aptly, in Paradise Bay. In November 1944 it was Waters' entry point to war. He admitted to feeling 'a bit of trepidation'. New Guinea had been mostly wrested back from Japan, but the Japanese still had other island bases. 'There were quite a few of them,' he recalled.

With 280 hours 20 minutes of daytime flying experience and 22 hours 5 minutes at night, Waters was posted to 78 Squadron RAAF. His total time as a pilot in command of an aircraft had been about 184 hours. This was about par for the era but on the low side by present-day standards. No RAAF fighter pilot would be sent to Afghanistan today with under 200 hours' experience as pilot in command.

But these were different times, and 78 Squadron RAAF had already won significant battle honours. Raised at Camden, New South Wales, in July 1943 in response to a demand for much-increased airpower against the Japanese, the unit was the first Australian squadron to be equipped with the new P-40N Kittyhawks.

When 78 Squadron first joined the war in the South West Pacific Area (SWPA), they were part of 10 Group, being the first squadron in 78 Wing in November 1943. They weren't originally designated to be in that wing, which was to have two Spitfire squadrons and one Kittyhawk. The squadron was the sole squadron in 78 Wing for the next two months, until it was joined by 75 Squadron RAAF in January 1944. It was to be the end of February before 80 Squadron RAAF joined them.

The squadron first saw operations off New Guinea in November 1943, providing air cover for strike forces into New Britain and adjacent islands as well as harassing enemy forces with bombing and strafing operations.

What was later to be dubbed the 'Big Do', a dogfight over Biak Island on 3 June 1944, involved fifteen 78 Squadron Kittyhawks pitted against a force of 41 Japanese Zeros, Judys and Oscars that outnumbered the Australians nearly three to one. In the ensuing combat, the Australians shot down seven fighters and three dive-bombers and damaged a fighter, for the loss of one Kittyhawk and its pilot. It was the RAAF's largest air combat in the SWPA in terms of enemy aircraft shot down. Seven days later, one of the pilots involved in the action, Flight Lieutenant Denis 'Denny' Baker, shot down another fighter over Japen Island in his Kittyhawk *Black Magic*. It would be the RAAF's last air-to-air combat kill in the New Guinea campaign.

When Waters arrived, the Allies had been in control of Noemfoor since August, having taken the island after two months of fighting. However, Japanese forces were stubbornly refusing to accept the reality of looming defeat, which now appeared all but certain. What was clear was that obedience and honour were crucial elements of the military culture of Japan, and they made the Japanese tough, determined soldiers, ready to die for the glory of the Emperor. Moreover, the myth that the Japanese soldier was small and near-sighted was quickly debunked.

As was standard practice, Waters received a comprehensive briefing on survival and indigenous attitudes and customs, as well as on Papua New Guinea weather and terrain. Last, but hardly least, was the treatment he could expect if captured by the Japanese. Intelligence officers always made it clear that as aircrew, pilots risked being summarily beheaded. However, most aircrew were bayoneted, pegged down over ant nests, shot, or had grenades thrown at them. Before they were killed, they were usually beaten senseless.

Waters was thus psychologically inducted into the deadly business that lay before him. Every pilot, when flying, carried a large machete strapped to the calf of his left leg and a Smith & Wesson revolver in a waist holster. The credo was that, if opportunity allowed, every bullet would be used against the enemy—except for the last. That was kept to be used on oneself.

The threat of execution if captured by the Japanese was chillingly real. Waters and the other Australians on Noemfoor would later learn that that same month, one of their comrades based on the island, Flight Lieutenant Arthur Douglas Nelson, of 80 Squadron RAAF, had been beheaded after his Kittyhawk was shot down over the Kai Islands. Nelson was known as 'Pop'—he was 23 years old.

Sobering as this was, there was also the more practical side associated with flying a combat aircraft in wartime conditions that Waters had to become familiar with. Pilots' seating arrangements consisted of a folded parachute with a rubber dinghy pack wedged between pilot and 'chute. Included in the pack was a compressed-gas cylinder enabling the dinghy to be inflated as necessary. As one pilot observed, they walked 'a bit funny' at the end of a long flight.

Also essential for pilots was a 'Mae West' life vest to keep them afloat if they were brought down over water. The vest's other function was to hold escape and survival gear, including emergency rations, compass, whistle and signalling mirror. Along with the gun and machete, a water bottle, oxygen mask, gloves, helmet, goggles and throat microphone, pilots felt they were equipped to meet any eventuality. A silk scarf doubling as an escape map added to a tenuous sense of security.

As MacArthur pushed on to the Philippines, the RAAF was assigned the role of mopping up Japanese strongholds. It was not only dangerous but Australian pilots were becoming increasingly annoyed with what they regarded as off-hand treatment by the Americans. This was a challenging environment for any new pilot.

After moving to Noemfoor, 78 Squadron, as part of 78 Wing, was to carry out patrols, sweeps and strikes to provide cover for Allied troops attacking Japanese posts and airstrips. In September, the squadron carried out strikes against enemy airstrips on the Vogelkop and Bomberai peninsulas and in the Kai Islands. These were the last enemy stronghold in the New Guinea area.

In the process, the squadrons forming 78 Wing were re-established as part of the First Tactical Air Force (No. 1 TAF) to provide a mobile force of fighter and ground attack aircraft. The Australians were under the command of the U.S. Fifth Air Force. As 78 Squadron flight rigger Bill Soden commented, 'We felt we were the poor relations, our U.S. counterparts had better aircraft than we did and were certainly better off in the food department.' The reorganisation came a few days after MacArthur waded ashore in drenching rain onto the Philippines island of Leyte, as the largest mass of naval assault craft and warships ever concentrated in the Pacific sailed into Leyte Gulf.

As the Allied forces pressed on, Flight Lieutenant Dick Sudlow flew from Townsville to Noemfoor. The 78 Squadron adjutant met the plane when it landed at Kamiri airstrip, took a quick look at his papers, jumped to his feet and said, 'Welcome to 78 Squadron, Commanding Officer.' No one had told Sudlow he was to take over command of the squadron. He was impressed with what had been handed to him. 'I quickly discovered I had inherited a unit which was running as smoothly as a well-oiled piece of top-line machinery . . . I wasn't about to ring in changes without good reason.'

However, after his first dive-bombing mission of a Japanese airstrip in the Halmahera (Maluku) island group, Sudlow reconsidered this from a personal perspective of safety. The P-40N Kittyhawk that he had inherited was silver with a blue, white and silver spinner and highly conspicuous in the air when caught by sunlight. During the raid, the Japanese quickly saw him, targeting him with fire behind, in front and either side. He was lucky that they were off line. On landing, Sudlow immediately ordered his Kittyhawk to be 'transformed from bright silver to fully camouflaged in probably the quickest time in the history of the RAAF.' It was repainted in the more common olive drab.

Waters was full of admiration for Sudlow, who, as squadron leader, 'reached great heights over enemy territory'. Waters was assigned to 'A' Flight under Flight Lieutenant Denny Baker, making his first familiarisation flight on 17 November 1944. Baker took him through squadron formation flying and shadow shooting during the next week. This practice, developed from the observation of bird flocks using a 'V' formation, honed flight discipline with the benefit of enhancing aerodynamic efficiency. The Kamilaroi in Waters would have understood.

Baker had previously flown Kittyhawks with 76 Squadron RAAF in the difficult times early in the war, when the RAAF had only three front-line fighter squadrons: 75, 76 and 77 Squadrons. He had served with distinction at Milne Bay as a

Flight Sergeant pilot and brought a wealth of experience to 78 Squadron when he joined in May 1944 to become the leader of 'A' Flight.

He cut a dashing figure. With a ready smile, he was a lithe 180 centimetres tall and weighed 63.5 kilograms. His background could not have been more different from Waters': he had been born into colonial privilege, his father having been a District Commissioner in Fiji. Young Denny had been educated at the elite Sydney Church of England Grammar School, otherwise known as Shore.

He would later write in the school magazine, *The Torch Bearers: War Service of Shore Old Boys, 1939–1999*, that he had named his Kittyhawk *Black Magic* because 'of my close association with the natives of Fiji, where I was born, and the "Fuzzy Wuzzies" in New Guinea with 76 Squadron'. While Waters had been a novice shearer on enlistment, Baker was a clerk with the influential blue-chip Perpetual Trustee Co. Waters imagined him the very image of what everyone thought a fighter pilot should be:

A completely devil-may-care swashbuckler. One of his favourite tricks was, when returning from a bash, he would call everyone in to what we used to call 'pansy formation'—that is, everyone would be in formation almost wing tip to wing tip, and when we would all be as close as possible, he would let go of the stick and start picking his finger nails. I might add that he would also have us down as low as it was possible to fly. His prop would be almost chopping the sea.

What most people would not know is that you can't trim a Kittyhawk, that is, they do not have an automatic pilot, but in the tropics

> *there is a hell of a lot of turbulence, so the slightest slip one way or the other could have been disastrous. Everyone went every which way when he pulled this stunt.*

Japanese activity in the immediate area was reducing, so missions from Noemfoor began ranging as far afield as the Maluku Islands—Ceram, Ambon, and the Kai and Halmahera island groups. These were offensive operations, aimed at keeping local Japanese forces contained. Along with strike missions, photographic sorties were undertaken to keep airstrips such as Utarom under observation and note any attempt to repair or re-use them.

Waters joined squadron operations for the first time on 24 November. He was part of a three-aircraft detail to dive-bomb the Moemi strip on Vogelkop Peninsula under Flight Lieutenant Harry Kerr. This was rated a practice strike for the new pilots, as it was considered a soft target that would give them some operational experience. Waters noted in his logbook that he had dive-bombed enemy territory. 'First time over E.T. Bombs fall wide of target.' The area was still a Japanese stronghold, and Waters was not yet battle hardened for an attack that was 'the hottest spot left in New Guinea'. 'We went over and all hell opened up when we got over there. We went over at 16,000 feet and dived down to treetop height, dropped our bombs and just cleared out.'

A day later, Sudlow led a formation of twelve Kittyhawks, together with another twelve aircraft from 80 Squadron, to dive-bomb the strongly defended Japanese naval base at

Sorong, on Cape Noejew, on the north-western point of then Dutch New Guinea. They encountered a hostile reception, but the operation gave Waters a chance to improve his aim. 'Fairly hot spot, medium to heavy A.A. [anti-aircraft fire, or ack-ack], put bombs on target area.'

The attack was repeated the next day, and Waters thought their reception from the Japanese was even hotter. 'There was flak! I got turned over twice . . . in the blasts of the ack-ack . . . and bloody hell! Flicked it, the plane, twice!'

Despite only being 20 years of age, Waters had prepared for this moment. Through his teenage years of working with teams of hardened men in the bush—men for whom surviving off the land was a hard-won skill—he had trained himself to deal with fears and doubts silently. He had learned from these men—not least of whom was his father—that doubt meant vulnerability. From everything that can be gleaned about Waters, this was his modus operandi. These initial operations were not just a new warfare experience for him. Through them, he began to forge bonds with his comrades. For fighter pilots, this heightened sense of danger quickly welded them into a tight unit. Rank aside, they were equals.

Waters shared a tent with Sergeant Stan Hattersley, who had gone through the conversion course at Mildura a few weeks before him. Born in Melbourne, Hattersley had come through the air cadets before enlisting. He and Waters quickly struck up a bond. 'My little tent-mate,' Waters called him. On the morning of 27 November, he and Hattersley, in formation with Kittyhawks from both 78 and 80 Squadrons, left Kamiri airfield on Noemfoor to launch another strike at the Japanese naval base at Sorong, in West Papua.

There was a little cloud, and the flight was uneventful. Just north of Doom Island, the Japanese ack-ack opened up on the RAAF Kittyhawks as they approached at around 8000 feet. Waters noted that it was 'still hot, AA intense'. Hattersley was trailing the attack group. Waters, with his ear attuned to mechanical problems, believed the Kittyhawk had engine trouble, but Hattersley kept in touch rather than turn back or land on Middleburg Island. 'We dropped our bombs,' Waters recalled, adding that Hattersley was the last pilot to go over the strip. 'They let him have it when he came in because he was trailing behind us. They hit him with everything.' Hattersley's Kittyhawk started weaving, with puffs of heavy ack-ack around him. Flight Commander Harry Kerr was among those who saw Hattersley's aircraft suddenly dive towards the water.

The reality of war struck home. Waters watched, horrified, as Hattersley's Kittyhawk ploughed into the sea. The official internal report by the Adjutant of 78 Squadron, Flight Lieutenant Albert Andrew, described the incident:

> *At 1100 hours on 27 November 1944, the above aircraft was seen 'weaving' at approximately 8000 feet, with about ten puffs of heavy ack-ack fire in its vicinity, and was subsequently seen in a vertical dive. It crashed into the sea approximately 1000 yards north of Doom Island, in the vicinity of Cape Noejew, Dutch New Guinea, when flames and smoke were noticed rising from the water lasting no more than one minute. The pilot is reported missing, believed killed.*

Other pilots from 78 Squadron made statements to the same effect, with Kerr stating that the Kittyhawk hit the sea at a speed somewhere between 450 and 500 miles per hour. At that speed, the aircraft would have disintegrated on impact and sunk, 'leaving no other signs but oil smoke for a short time'.

For Waters and his training mate from Mildura, Frank Smith, it was only their third time over enemy territory. He was full of praise for what Dick Sudlow did next:

> *That commanding officer of ours, as far as I am concerned, he is one of the bravest, and that man should have been decorated several times. He flew right down with all those war ships and everything like that and circled that spot where that boy went into the water, and they threw everything at him, and he came back. I used to fly number two with him a lot of times in the earlier days and he was an inspiration to be with.*

Aside from Sudlow's spur of the moment response, Kerr said that as no parachute was observed, it was decided that no searches would be carried out, as the crash occurred in 'close proximity to a heavily defended enemy area and the risk of losing additional aircraft and pilots on a search was too great.' Hattersley was nineteen years of age, the youngest pilot in 78 Squadron to die. It would have been a sombre flight home.

Two days later, Waters was back in the cockpit as part of a long-range dive-bombing raid on the Galela strip in the Halmaheras. In contrast to the 27th, there was no ack-ack, which created a strange quietness. The damage the raid wrought could not be assessed owing to bad weather and thick jungle on the strip's edge. They broke the return journey at Morotai before returning the next day.

Waters was now receiving letters from his mother, Grace—and Margie. It seems from family lore that Grace was adamant that her son should not marry a white woman. Grace wrote to Margie to explain her misgivings, which, in the context of 1944, are not difficult to understand. Waters would later describe how he shared his mother's letters with Flight Lieutenant Johnny Griffith. Whether these were Grace's letters opposing his relationship with Margie is not clear. What was clear was the strength of his relationship with his mother, or, as he put it later, 'the way I felt about her she felt about me, apparently; well, I know she did.'

Although he had been on Noemfoor less than a month, Johnny Griffith had taken Waters under his wing. Because of the experience Griffith had accumulated, Waters saw him as a mentor at a time when he was still feeling his way. He regarded Griffith as 'a really good friend'. Griffith, who had turned 29 just a few weeks earlier, had some advice for him from hard-won experience about unnecessary risk-taking. He told him, 'Don't be a hero, don't be a war winner, there's plenty of those fellows here; just do your duty, pull your weight and you'll come through it OK. Remember, you've got two parents who idolise you.'

These were thoughts Waters could use to sustain himself as he integrated into his environment. Life was divided between flying sorties and relaxing on an island where paw-paws, bananas and coconuts were plentiful, and where fish could be caught by dropping either a hand grenade into the water or a 500-lb bomb from a Kittyhawk just off the edge of the coral reef surrounding the island. If there was a complaint about the food, it was the scarcity of fresh meat and bread—as Australian service personnel had long known, there was a limit to the amount of bully beef they could eat. Bully beef aside, there was a dissonance between this seemingly idyllic lifestyle and the realities of war as Stan Hattersley's death sank in.

On 2 December, Griffith, who was approaching the end of his second tour of duty, drove Waters and other pilots to the strip, promising that he'd be there when they returned to take them for a swim. At the last minute, Sudlow asked Griffith to lead the flight, with Waters flying No. 2 for a mopping-up raid to stop the enemy from smuggling supplies in by barge to their base. Waters recalled that Griffith said he would be only too pleased to do it, as he did not enjoy just lying around the camp:

> *When we got out from base, we ran into a tropical storm, an electrical storm, it was down to about 200 feet above sea level and could have been 120 feet wide. With the Kittyhawks you couldn't get over a storm like that because they couldn't go up to 35,000 to 40,000 feet. So he called us and gave us the thumbs-down sign and said we'd go back. It was not worth risking us, as we did not have night flying instruments. So we went back.*

Waters was in his tent that afternoon when Griffith walked past, commenting that he was going to fix his logbook and put a few photographs in it. It was clear to Waters that Griffith was winding down and looking forward to shortly returning to Australia. The day was windless when Griffith went to the photography tent to paste in some photos. With no warning, a large bough from a 'jungle giant' tree overhanging the tent broke off and smashed through the tent from high above, hitting Griffiths directly on the head. The sound of the falling limb brought others out of their tents. In the crushed tent, Griffith lay dead, killed instantly by the weight of the limb. He had flown two operational tours, the first with 77 Squadron in the difficult days of 1942 and early 1943, as well as the 'Big Do' of 3 June 1944. He thus became the last of the pilots from this encounter to die.

Waters and the rest of the base were left stunned. It did not seem fair, and it was especially moving for Waters, given that Griffith had erred on the side of safety that afternoon in bringing the squadron home and shortening the raid. 'It shattered me especially, as he had said, "Don't be a hero, don't be a war winner." And another thing, he couldn't be certified as "killed in action". Incidents like that got to me more than any other.' In his logbook, he noted of Griffith's death simply: 'Bad show.'

14

HERE TODAY, GONE TO MOROTAI

Thump! Thump! Thump! Swaying as he jabbed, Waters' gloved fists pounded the punching bag. He danced on his feet as he let rip with hooks and crosses. There was something rhythmic and purposeful in his movement. Waters' squadron mates took note: here was a boxer with skill, someone who was not a mere backstreet brawler. He began sparring with them, in the process showing them the finer points of boxing, and passing on the lessons he had learned from the old tent boxer at Nindigully. With a boxing tournament in prospect, his new mates realised that he would be worth backing. They might just make a few quid.

When the men were not flying, the punching bag soon became a popular alternative for those spare moments when they weren't swimming in the crystal-clear water over the reef. And if they weren't playing cards there was always the chance of cricket on a makeshift coral pitch prepared by taxiing an aircraft into position and using the draft from the engine, gunned to test revolutions, to blast the pitch clear.

There was more time for these activities now, as targets in the Vogelkop Peninsula were mostly bombed out and Waters was involved in standard training exercises. With his ear for malfunctioning engines, he knew he had to return from one of these exercises on 6 December; he duly noted 'engine trouble' in his logbook. Two days later, Waters took part in further squadron formation flying exercises. Later that day, Harry Kerr led Waters and others in having some fun with a 'line-astern chase' and some aerobatic rolls and loops.

Attention now turned to the Halmahera group, where the Japanese regularly repaired the strips they used as staging points for their small bomber fleet to carry out night nuisance raids. On 11 December, Waters and three other Kittyhawks bombed and strafed Idore, his bombs falling on target as the aircraft strafed and hit three huts, one footbridge and five enemy barges. He noted that there was no ack-ack. At Hatetabako and Miti on the 12th and 13th, as the squadron dive-bombed a bivouac area near the Lolobata River, he recorded that the ack-ack was light and inaccurate. Of the 46 bombs dropped, twelve exploded on target.

Waters' Kittyhawk also developed engine problems on the 13th, forcing him to spend the night on Morotai, the northernmost island in the Halmahera group. The squadron had begun staging through airfields on Morotai from early December, two months after American forces streamed ashore to surprise the Japanese. They established a strong perimeter defence around the new base, fighting off counterattacks to consolidate their hold. The decision to eventually move to Morotai came as no surprise to 78 Wing. Waters returned to Noemfoor on 14 December. The catchy phrase 'Here today. Gone to Morotai' was noted appropriately in his logbook.

Morotai is a rugged island of thick jungle with an area of just 80 by 42 kilometres. Japan had invaded the island in early 1942 and to MacArthur, it was the perfect location to create a base from which to launch the liberation of the Philippines. Two Allied-held airfields, Pitu and Wama, were at the southern end of the island, just 32 kilometres from the Japanese-held northern tip of Halmahera, the main island in the group. Morotai had become a refuelling and re-arming stop for attacks on the Halmahera airstrips at Miti, Galela, Lolobata and Hatetabako, interspersed with days of squadron formation flying to maintain the skills of pilots.

There were now up to 60,000 Allied troops on the island, which had become an important hub of Allied activity south of the Philippines and one of the largest bases in the South West Pacific Area. So big was the base that it was equipped with a 1900-bed hospital. While the Americans had built a protective barrier to secure their hold on Morotai, thousands of Japanese troops from the Fourteenth Army still remained on the island. Cut off by the Allied navy and air forces, they were well armed, but fuel, food and medicine were running out. In the distance, the Japanese could be seen tending their gardens, subsistence style. The American policy was not to endanger soldiers' lives fighting an enemy that was already beaten.

As the war entered its final year, the Australian approach under General Sir Thomas Blamey was to fight on—even though any strategic gains would make little difference to the outcome. The risk was that more lives would be lost unnecessarily. Those doing the fighting came to see the futility of these campaigns. Waters was developing his own view.

Waters was up in the air again on 17 December when Denny Baker took his 'A' Flight for an hour-long formation flying exercise, followed two days later by Dick Sudlow taking the entire squadron of up to 24 Kittyhawks on a formation flight. On 21 December, Waters was among 25 Kittyhawks and one Wirraway that left Noemfoor permanently for their new base at Morotai. While C-47s transported lighter equipment, the pilots had to look after their own gear. With little room to spare on Kittyhawks, resourcefulness was called for. Some pilots stuffed their belongings into the wing ammunition bays and stashed beer cartons in beside the radio transmitter. Sudlow noted that some even resorted to lashing gear tightly to the belly tank, hoping that they would not encounter enemy aircraft on the way. He was similarly compromised. 'I would have had to shoot at them with bits of shaving gear, buttons and shoes.'

The new Australian camp was only 360 metres from the defensive perimeter, beyond which the Japanese had been pushed back. With the Australians greeted by the tropical wet season, living conditions were difficult. And then there was the mud—thick and sticky. Unmade roads became impassable bogs, littered with vehicles stuck fast to their axles. Noemfoor suddenly seemed an oasis in comparison. Despite the rain, it was straight back to work, albeit with the operational sorties being of shorter duration. Focused on the Halmahera Island area only, it meant operational flying hours fell, but the number of strikes increased.

Routine strikes did not lessen the danger that 78 Wing faced. They had lost Stan Hattersley at the end of November and Johnny Griffith at the start of the month. Two pilots from 80 Squadron attacks lost their lives during the month. On 13 December, 22-year-old Flight Sergeant James Lennard was killed over Halmahera when his Kittyhawk was hit by ack-ack while strafing enemy positions at Galela Bay. Nine days later, 20-year-old Flight Sergeant Cliff Tothill, in his first operation with 80 Squadron, died during a strafing run when his Kittyhawk flipped over and ploughed into the sea. Four deaths in less than a month underlined the danger still alive in the skies over the south-west Pacific.

On 23 December, a formation of sixteen Kittyhawks dive-bombed and strafed the main Japanese base at Hatetabako, running into ack-ack. Waters noted in his logbook: 'Pretty hot. Two kites holed.' One of them was Denny Baker's *Black Magic*. Later that day, Waters was part of another attack, dive-bombing and strafing barge hide-outs in mangrove-fringed Goeroea Bay. Waters wrote that there was some heavy ack-ack as they strafed and burnt two huts, with smoke rising to 800 feet.

They were back to Goeroea the next day, Waters observing that the Kittyhawks had delivered a 'terrific pounding'. Christmas

Eve followed the same pattern, with the squadron returning to Goeroea and strafing more barge hide-outs and destroying more buildings. Later, Waters recalled that the squadron had had some luck in the attacks, 'as there were new aircraft still in their crates by the side of the strips, but they didn't have the pilots to fly them.' They made an irresistible target.

There was little time to celebrate Christmas—just a day off, when the tradition of officers serving the other ranks Christmas dinner was observed. Boxing Day saw Waters back in his Kittyhawk strafing Galela again. Another dive-bombing and strafing run followed a day later at a site on the Soebaim River, successfully hitting barge hide-outs, which Waters thought was 'pretty fair bombing'. He was among Kittyhawk pilots who returned to the Soebaim River area on 30 December, remarking that he had not seen anything worthwhile. He returned with one bomb not dropped.

To mark the last day of 1944, Waters and eleven other pilots were sent to again dive-bomb the Hatetabako strip. While he made no entry in his logbook about the outcome, the squadron's operations book recorded that the bombing was accurate. Until 31 December, enemy raids were carried out over Morotai every night. On one occasion, shortly after the arrival of the advance party, a bomb burst on the camp site and within 75 metres of the tent area. There were no casualties, but the danger was brought closer to home.

Waters marked New Year's Day 1945 by writing in his logbook that he had completed sixteen strikes and seventeen sorties, becoming an integral member of the squadron. By now, it was likely that he had been introduced to an unofficial practice that was certainly not taught at training and conversion courses in Australia. It became known as the 'Aussie revenge' and involved Kittyhawk pilots taking empty bottles, with razor blades forced into the bottle necks, on missions and hurling them out while flying over a target area with the cockpit open. The falling bottle made a screaming sound as it fell from between 5000 and 6000 feet, the more so if something was inserted to partially block the neck. The piercing noise would cause the Japanese to dive for cover, and while they had their heads ducked down, other planes would seize the opportunity to fly down and strafe.

Despite the operations over the Christmas–New Year period, the ground staff had nonetheless found time to set up an outdoor cinema to utilise the squadron's film projector. Films helped relieve the tedium when the men were not flying. Generally, the screen was just a sheet erected between two coconut palms. As Morotai was an American base, there was a plentiful supply of Hollywood movies. There being no seats provided, each person would bring his own chair, box or upturned helmet. An honour system for seating was rigidly applied, with those staking their place early enough assured that it would be respected. Dick Sudlow recalled that many men from nearby units attended the squadron's film shows. 'I am sure they did a great deal for morale and probably ranked second in popularity to mail from home.'

According to one pilot in 80 Squadron, the evening's entertainment was provided by both the film and the audience. Much amusement was derived from the romantic overtures by male stars. If he appeared timid or reluctant in his approaches to the object of his desire, 'he was encouraged most vigorously by the audience . . . or should the actor appear too masterful or daring, he was most roundly reproved in robust style.'

Behind the screen was thick jungle, and it is said that Japanese soldiers would emerge unseen from wooded safety to watch a movie from the other side of the screen. This became clear on one occasion when one of the Aussies took a shot at a character on the screen who had occasioned his displeasure. The Japanese behind the screen yelled out in alarm and ran off back into the jungle, adding to the evening's entertainment.

The squadron's operations from Morotai were similar to those from Noemfoor, though with fewer long operations. Several targets were in the Halmahera group, with particular attention being paid to nearby Japanese positions. On 2 January, Sudlow led twelve Kittyhawks to dive-bomb the strip at Hatetabako. Waters was among those dive-bombing the heavily defended target area. Sudlow explained later that the purpose of such ops was to check that no enemy aircraft had been flown in and, if they had, destroy them. Sudlow would put the squadron into line-astern formation at about 18,000 feet, enabling each pilot to dive independently while at the same time keeping the attack concentrated:

> *To do this we needed to be very low to see whether or not the dispersal bays were empty. We would fly down the strip at full speed below the tops of the trees on each side. The Japs knew we were regular callers and it became a cat and mouse game between us. We made our runs*

> *from different directions, slipped out from behind high ground near the strip, and used diversionary tactics like shooting up their camp with two aircraft while two others swept down the strip. Sometimes we made it without having a shot fired at us, but on the whole their heavy guns got off a round or two. Fire from the lighter machine guns and cannons was difficult to detect and we had to hope we were making it difficult for them to line up on us.*

Waters commented that he met 'fragmented clusters' of fire. Surviving this, he added: 'Good bombing.' The attack successfully destroyed a gun pit from where heavy ack-ack had been trained on the squadron, leaving two aircraft holed. Not noted in his logbook were comments he later made to his daughter about the shock of witnessing at close range the deaths of Japanese soldiers that followed such low altitude strafing.

Waters flew again on 6 January, when his Kittyhawk was one of six that bombed and strafed the personnel area at the Loloda village, damaging or destroying up to sixteen huts. Again, 'Good bombing!' was his logbook comment. On the 8th, Waters was part of a sweep on the west coast of Halmahera Island, from Cape Ngolopopo to Cape Libabo. He noted that the mission, which saw some strafing of machine-gun positions and installations, was 'boring!' This reflected the increasing discontent among the Australians about the limited roles they were playing. Mopping up, while ever dangerous, was not the cutting-edge action they believed they had trained for.

Animosity towards the Americans was growing, as many believed they were being given a back seat. 'The Yanks, all they were interested in was getting back to the Philippines, and we had to clean up in between,' Waters, still smarting years later, would recall. A regret was that by the time he joined the war effort in late 1944, the battle in the air had all but finished, so he was never able to participate in a dogfight for real with a Japanese fighter plane. The chance to test his mettle and achieve the status of an 'ace' was no longer possible.

Back in the air on 9 and 10 January, Waters joined an attack across the bay to Galela when 20 Kittyhawks from 78 Wing, together with Beaufighters from 77 Wing, attacked the main enemy bivouac and supply area near Galea village, on the north of Halmahera Island. The Japanese were using Galea as a base to reinforce and supply their remaining forces, which still occupied a large part of Morotai Island outside the heavily defended perimeter.

This was a combined operation with the Royal Australian Navy, which sent the sloop HMAS *Swan* and corvettes HMAS *Cowra* and HMAS *Kapunda* to bombard enemy shore positions. Thirty-two Kittyhawks then bombed and strafed the area. The raid was rated a great success—'500%', noted a delighted Waters in his logbook. A similar strike was repeated a day later, again with Waters flying. On the 11th, Waters was among twelve Kittyhawks that bombed and strafed Japanese stores and huts five kilometres inland, near a bridge over the Fiang River. It had been a week of mixed results. The next day was Friday, a day off for Waters. Friday was also the day that he would put his boxing prowess on the line for the first time on Morotai.

15

FIGHTING FIT

The boxing stadium at Morotai stood in a coral pit about a half a kilometre from the beach, fringed by coconut palms and jungle. Here up to 10,000 Australian and American servicemen would flock on Friday nights to drink beer, gamble in Dutch guilders and, for a moment or two, forget the war. Nearby, at Barney's Casino, 'two-up' was under way as the arena quickly filled. Over the loudspeaker, the week's sporting results, which had come in over shortwave radio from Australia, were announced.

By 7 p.m., every seat was filled. They sat on kerosene tins, stools, bomb crates, canvas chairs, and a few hundred planks perched on top of old drums. On schedule, 20 minutes later, the bouts began in the brilliantly lit ring. In one corner was the American Stars and Stripes, while opposite was the Australian flag. The tropics is hardly the ideal place for such rugged sports as boxing and wrestling, but on Morotai they thrived. Owing to the enervating heat, bouts were kept to three rounds.

Throughout the war with Japan, Australian and American officers cooperated to provide many combined amenities and activities in the SWPA. Both at home in Australia and in the islands, the influx of American servicemen boosted interest in boxing, and some of the black boxers in the SWPA base areas were outstanding. By November 1942 some RAAF personnel were organising boxing tournaments at Port Moresby, with Americans in the area invited to take part. In early 1943, interest in boxing increased after American forces took on a greater role. Two new stadiums opened, one seating up to 8000 spectators.

As with international professional boxing at the time, African-American boxers eventually dominated Port Moresby's boxing scene. Betting on the outcome was common. A letter to the *Sporting Globe* noted that the Americans thought 'nothing of wagering £30 or £40 a head on their man' and added that the Australians also bet heavily. But the Port Moresby boxing scene inevitably fell away in early 1944 with the closure of the stadium owing to illegal gambling and the decline of Port Moresby as a major Allied operational base.

On Morotai, American, Australian, English and Dutch boxers took part. Len Waters was one of them. Boxing had been a way of life since Nindigully days and he was good—very good. His comrades in 78 Squadron knew it. Armourer John 'Curly' Wheatley, of 78 Squadron, recalls that Waters taught boxing at both Morotai and Noemfoor. 'He was a good boxer, he was teaching others to box.' He had lightening quick hands.

A lean 75 kilos and lanky 179 centimetres tall, Waters was a middleweight nicknamed 'Bones'. He had that toughness that comes not from the gym but from a hard physical life. In the boxing ring on Morotai, his comrades thought he was worth backing. The program usually featured ten bouts, each comprising three three-minute rounds. At the end of each bout, thousands of guilders changed hands among the troops. All boxers were paid from a shower taken up midway through the night. Usually they received about 20 guilders each (about $250 in 2018).

On the evening of 12 January 1945, Waters stepped into the ring at Morotai. There was an ebullient mood, as the Allied amphibious invasion of Lingayen Gulf in the Philippines had ended successfully just three days earlier. Victory was closer. Celebrated newsreel cameraman Bill Carty, who worked for the Australian Information Department, was on Morotai at the time and filmed the fights with his Bell & Howell cine camera. There, with floodlights hovering over the ring, he filmed Waters fighting an African-American. The clip runs for only 25 seconds, but it shows a confident Waters. He won this three-round event and would continue to progress through the bouts over coming weeks.

Waters was back flying the next day, allocated to base patrol. After the euphoria of the previous night, he rated the job 'very boring'. But that day there was to be an unfolding tragedy for 78 Wing. Four 80 Squadron pilots disappeared on a ferry flight from Noemfoor to Morotai. Possibly owing to bad weather, their Kittyhawks overshot Morotai and when their fuel ran out they came down off the Talaud Islands. Despite intensive searches, there was no trace. It later emerged that one pilot, Flight Sergeant Ron Parry, was lost at sea, while the other three—Flying Officer Laurie Hann, Warrant Officer Peter Waters (no relation) and Flight Sergeant Leon King—were taken prisoner and held for some weeks before being executed by the Japanese, bayoneted to death on 23 March 1945 after being severely beaten.

It was just the next day, 14 January, when another 80 Squadron pilot, Flight Sergeant Neville Thornley, was shot down in a joint raid with 78 Squadron on Hatetabako airstrip in the Halmaheras. His Kittyhawk plunged into the sea after being hit by enemy ack-ack. Waters was on the same raid. Leaving the target area after dive-bombing the strip, he noted, 'Still shooting at us.' This was a devastating few days for 80 Squadron and a sobering experience for all. Next day, Waters was part of a similar raid on the Wasile pier area that was deemed successful. Less successful were raids on the 16th, to Dodinga Bay, in the western Halmaheras, and on the 18th, to Baroe village, a hide-out for barges in Dutch Borneo (in what is now the Indonesian province of East Kalimantan).

Frustration was growing. It was increasingly clear that their operations were having little, if any, bearing on the war's progress. The Americans were back in the Philippines. The isolated pockets of Japanese in their area of operations were no longer influencing the outcome. If Waters was feeling some discontent about the nature of operations, a little magic was coming his way. Flight Lieutenant Denny Baker, after finishing his second tour, was about to return to Australia. Flight Lieutenant Joe Black took over 'A' Flight. The difference was stark. 'A nice bloke and a good pilot but as much alike as chalk and cheese to Baker,' was Waters' assessment.

The question of who would take over Baker's Kittyhawk, *Black Magic*, remained. It was the practice among pilots to give their planes a name, perhaps revealing something of themselves in the process. *Watch My Form*, with its provocatively posed naked young woman, was another Kittyhawk in 78 Squadron. Then there were *Hot Stuff!*, *Stormy Weather* and *Pistol Packin' Mama*. Painted on the engine cowls of aircraft, the images became known as nose art. Pilots often treated their planes as if they had human personalities. Many spoke of their aircraft as their 'best friend'—reflecting the bond forged between man and machine.

Black Magic was a name that had particular significance for Baker, and the fighter had served him well since May 1944, during the hottest part of the campaign. Now it was time to farewell his Kittyhawk. Someone else in the squadron would take it over. To this point, Waters had flown nine different Kittyhawks in 78 Squadron and had yet to call one his own. It was an obvious choice: Kittyhawk A-29-575 HU-E, with *Black Magic* emblazoned on its cowl, went to him and would remain his for the rest of the war. The ground staff derived much amusement from the allocation, and Waters likewise thought it fitting.

He took *Black Magic* for a 45-minute test flight on 20 January and immediately felt at home. Recalling the eerie coincidence later in life, Waters commented: 'Was that fate or what?! What an omen—and I'm not a believer.' Waters clearly felt an affinity with *Black Magic* from the start. Although he was 'not a believer', superstition was common among pilots in war—from lucky charms or mascots to peeing on the rear wheel before a mission. Pilots have even been known to put their chewed gum on the wing to tilt the scales of luck in their favour.

Leading Aircraftman Arnie Nunn, a member of the ground crew of No. 114 Mobile Control and Reporting Unit, saw the bond that soon developed between Waters and his Kittyhawk: 'I used to walk around it with Lenny. He reckoned it was a great plane—he loved it.'

Next day, 21 January, Waters climbed into *Black Magic*'s cockpit to undertake the first operation in his new fighter. He was among nineteen Kittyhawks that left to bomb and strafe building yards on Tahoelandang Island, but, failing to locate the target because of the weather, they returned to base. Being the wet season, this was not an uncommon occurrence owing to low cloud.

On 24 January, Dick Sudlow led another eleven Kittyhawks, including Waters in *Black Magic*, to bomb and strafe a bivouac to the east of Kaoe No. 1 airstrip in the Halmaheras. Waters wrote in his logbook, 'Bags of A/A, 4 kites holed.' A day later, nineteen Kittyhawks set out on a mission to Tomohon, on the northern tip of the Celebes, targeting Japanese officers' quarters. The weather was so bad that a nearby alternative target at Manado was attacked instead. They met with heavy ack-ack. Despite this, Waters recorded in his logbook, 'Good bombing.' But there was much more to that brief entry. Waters was among those who bombed three bridges in the area. Up to that point, Manado had been an important Japanese coastal base in the Celebes. Neutralising it was a high priority. Waters would later recall that the Japanese 'were still very well armed over the Celebes Islands.' So strong were the enemy defences that during the raid, 'I nearly bought it'. He later declared what happened:

> *It was fairly hot there, because we were pushing the Japs back all the time and of course, they were still resisting. We had raided this place before. It was a little bay, a depot, like a base. It had motor torpedo boats and barges and that sort of thing and we dive-bombed and then we had to go down and strafe afterwards.*

Waters was leading the flight at the time. He described how, having dropped his bombs at 3000 feet, he began to pull out of the dive in order to come back around to strafe. '[But] I felt this clunk underneath me and thought, "I've got a hit there somewhere."' By this time, the pilots knew the type of anti-aircraft fire the Japanese were using, and he believed it to be a Japanese type of 'pom-pom'—a 37-mm shell:

> *I knew it was pretty close to where I was sitting because I felt the jar and I was hoping, praying that it wasn't a high-explosive shell—I thought that it is a two-hour flight from the Celebes to Morotai and I could almost hear the thing ticking behind my skull because one in five is a high-explosive shell . . . I felt this slug . . . lodged between my*

armour plating behind the nape of my neck and the 75-gallon high-octane fuel tank in the fuselage.

It was a long flight back. When coming in to land on arrival at Morotai, Waters alerted the other pilots in the flight as well as the ground crew:

I told the others to land and clear the strip, because I didn't like what had happened to me. I came in on my own and I just taxied to the end of the strip and the armourers came over and I said to them, 'There is something underneath here.' Luckily, underneath the belly of a Kittyhawk is fabric, between the armour plating and the 75-gallon fuel tank.

Now, if it had landed six or eight inches one way or the other, I wouldn't be here talking about it today. The armourers looked up inside, ripped it open and it was there—it was a live 37-mm shell. Incidentally, it was a high-explosive shell. I tell you, it's the smoothest landing I've ever made! I guarantee I could land it on eggs because I didn't want to jar out what was there.

Waters' lucky escape called for a drink in the mess afterwards to celebrate a safe landing. Understandably, nerves needed soothing. At that time, the beer ration was only two cold bottles a fortnight. The 78 Squadron medical officer, Dr Cyril Chambers had a solution. He had the makings of 'jungle juice' in his medical supplies and quickly made a brew. The basis was medicinal alcohol; the finished product tasted much like aniseed crème de menthe. 'I had a couple extra that night,' recalled

Waters, convinced that a drink was clearly justified. He was soon impressed by Chambers' efforts:

> *If you put it in a bottle, you could have sold it—I said to him, 'That was a real good brew you put on tonight, Doc. What intrigues me is how you got the colour.' He said, 'That was quite simple, I just used tinea paint!' Naturally the next morning we were all a bit seedy and I went across to see if there was any of the brew left and to my surprise, the galvanisation of the old milk bucket he made the brew in was starting to peel off.*

On the 27th, the Australians returned to Tomohon to attack the same quarters. A force of 32 Kittyhawks from 78 Wing, sixteen from 78 Squadron, including *Black Magic*, completed the raid successfully.

February brought no relief from the heavy tropical rain and steamy conditions. And still there was mud. Despite this, the Australians continued harassing Japanese positions in the Halmaheras and the Celebes. On 3 February, Waters, along with Pilot Officer Peter Finch and Flight Sergeant Allan Beinke, again dive-bombed the Wasile pier area on the Halmaheras coast, an early-morning operation on which the pilots again met with ack-ack.

That same morning, 78 Wing's devil-may-care Wing Commander, Geoff Atherton, led a low-level sweep over Hatetabako Aerodrome on Halmahera Island. Over the target, ack-ack hit his Kittyhawk behind the cockpit and in the radiator. With glycol streaming from the engine and smoke obstructing his vision, Atherton headed out to sea, where he prepared to ditch as the aircraft's oil and glycol temperatures rose alarmingly. 'Off the clock,' he noted.

Locking back the canopy after it refused to jettison, Atherton disconnected his helmet and microphone, tightened his straps, loosened the dinghy, and partially inflated his Mae West. He approached the water with full flaps at 110 mph, cut the ignition and touched down tail first at around 90 mph, skating for some distance before a wing dipped, bringing him to a halt. He just had time to step out onto a wing and free his life raft before the aircraft sank within fifteen seconds.

Luck was on his side, as one of the accompanying pilots was able to organise his rescue. Two 75 Squadron Kittyhawks arrived as top cover. As he drifted closer to Boebole Island, Atherton came under fire, forcing him to paddle further away. Ninety minutes later, he sighted a Catalina about 24 kilometres away. Signalling with a mirror, he caught the attention of the pilot, who picked him up and took him back to Morotai. Angered at having been fired on, he grabbed a Kittyhawk and returned to strafe the area from where the shots had been fired. Somewhat mollified, he returned to Morotai.

Such mishaps underlined to Waters that he could not let his guard down, whether it be in the Halmaheras or the Celebes.

On 8 February Waters joined a dive-bombing raid on a wireless/telecommunications building on Woda Island, off the west coast of Halmahera Island. After successfully completing the raid, he and three other Kittyhawks on the mission returned via Soebarim, on the east coast. There they undertook a barge hunt, sighting around ten that were covered with branches and leaves and screened by a heavy outcrop of palm trees. Eight were strafed and hit at low level.

As the noose tightened on the remnants of the Japanese forces, information from the locals suggested there was a large enemy concentration in Tondano, in the Celebes. At the same time, further intelligence suggested the Japanese were spreading their forces away from the larger towns into smaller villages to make them less of an attractive target. A plan was developed to strike a single blow at this concentration of troops. Each of the three 78 Wing squadrons contributed 20 Kittyhawks, including Waters in *Black Magic*, to the mission on 11 February.

The first wave of 40 Kittyhawks, from 78 and 80 Squadrons and led by Wing Commander Atherton, dive-bombed ack-ack positions and barracks with 250-lb bombs. They also hit the town's hydroelectric plant with depth charges, while 75 Squadron followed to attack another part of the town before three waves of Beaufighters dropped napalm and high-explosive bombs to finish off the job. A heavy pall of smoke covered the area.

Three days later, Waters and six other Kittyhawks from 78 Squadron returned to Tondano to again dive-bomb the power station to ensure it was completely disabled. These were the last Celebes targets attacked, all future efforts being directed to the Halmaheras group. For the rest of the month the main target was the Wasile area, with Waters joining in operations to the Kaoe airstrip and Saloean on the 18th and 21st.

Waters could see that operations were winding down. He recalled later that 'most of our work had started to become routine, cleaning up and preventing barges from supplying bases.' By then, Japanese soldiers on the islands had lost contact with Tokyo. They were isolated, left to defend for themselves on Morotai, the Halmaheras and the Celebes, with no direction.

There were two more dive-bombing and strafing missions in March, but by now, most worthwhile targets in the Halmaheras and the Celebes had been crippled. The capacity of the Japanese to counterattack had been severely curtailed. Bursts of ack-ack were about all they could deliver, but those could still kill. It was a no-win situation. Although 78 Squadron's operations record book for February asserted that 'the morale of all pilots is excellent and that of the ground staff satisfactory', frustration festered. As Waters commented, 'January and February started to become boring, and I was very pleased when I was granted leave.' In mid-March, he bade a brief farewell to *Black Magic* before boarding a C-47 bound for Australia.

He was unaware of Dick Sudlow's positive official assessment of his performance at the end of January, by which time he had flown 62 operational hours. 'Sgt Waters adapted himself to operational flying very quickly and should develop into a sound and reliable pilot. He is a good solid type, popular with his fellow pilots but requires further experience before being fit to hold a commission.'

Sudlow was seeing potential. This was the first suggestion that, in time, Waters could be considered for commission to officer rank. He could be well pleased with his transition from training to combat, from rookie to seasoned fighter pilot. He had fitted in seamlessly, but it had not been easy; already, he had seen the deaths of two close comrades and had had a close shave himself. And he was only twenty.

16

WIND-DOWN

By the time Waters reached St George in late March 1945, his relationship with Margie was over. His mother, Grace, could foresee only pain and hurt in a mixed-race marriage. She had written to Margie spelling out her misgivings, saying she did not think it right for a white girl and an Aboriginal man to marry.

Living in Sydney, and serving in the WAAF, Margie had not met Len's family. The prospect of marriage was now no more. Margie and Len had written frequently to each other, and he had kept all her letters bundled together with a ribbon. The relationship was serious, but family say that while he was hurt, he understood.

A telegram to Grace and Don told them that their son would be arriving on leave. A train from Brisbane to Thallon and a hitched ride from the station brought him home. When he walked up the path to the family's house on The Terrace, nothing much had changed: just over the road the Balonne River meandered past, and the wide dirt streets had the usual few pedestrians and dust-covered cars.

After a tumultuous few months in the front line of jungle war, St George was another world: a sleepy country town on a plain with a few sparse trees and none of the frenetic activity of Noemfoor and Morotai. There, the sounds of thousands of troops and the whirring of Kittyhawk engines were an ever-present reminder of the urgency of war. In St George, the silence was deafening; in the past few years the population had grown to perhaps 1000 residents, untouched by a world in conflict except for some trenches in the school grounds, and when they read the newspaper or watched the Fox-Movietone newsreels at the shire hall.

In its Social Notes, *The Balonne Beacon* recognised service-men and women back in town on leave. On 5 April, it reported: 'Flight Sergeant L. Waters is at present on leave in town with relatives.' Waters would later reminisce that 'Naturally it was nice to be with the family once again. I took my mother to the pictures on the Saturday night after I got home.' Waters would have cut quite a dashing figure in his blue uniform and forage cap. After the usual newsreels, mostly about the latest developments of the war in Europe and the Pacific, the main feature that night was a comedy-drama, *Holy Matrimony,* starring the armed services' favourite entertainer, Gracie Fields. It provided light escapism from the deadly serious business of war.

On the way out, Waters and his mother chanced upon an attractive sixteen-year-old with dark curly hair. Gladys Saunders was her name, and Grace introduced the young woman to her son. Gladys was a housemaid at the newly refurbished Australian Hotel and knew Grace through her family. Her father, George Saunders, had earlier suggested that she contact some friends of his when she arrived in St George from Charleville to work. He had been best man at Don and Grace's wedding, and they had been witnesses at his wedding. As well, Grace was godmother to Gladys' second cousin, Billy, whose family had known the Waters at Nindigully, and had followed them to St George after the school there closed in 1939. Contact was made, and sometimes after finishing work at the hotel, Gladys would walk up the road to 'have a yarn' with the Waters family.

Len and Gladys were instantly attracted to each other. As Gladys recalled:

> *Well, he looked very smart, he was really handsome. Anyone would have fallen for him. He was lovely. Yeah, I liked him, I liked him from the beginning. I thought he was going to be a smart alec and spin me a tale, then love and leave you, sort of thing.*
>
> *He was in uniform . . . and he was very nice. [Grace] had told me about him beforehand. Her and my father were very good friends, and she called at the hotel when she knew I was working at the Australian Hotel to introduce herself [and] to tell me that she'd like me to meet her son, Leonard.*

They agreed to write to each other after Waters returned to the islands. The pain of breaking up with Margie was receding.

There was another change the family noticed: Waters had been a non-drinker before the war, but now he surprised them by going to one of the town's pubs for a drink. 'It was a shock to Mum,' Kevin recalled.

Waters had a yen to use some of his precious leave time by doing some bush work for the Mitchells at Balagna station, a complete yet familiar change from flying a fighter. Kevin was a 'cowboy' on the property at the time, mustering and rouse-abouting. He remembers the Mitchells picking up his brother at the front gate and welcoming him warmly. Waters was to miss catching up with their son and his close mate, Wal Mitchell, who was on a bomber navigation course in Canada.

The family put him up in the main homestead rather than the shed where the station hands bunked. Kevin recalls that his brother 'spent a week on Balagna working. He was out riding and mustering. He didn't speak too much about the war but he did tell us about the time he nearly got killed when the shell lodged behind him. He was thankful to get home and land safely.'

*

Gladys Saunders had had her own war experience before arriving in St George. In December 1943 she decided to leave Charleville, because 'Dad kept drinking and the fights were getting worse'. She caught the train to Townsville and stayed with some girls she knew from Charleville. 'The war news was getting very bad. The Japanese had bombed Townsville, it was very frightening.' When she told her friends she wanted to join the services, they laughed at her. When one remarked,

'They wouldn't take the likes of you!' Gladys was affronted: 'I decided I'd prove to my so-called friends and anyone else that I was as good as anyone else, if not better. So I forged my birth certificate and my identification card and got some references, even my Mum helped me.'

She wanted to join the WAAF, but she was turned away because it was clear her papers were not genuine. Undeterred, she looked elsewhere. Nearby was an office of the Women's National Emergency Legion. While not part of the Australian military, it cooperated with the Department of Defence, forming units for nursing as well as transport, some of which were attached to the U.S. Army. The recruiters were less diligent than other arms of the defence forces. 'I had the cheek to front up with my forged papers to see if I could be employed as a bus, truck, or sedan driver as a civilian employee with the United States Army. What a shock! They accepted me.'

Her American pass, issued on 20 December 1943, showed that her date of birth was 4 February 1926, making her seventeen rather than her actual age of fourteen years. They had not been bothered by the forged birth certificate and identification card. Gladys lived on the American base at Victoria Barracks, with good meals and generous pay and a uniform thrown in.

Her work involved driving a bus to the 13th Station Hospital, where she would report to the front desk. On one of these trips, a tall American in uniform and cowboy hat was pointed out to her. Asked if she knew who he was, she said no. It was John Wayne, the actor: 'I had the pleasure of meeting him.' But it was her friend Edie Thomas who had the more exciting encounter.

Edie was working on the American telephone exchange at the base when a call came through. The voice said, 'You don't know who you're talking to, do you? This is John Wayne.' Edie responded, 'And I'm Greta Garbo'. Wayne made arrangements to meet her at the exchange, and he did. Gladys was not just a little envious.

*

By the time Waters returned to Morotai, he had Gladys on his mind. His mother had asked Gladys for a photo of herself to send to her son. It was a hand-coloured portrait taken at Broadway Studios in Charleville. On receiving the photo, Waters was soon telling his mates that this was the girl he was going to marry. On Morotai, there was now much time to yarn about such things, as operations had slowed. This wind-down of activity was somewhat of an anti-climax.

Dick Sudlow was convinced that the operations his men were undertaking were having little, if any, bearing on the war's outcome. Japan was now their focus, not the islands in the south-west Pacific. Sudlow concluded that the isolated pockets of Japanese in their area were inconsequential: 'Although I was not directly involved with the controversy I certainly had my doubts about the usefulness of many of the missions we were flying, so I took it on myself to abandon a mission if I had the slightest fear that weather conditions might deteriorate and present a hazard. I could see no point in risking pilots' lives unless there was a good reason to do so.'

It was not surprising when a halt on all operations was

called on 10 April to allow concentration on the next stage of the campaign, which was to be the invasion of Borneo. Discontent among senior RAAF officers culminated in the 'Morotai Mutiny' shortly after.

Morale plummeted to a dangerously low level among personnel based on Morotai, ground staff and aircrew alike, but particularly Spitfire pilots, who had had little opportunity for the air-to-air combat they specialised in and whose aircraft were ill-suited to ground-attack missions against Japanese positions that the Americans' island-hopping campaign had bypassed.

On 19 April, Group Captain Clive Caldwell, having returned to the islands to command 80 Wing, and seven like-minded senior officers from the 17,000-strong First Tactical Air Force tendered their resignations in protest at what they saw as the side-lining of RAAF fighter squadrons to the strategically wasteful yet dangerous ground-attack mopping-up raids after the destruction of Japanese air power in January 1945.

The crisis forced an immediate government inquiry, which ultimately confirmed the officers' claims that the operations their men were fighting were not militarily justifiable. Changes in command followed. However, the 'mutiny' set the pattern for lingering discontent.

Waters arrived back in the midst of the mutiny to find his flying limited to training. On Anzac Day, 25 April 1945, he flew as part of a squadron formation, but it was another five days before he was again airborne, this time in a 78 Wing formation. This involved Wing Commander Geoff Atherton taking the Kittyhawks through their paces in a test of battle climbs, tight formation flying and turning and diving manoeuvres. All kept their positions within the formation. Atherton had all the pilots, including Waters, tested in as many aspects of their flying ability as possible. He later commented to Dick Sudlow that 'it was a pleasure to fly with a squadron that flew so well and knew what to do in a squadron formation as well as a wing formation.'

In May, Waters flew just eight times, all training flights involving squadron formation and manoeuvres such as battle climbs. Not being an officer, he was not privy to the machinations of higher command that had led to the so-called mutiny. Waters understood the consequences of the breakdown of RAAF command in the islands, but he and his mates saw it more as a result of the high-handedness of the Americans trying to 'snatch the glory' through their control of the media:

> *The Yanks, all they were interested in was getting back to the Philippines, and we had to clean up in between. If there was anything too hot for them to go into, they'd send us in and if the effort was successful, you'd still hear over the news that night that there was another successful raid by the American air force in the islands.*

They might have been allies with a common enemy, but Waters' experience underlined the simmering tensions between the Australians and the Americans owing to the overarching control that the American command exercised in relegating the Australians to a secondary role. Although he admitted to important exceptions at a personal level, he would harbour this antipathy for the rest of his life.

17

ONE OF THE BOYS

When Waters climbed into the ring for the final of the inter-services middleweight contest, he knew he faced his toughest opponent yet. An imposing African-American was in the opposite corner, a soldier with the 93rd Infantry Division. There were some 'fit fighters amongst them, too', he later recalled. His mates in 78 Squadron had backed him throughout the fights and won thousands of Dutch guilders on his victories. They again backed him in the final.

From that first bout in January 1945, Waters had continued winning. Fellow 78 Squadron pilot Max Davey recalled that Waters was 'an excellent boxer, having fought many elimination bouts, held each Friday night in front of huge crowds, his opponents consisting of Australian army and navy boxers, and the best fighters the American marines and navy could produce.' This would be his fifteenth fight, and he was determined to keep his unbeaten record on a tropical night before thousands of cheering fight fans. The American fought out of the corner draped with the Stars and Stripes; Waters out of the corner sporting the Australian flag.

One of his 78 Squadron mates, Flight Lieutenant Bob Crawford, was among those who backed Waters in the ring that night. 'The squadron had all the money on him, and at one stage in the second round it didn't look as though we were going to win, but Len came through and was the victor and we all won money.'

Waters proudly recalled: 'I won the middleweight title at Morotai. I held it for 1944 and 1945. I had fifteen fights and I didn't lose one. There were only about five or six negroes in the American boxing team, but I beat them all.' No official record of the fight was kept, as it was considered a sporting event, but he was presented with a handsome trophy in the shape of a wooden shield with two aluminium plaques fittingly held in place by aircraft rivets. The top scroll was engraved with the words: 'MOROTAI. BOXING. CHAMPIONSHIP', and the lower reading: 'Middleweight Division Won by FLT/SGT "Len" Waters. 1944-45 N.E.I.'

Many years later, Waters was asked about the fight in conversation with friends in Sydney, and explained that his opponent kept hitting him with low punches. Despite two warnings from the referee, he continued. Just as Crawford's recollection confirms, Waters admitted that he was in trouble, but after another low blow the referee issued a third warning and stopped the fight. He may have won on a foul, but he won nonetheless.

The fight highlighted the issue of racial discrimination generally. Waters was adamant that in his time in the RAAF since August 1942 and, more particularly, in 78 Squadron since November 1944, he had experienced no discrimination. But that was not what he saw in the tense relations between white Americans and African-Americans on Morotai. 'Everyone felt sorry for them the way the white Yanks used to treat them. No one was allowed to hold a rank above captain in the 93rd Division,' Waters observed later. While the enlisted men were black, most of the officers were white. It was generally thought that being assigned to command a black unit was the kiss of death for a white officer. As well as the 14,000 enlisted men in the division, there were 883 officers, half of whom were black but were restricted to lieutenant rank.

From its beginning as an all-black outfit formed in the United States during World War I, the 93rd Division had been burdened with overt discrimination. This continued to play out during World War II in the South West Pacific Area—not least on Morotai, where they were intent on proving they were just as good as an all-white division. A race war threatened to erupt before cooler heads prevailed. Segregated units only exacerbated the situation.

This all happened within a few hundred metres of the Australians on Morotai, who had a very different situation: they had a lone Aboriginal fighter pilot. The Australians could clearly see how differently racial tensions played out in

American units. This was an uncomfortable reminder of race relations at home—something even reflected in the RAAF's own magazine, *Wings*. Just a few weeks earlier, a flight lieutenant from 326 Radar Station in Western Australia had written an article headed 'Black RAAF'. The artwork, a caricature of an Aboriginal face. It began with a reference to an Aboriginal man named Peter and his 'unofficial appointment to the non-existent rank of Acting Corporal, Unpaid'.

> *Peter by virtue of his energy and thoroughness, was appointed boong boss and was duly presented with two stripes by a corporal proceeding to the city for a bowler hat . . . A minor crisis arose when Peter realised that his shirt, carrying the one and only set of stripes, had to be washed occasionally.*

The article went on to describe an outdoor film evening to which 'the natives' were invited—but directed to sit 'down wind'. Peter then 'ushered the tribe into the improvised open-air theatre. The neatly dressed women, in floral print dresses, with glossy curly hair, were given seating accommodation on an old tent fly . . . Most of the children were naked but all had been carefully washed and powdered.'

To this RAAF officer, Indigenous Australians were people to be lampooned and dismissed with patronising contempt. This was a dangerous message to send to the airmen who were readers of *Wings*. In the theatre of war, however, another factor came into play: the national ideal of egalitarianism. The men of 78 Squadron formed a tight unit. Familiarity and dependence on each other in life-or-death situations broke down racial and social barriers. The danger they shared created deep bonds between them. This cohesion welded the men into a tight team, leaving no room for divisiveness. With their segregated units, the Americans were unable to experience this bonding across racial lines. In fact, the differences were magnified.

On the battlefield, racism was out of place in the Australian services. As fellow pilot Peter Finch put it, Waters would stop a bullet as easily as the next person; Waters himself said that bullets did not discriminate. Bob Crawford reflected this pragmatic attitude: 'I don't think anyone ever knew he was an Aborigine—he was one of the boys, he was just there—we all dressed the same, just shorts, boots, a shirt, sometimes no shirt, no rank, no nothing, we were all just one big happy family.' As Dick Sudlow put it, 'Len fitted very comfortably into his slot in the squadron as one of the team.'

Waters was respected for his mechanical nous just as he was for his boxing skill. With his background as a flight engineer working on Kittyhawks, he had an ear for trouble: 'I knew if the plane was airworthy.' He would warn his fellow pilots on the tarmac as they warmed up: 'I wouldn't take that aircraft up if I were you, there is something wrong with it.' This they appreciated.

Waters' standing within the group was reaffirmed on Anzac Day 1945. He had returned from a squadron formation, his sole flight for the day. A new batch of Doc Chambers' infamous brew beckoned Waters and the rest of the pilots from the flight when they walked onto the sawdust-covered floor of the mess:

> *Our old doctor used to make us a couple of buckets of jungle juice. We could have a drink and relax after a flight when we came back. We were over in the recreation tent—it was the officers' and pilots' mess. We were just lounging around, laying down back on our parachutes, and the flap came back on the tent and Jim was standing there, my brother. I thought I was seeing a ghost! It was a fantastic surprise. We'd been apart for about three years.*

Amid this sudden elation, Jim was immediately welcomed to the mess, and he and his brother caught up and shared experiences and news of home. Importantly, there was no differentiation between the brothers in the mess. That Jim was a private in the AIF and was not in the RAAF was irrelevant to 78 Squadron pilots: he was putting his life on the line, just as they were. Although he was considerably darker than his brother, it posed no problem here. He was just one of the 'fellas'. In his battalion, Jim's nickname was 'Darkie'. Waters recalled: 'Jim was three-quarter caste—my mother was the same colour. My father was almost a white man, and you would never have taken him for an Aboriginal. When Jim came there, and even after that, there was no discrimination in any shape or form.' Waters' comments on his brother's darker skin perhaps underline his own sensitivity to the question of colour. He had had a momentary concern that this might be problematic for his fellow pilots. To his relief, it was not.

Jim Waters had arrived on Morotai with the 2/23rd Battalion AIF, which was part of the 9th Division's 26th Brigade. The island was a staging post in preparation for the 7th and

9th Divisions' amphibious landings on the islands of Tarakan and Borneo under Operation Oboe. After their brief catch-up, Jim Waters returned to his unit in preparation for the brigade's landing on Tarakan on 1 May:

> *They were on their way to Tarakan, they didn't know where they were going, but our upper echelon of officers had an idea because there had been quite a bit of softening-up by the Liberators and heavy bombers that the Australians had, and the Yanks were coming down from the Philippines and bombing. Anyhow, Jim said, 'There's a big bash on, I don't know where we're going.' I said we had a pretty fair idea.*

Jim Waters did not have to wait long before finding out. Estimates of enemy strength before the Tarakan assault showed that there were not more than 48 Japanese fighters and 21 bombers in the whole of the Dutch East Indies, while enemy troops on Tarakan were estimated at 4000, of whom only 1500 were considered to be combat troops.

On 1 May, the 2/23rd Battalion, as part of the 26th Brigade, was tasked with capturing Tarakan. After a massive pre-invasion air and naval bombardment, the battalion, along with the 2/48th, landed on the beach about 8.15 a.m. and began their advance towards the strip. Jim Waters took part in the landing that first morning. The hope was to capture it so RAAF squadrons could move in to support the ground troops. This was not an easy task, as Japanese forces turned out to be much stronger than anticipated. Fighting continued throughout the day as the 2/23rd came up against Japanese snipers. By nightfall they had dug in along the main road to Tarakan town, which they went on to capture two days later.

Meanwhile, Len Waters languished on Morotai, increasingly frustrated by the lack of involvement in operations. The main RAAF contingent, around 4700 personnel, had left for Tarakan on 27 April, while on Morotai, the rear echelon of 78 Squadron—nineteen officers and 37 NCOs, mostly pilots—had to settle for the odd training flight and routine equipment testing. Their expectation they would be joining the rest of 78 Squadron in seven to ten days quickly evaporated. In his summary for May, Dick Sudlow explained that the squadron could not go to Tarakan because, through unforeseen circumstances, the strip on the island had not been finished. 'It has been difficult to keep the morale up, with no operations to sustain interest.'

At this time, a new pilot arrived to take his place with 78 Squadron—Geoff Cutler, whose older brother, Roden Cutler, had earlier in the war been awarded the VC while fighting with the AIF during the Syrian campaign. Waters remembered how Cutler quickly fitted in, becoming one of the boys as they got about Morotai in shorts and not much else because of the tropical heat. Cutler quickly developed a deep suntan as did his comrades. Waters, with wry amusement, noted that they all referred to each other as 'boongs'. It was in this light-hearted vein that racism was turned on its head in the cloistered environment of a south-west Pacific wartime base.

With ample time on their hands, they quickly became good mates. For the month of May, Waters flew just eight times, and for Cutler, having arrived with the expectation of operational flying, it could only have been a let-down. Inadvertently, he was drawn into a controversy involving Waters' promotion to Section Leader. 'There was another young fella in the flight, in the squadron, he was a bit jealous of me being promoted,' Waters recalled. 'He said that Cutler was sour on me—Cutler was a Flying Officer and I was a Flight Sergeant. Of course, he was a silvertail too. That's how we referred to them. He came from the upper crust.' The 'young fella' said to Waters, 'Cutler is sour on you, the things you do when you're leading the flight.' Waters decided to confront the issue head-on and approached Cutler in front of others in the squadron. Raising the issue in public confirmed not just Waters' growing confidence but his status within the squadron:

> *So I put it to him one night when we were having a few drinks, and I said, 'I believe you're a bit unhappy with me and the things I do.' And he said, 'I don't know where you got that idea from, I'll tell you now, I'd rather fly number two to you than anyone else in the Squadron.'*

Years later, Cutler confirmed this statement. 'Len Waters was a great man and a great pilot. Of all the pilots in 78 Squadron, I preferred flying number two to Len because to me, he was the best.' There had been no rank distinction, he added. 'As for Len being an Aborigine, we were all dark back then, given the heat and the outdoor lives that we led. I honestly didn't realise that Len was an Aboriginal until it was pointed out to me.' Waters would later comment: 'Funny thing was, with me being the only Aboriginal pilot and all, Cutler was a bloody sight blacker than I was!' Waters and Cutler would remain good friends for years to come.

There were celebrations to mark the end of the war in Europe, which saw nineteen Kittyhawks do a 'pansy formation' in the shape of a 'VE' on Tuesday, 8 May 1945. Waters celebrated appropriately with a few beers. Even with beer costing one shilling and threepence a bottle, the squadron drank to the occasion. It was a sign of hope that the war in the Pacific would soon come to an end. But such was the boredom that giving their own Kittyhawks a wash and polish helped to fill in time. The aircraft needed it—the tropical weather and continuous operations over the past year had taken their toll.

18

COMING OF AGE

Flight Lieutenant Joe Black's time as Officer Commanding 'A' Flight was up. He had finished his tour of duty, and it was time to return to Australia. Dick Sudlow needed a new OC. His choice was Flying Officer Fred Jones. Before the appointment was officially announced, Waters took the unusual step of approaching Flying Officer Lyall Ellers and asking if he would be happy to be the OC of 'A' Flight.

Ellers said he would, without knowing the reason for Waters' query. Armed with this, Waters and two colleagues went to Sudlow and argued the case for Ellers over Jones. Sudlow reconsidered his decision and appointed Ellers. Ellers was later somewhat critical of Sudlow for a decision that he saw as giving in.

Just why Waters took this action is unclear. Like him, Jones had joined the RAAF as ground crew, as a general fitter, in August 1942, re-mustering to aircrew in June 1943. In ground crew, Waters and Jones overlapped for two months at Ascot Vale. In aircrew, they continued to overlap, first at Somers for six weeks, then at Narrandera, learning to fly Tiger Moths. Waters followed Jones, who was on Course 42, to Uranquinty, where their paths again crossed, this time for four months. Finally, after both had been awarded their wings, they were together for a month on the conversion to Kittyhawks course at Mildura. Whether they ever met is uncertain, but likely. Jones joined 78 Squadron in late September 1944, about six weeks before Waters did.

If there was an incident involving them, it may well have occurred during aircrew training or indeed on 78 Squadron, between November 1944 and May 1945. But there is no record of such an incident in either man's service record. Jones's record shows that when he finished his tour of duty with 78 Squadron on 30 June 1945, Sudlow gave him a glowing assessment. 'An extremely keen and hard-working officer. Shows initiative and with more experience should prove a sound leader,' he wrote.

Perhaps Waters thought Jones not operationally experienced enough to justify being placed in charge of 'A' Flight, his record showing just 36 strikes and sorties and five other ops—less than half Waters' record. Ellers, on the other hand, was already a pilot of considerable experience, having flown Wirraways and Boomerangs with other squadrons. He had completed an operational tour in New Guinea with 4 Squadron RAAF, during which he completed 47 operational sorties, 71 operational travel flights and 30 training exercises. 'Operational travel' included flying personnel around in Wirraways and Tiger Moths, some of it over enemy lines. Among these flights were searches for downed crew.

Thus the record shows that Ellers had much more experience than Jones. Just why Sudlow chose Jones in the first place is unclear, as he must have known of Ellers' previous operational experience. Given Waters' proclivity to generally take a low profile, it would seem he felt strongly enough to take the initiative, first to sound out Ellers and then to take the matter to Sudlow. This was out of character, but clearly Waters felt he was by then sufficiently respected, and experienced enough as a pilot, to voice his concern. And Sudlow listened.

With this decision in play, Waters had to cool his heels on Morotai as more and more delays occurred on Tarakan. By 1 June there was still a way to go before the Tarakan airstrip would be serviceable. Heavy traffic churned up access roads to the strip, with torrential rain washing them away. In a week of little rain, some progress was made, only for the road to become a quagmire again after a deluge mid-month. Frustrating as it was, work continued on the strip to make it operational in the face of unforeseen problems that included a high water table and a lack of paving materials.

Throughout May and early June, the AIF advanced into the island's steep inland areas. By mid-June, the fighting had mainly subsided and the 2/23rd Battalion began mopping up operations in the central sector of the island, fending off skirmishes and conducting patrols looking for stragglers.

For the RAAF, Tarakan was soon regarded a failure: aircraft were not able to land there to give air cover to the troops before they had the island sufficiently under control. Sudlow commented in the squadron's operations record book that, 'Viewed from all angles it has been a very unsatisfactory period. Since April 10 pilots have had very little flying and the ground staff have not worked on aircraft since that date.' Waters recalled that the squadron had been told that they were to join the fighting shortly after the landing. 'They were going to give us six days for the 9th Div. to take the beachhead and the strip; we would be going in to give them close support to take the rest of the island.' They finally landed there nearly eleven weeks later.

In the meantime, Waters had a significant occasion that could not go without being celebrated. On 20 June, he turned 21. The boys in the squadron drank his health as beer and spirits flowed at the mess. If the war had done anything, it had introduced him to alcohol as something to be shared and enjoyed with his comrades. The culture in the squadron, as in all its counterparts, was a periodical drinking pattern termed a 'grog bash'—in effect, a group binge as a way of relieving built-up tension from operations. There was some pressure to join in, but his mate Frank Smith worried from early on that Waters was a 'fragile drinker'.

Finally, on 18 July, Waters took off from Morotai, heading for the base on the southern Philippines island of Tawi Tawi to refuel after a flight of more than three hours. The island was so small that aircraft had to wait in a holding pattern owing to the shortage of runway space. And then it was on to the short, rough landing strip at Tarakan, almost another two hours away. The next day, he once more met up with his brother. 'Jim and I were all right after that. He wasn't stationed too far away from us. We were actually in Tarakan city, in a big girls' college—first time we lived in a building.' While buildings in the town were badly damaged from bombing, engineers rigged up canvas roofs, and the men enjoyed the amenity of having solid walls and tiled floors rather than tents with dirt floors that were subject to flooding.

From that point on, the two Waters boys spent as much time together as possible. 'We used to go up to the perimeter and pick Jim up and drop him back again later that night,' Len recalled. Just as on Morotai, Jim was welcomed warmly by the rest of the squadron. Yet again, egalitarianism in the theatre of war proved strong. Jim had not long seen action in the Battle of Balikpapan, the concluding stage of Operation Oboe 2.

In years to come, in reflective moments, Jim would talk of the horrors he had witnessed, of seeing enemy soldiers being virtually sliced in half by machine-gun fire and of staunching the bleeding of one of his comrades by packing the wound with mud held in by a towel he quickly tore in half, before carrying him back to camp and hospital. This appears to have saved the Digger's life—and Jim kept the other half of the towel for the rest of his life.

Although cut off from their homeland, the Japanese continued to operate the oilfields at Balikpapan, on the mid-east coast, where there were an estimated 6000 enemy troops. The role of 78 Wing in Operation Oboe 2 was to provide close support and cover for the 7th Division in the region, all the while rendering airstrips in the area unusable. The objective in these operations was to keep the Japanese army units on the move, denying access to village food supplies and driving them back into the jungle where they would become targets for the indigenous Dyaks, who supported the Allies' operations. To aid this, commandos were dropped behind the lines to make contact with the Dyaks and organise them into a guerrilla force. The Japanese feared them.

During July, the Japanese at Sandakan and nearby areas in Borneo came under constant bombing and machine-gun fire. As with Balikpapan, the tactical plan was to prevent the enemy consolidating positions or concentrating in any one area. Aircraft from the First Tactical Air Force were used to attack any sign of concentration. Attacks were made on stores, keeping the enemy on the move and preventing them from growing food supplies.

At the same time, the AIF was finding dislodging the enemy on Tarakan difficult. Sudlow was taken on a tour of the front line on a day when the American Liberator bombers were to bomb a Japanese stronghold. 'The precision bombing by the Liberators was magnificent to watch, every bomb plumb on the target. Of course, they had bomb sights to help. Our dive-bombing was only as accurate as the pilot was skilled,' Sudlow recalled.

As CO, Sudlow was required to write reports on each pilot in his squadron. On 14 July, he turned his mind to Waters, assessing him as 'an average operational pilot. Not particularly energetic but does his work satisfactorily.' To be rated 'average' among these battle-hardened veterans was confirmation that Waters had made the grade as a combat pilot. Sudlow himself commented that his assessments of his own flying ability progressed from 'average/good average' during training to 'above average' in 78 Squadron. Undoubtedly the greater number of hours he flew sharpened his skills.

He listed Waters' total hours since completion of training at 197:15, and total operational hours at 85:30. Waters was indeed among the elite. Sudlow's comment that Waters was 'not particularly energetic' could be explained by the fact that at this stage of the war, pilots were keen to minimise the risks. Sudlow himself took steps to avoid losing any more pilots as the war drew to a close.

On 21 July, Waters joined seven other Kittyhawks bombing and strafing barracks at Sandakan. In a departure from normal practice, the Kittyhawks were each armed with a single 500-lb bomb under the fuselage, rather than the usual 250-lb bomb under each wing. The heavier bombs came from the Americans in preparation for the attack on a group of buildings and huts on the northern boundary of Sandala Estate.

They took off at 6 a.m. and were met with fine weather and good visibility. Waters was wingman to Sudlow for this, his 38th strike. However, on this occasion, he did not fly *Black Magic* but another Kittyhawk, as he headed to the eastern end of the town. The change of fighter did not impede his accuracy. 'Direct hit on barracks,' Waters recorded in his logbook. His was one of three direct hits, the remaining bombs falling in the target area but overshooting the buildings. Enemy activity on the ground was scarce, the only Japanese presence being a few fires for cooking.

Two days later, Waters joined another six Kittyhawks to again bomb and strafe Sandakan. He noted that the bomb he dropped overshot the target but his strafing was a little more successful, hitting a hut, but added that not much damage could be seen. On the 25th, Waters was re-united with *Black Magic* for another attack on Sandakan. He joined his fellow pilots in breakfasting early before being driven down to his Kittyhawk, which had been refuelled and re-armed by the time he arrived. Waters took part in the normal discussion between pilots, armourers and airframe crew before going through his usual pre-flight check in preparation for the attack by ten aircraft to once more bomb and strafe Sandakan. In the event, they were forced to turn back by bad weather when just 50 kilometres from the target. The flight deviations that were needed to avoid the worst spots had run fuel too low to continue. However, by now Sandakan had been practically wiped out.

On the 27th, Waters and another eleven Kittyhawks flew to Sepinggan, near Balikpapan, to be briefed on operations. Six of the aircraft were assigned to the airfield at Oelin and six to the airfield at Tabanio. They shot up the hangars, huts and control tower at Oelin and reported that the Tabanio airstrips were unserviceable. It is not clear which target Waters attacked, but he noted in his logbook: 'Pretty good show. Very intrepid.'

Later that day, Waters wrote in his logbook that he had led the formation of ten Kittyhawks that headed for Riko Village, where the Australians dropped sixteen bombs, causing heavy damage to pillboxes and tents. Waters was among aircraft that strafed enemy ground positions. When the Kittyhawks left, fires were spreading throughout the village. He noted, 'Army very pleased, 5 Japs killed.' All aircraft stayed at Sepinggan overnight and returned to Tarakan the next day. It was, according to Waters, a 'good trip'. He would later say of his raids on Balikpapan that, overall, they had brought mixed results.

On 2 August, he climbed into *Black Magic* and joined two sections of four aircraft to fly to Balikpapan, with Waters leading the second section. But the weather was against them, rain and wind battering the aircraft on the way down to Sepinggan for briefing, refuelling and bombing up. 'Attempted two bashes from Balik, weathered out each time,' Waters recorded. Back at Sepinggan overnight, the weather again forced them to abort the mission the next day and jettison their bombs.

Waters did not fly on the 4th, a day on which 80 Squadron provided support for the army by successfully strafing the same general area north of Balikpapan. It was on the way home that the weather worsened, with dense cloud and rain to 18,000 feet. With visibility down to zero, two of the formation that entered the cloud failed to reappear. With no communication from either of them, the alarm was quickly raised. A search by Spitfires from 452 Squadron failed to find any trace of the missing Kittyhawks. To add to the tragedy, one of the Spitfires crashed on take-off and the pilot was killed. It was assumed that the two Kittyhawks had collided and crashed in the heavy cloud.

Two days later, on 6 August, Waters undertook a photo reconnaissance mission to the Brantian Estate palm oil mill, south of Sandakan. He flew *Black Magic* while Pilot Officer Roland Hill provided cover. On the way to the target, cumulus cloud from 2500 feet to 6000 feet reduced visibility. Hazy conditions prevailed over the target, but as they were there, Waters made two sweeps at 2200 feet before returning to base with seventeen photographs. Although the photos did not overlap, they indicated that buildings on the estate were in good condition and clearly in use.

While Waters did not know it, this was to be his last flight in his Kittyhawk. The name *Black Magic* on the cowl was by now almost illegible owing to the ravages of the tropical weather. The fading of the name was perhaps fitting. That same day, the Americans dropped the atomic bomb on Hiroshima. This was a heartening sign for the men that the end of the war was indeed in sight.

If the enemy's anti-aircraft guns were all but silenced, there was still an exception to be found at Samarinda, one of the last major bases the Japanese held on Borneo. On 9 August, one of Waters' mates, Pilot Officer Ted Quinn, of 80 Squadron, took off on a bombing and strafing mission with seven others to attack Japanese installations at the Dutch concession of Louise. They dived and bombed from 6000 feet with spectacular success. But when it came to his turn to dive and strafe, Quinn's aircraft was hit by small-arms fire just behind the cowling. Flames could be seen underneath the fuselage. It was thought he was unaware of the damage as he completed his strafing run, but he was then seen to belly-land and skid into an oil pumping plant. The aircraft and the oil plant burnt fiercely. Waters bitterly recalled that Quinn had not originally been scheduled to fly that day:

> *One of the pilots had engine trouble on take-off and he had to return, more or less did a circle and landed. When this other fellow returned to base, Quinny called out to the squadron leader, 'I'll take his place.' He had his motor on, took off, caught up to the squadron, and they went down and did the raid. There was only one casualty on that raid and it was Ted Quinn. So Teddy Quinn was killed on the last raid.*

It was to have been the last flight for Quinn, who had completed his tour of duty and was due to return home to his farm in South Australia. As it happened, he was the last RAAF pilot to die in action in the war. There was bitter irony in his death coming on the same day the Americans dropped the second atomic bomb on Nagasaki. Quinn's death hit Waters hard. Along with Frank Smith they had formed a strong bond during training on Course 44.

As with the deaths of Stan Hattersley and Johnny Griffith early in his tour of duty, Quinn's death affected him more than other incidents he had witnessed. With the expected end to hostilities, there was no further point in risking lives. Waters himself had been holed seven times in all. He and Frank Smith confronted CO Dick Sudlow:

> *When we heard about him buying it, we had a look and they had us down for a flight each the next day. We went across to the CO to lodge a protest. We paraded before our Squadron Leader and asked could*

> *we be excused from flying as it shook us up quite a bit, losing our mate. We said, 'We don't feel like going on a raid where Quinny had just got shot.' We had finished our tour, whether the powers that be knew what was going on I didn't know, but he said, 'Just leave it as it is on the notice board.' He took us over to see the Wing Commander, [who] more or less said the same thing, 'just leave it on the notice board. You never know, you mightn't even have to fly tomorrow.'*

And indeed they didn't. The war was all but over. If the two atomic bombs had not brought Japan to its knees, then the news on 8 August that the Soviet Union had officially declared war on Japan meant defeat was inevitable: Japan knew it simply could not win a war against two great powers. All airborne operations stopped. The end to hostilities came officially on 14 August, when the First Tactical Air Force sent out a message to squadrons:

> *Secret: offensive operations against enemy cities land communications and other land targets except direct support for allied ground forces in contact with the enemy will cease until further orders. Reconnaissance and photo missions anti shipping strikes and fighter attacks against airborne enemy aeroplanes will continue. Forces charged with air defence will be especially alert.*

The warning to air defences to be on the alert was to guard against the possibility that a few Japanese airmen would make suicide attacks rather than surrender; but this did not eventuate. As the Official History of World War II observes, the

Japanese loyally obeyed the order of their Emperor. The next day, 15 August, the Japanese surrendered.

Celebrations on Tarakan began immediately—and energetically. Pilot James Harding, 80 Squadron, recalled that whatever there was to be drunk did not last long. 'The word from "above" was that tomorrow's weather had been declared too bad for flying, and so it miraculously came to pass despite the blue skies, gentle winds, and the opinion of the meteorological people. After all, what did they know!' And that was not all, as Dick Sudlow remembered:

> *I reckon every gun on the island—army twenty-five pounders, ack-ack guns, tank guns, forty millimetre Bofor[s] guns, machine-guns, rifles, revolvers, were fired into the air with rare abandon, and every shell and every bullet had to return to earth somewhere. Somehow we survived all that lead.*

Victory was marked with a solemn thanksgiving service at the local war cemetery, conducted by the joint RAAF chaplains. On the 17th, Waters joined his fellow air and ground crew for a squadron dinner in the airmen's mess to celebrate and toast Dick Sudlow's farewell. Waters now knew he would not be adding to his combat service record, which showed 41 strikes and attacks and 54 other operations. He had flown 105 operational hours plus 42 'other' hours. Sudlow, who had watched him closely during their time together in the islands, held him in high regard, rating him in his logbook as 'Average plus'. Such RAAF understatement was typical.

19

TRUE AUSTRALIAN BLOOD

Abruptly, 78 Squadron had gone from a war footing to having no enemy in front of them, other than those still hiding in the jungle and unaware that hostilities had ended. Flying was reduced to two days a week and involved dropping leaflets to inform the Japanese troops of the surrender. The contrast for Waters was surreal. He had gone from front-line action and the constant hits of adrenaline to wondering how to fill in his time.

Sporting events were hurriedly organised. Volleyball and badminton had been popular on Morotai and also on Tarakan. The net that was erected was used for both sports, but because the shuttlecock was a bit too light the players added some extra tape to make one end heavier. Those playing were mainly the pilots and, according to Lyall Ellers, Waters was regarded as skilled at both games. For so many thousands of young men cooped up on an island, such games with a strong competitive edge were a means of redirecting all that pent-up energy.

On 25 August the entertainer Gracie Fields, on a victory sweep through the South West Pacific Area, arrived on Tarakan to perform for the massed troops, who gathered for the 'Victory Revue'. Such was the demand for the 7000 seats in the open-air theatre that each unit's attendance was limited to 50 per cent of its strength. Gracie wowed them, and they were vociferous in their clamour for her not to leave the stage. Of course, Waters had a soft spot for 'Our Gracie'. She had starred in *Holy Matrimony*, the film he had seen the night he met young Gladys Saunders in St George earlier in the year. Thoughts were turning to home.

His brother Jim was still at Tarakan, having survived the landing on Borneo. The two sat down to talk about what might lie ahead. Then a conundrum arose that Waters had not foreseen. A British Commonwealth Occupation Force (BCOF) was being formed to go to Japan, and volunteers were sought. Ultimately, about 16,000 Australians served in the BCOF, including an infantry contingent of 4700 men. RAAF squadrons 76, 77 and 82 were also posted to Japan. Waters was keen.

> *I said to Jimmy, 'What say we join the Occupation Force, go over there and have a look at the enemy at their expense?' He said, 'No, I've seen enough of the slant-eyed bastards. I'll be going home on the first boat I can get on.' So I said, 'Oh well, I'll go home too.'*

Waters later contemplated what could have been his fate had he indeed joined the BCOF. In 1950, after four years of service in Japan, the lone RAAF unit still in Japan, 77 Squadron, was diverted to support United Nations forces in South Korea after the invasion by North Korean forces. 'You know how fate is. Had I gone over there and done operations in Korea, I could have been buried on the side of a hill in Korea.'

He thought of Ron Guthrie, who had been an early Allied casualty after being shot down. Guthrie had been keen to serve in the Korean War, as he had been frustrated in his desire to see combat in World War II. What he was unaware of—and would not know for another twenty years—was that his father had intervened. A former Light Horseman in World War I, he had personally approached his local MHR, who handily was Prime Minister Ben Chifley, to request that his only son not be sent to a war zone. This sealed his fate. At the end of World War II, when the RAAF no longer wanted fighter pilots, Guthrie re-categorised to air traffic control before returning to flying. As Guthrie recalled, 'In those days, 1946–48, the RAAF was called the "interim air force", it was a sort of a stop-gap between the war and the future. We got by until some permanent decisions were taken by the government on the size of services and type of aircraft.'

The outbreak of hostilities on the Korean Peninsula meant the RAAF suddenly needed fighter pilots, and Guthrie jumped at the chance. He joined 77 Squadron as the only pilot with experience in jet fighters. He flew fourteen combat sorties before being shot down by a Russian MiG-15 on 29 August 1951 while flying a Meteor and attacking another MiG-15. He ejected at an altitude of 38,300 feet while flying at a speed of Mach 0.84, with the temperature at minus 50°C—dressed in a lightweight cotton flying suit. At the time, it was the fastest and highest bailout attempted successfully, and Guthrie took 30 minutes to reach the ground, where he was duly taken prisoner. He spent two difficult years as a POW before being released and returned to Australia.

In later years, Guthrie's experience clearly gave Waters a level of comfort in his decision to forgo service in Japan. The decision made, Waters left for Australia on 27 August 1945, flying out on a C-47 transport. Jim Waters had to wait behind for an army troop ship. Unbeknown to Len, his brother had a change of heart.

> *I wasn't home a week and Mum got a cable from Jim to say he had joined the Occupation Force and [would go] to Japan. He was eighteen months over there and had a ball, and I could have been there with him. But then . . . I suppose if I had gone over there I might have still been a single man.*

From February 1946 to January 1947, Jim Waters served with the BCOF in the 122nd Transport Platoon. In early 1946 Len belatedly applied. 'I tried to join the Occupation Force. They didn't accept me. I reckon they'd had enough of me.' Not long after the war finished, and while Jim was in Japan, the army reinstated the rule about members being substantially of European origin or descent. This meant that only a few Aboriginal or Torres Strait Islander men served in the Occupation Force.

In March 1946, the army announced that it was 'not accepting Aboriginals [*sic*] for service with the interim forces,' meaning they would not be chosen for Japan. The clear implication was that men who had fought for Australia during the war were not welcome for peacetime service. Pastor Doug Nicholls, secretary of the Australian Aborigines' League, pointed out that about 1000 Aboriginal men—the known figure at the time—had been members of the three Australian services during the war: 'The statement that men of our race who served in the war are not wanted in Japan is embarrassing and undemocratic.' Jim got in just in time.

One of the men affected by the ban was Sergeant Reg Saunders, a Gunditjmara man from Framlingham in western Victoria. By coincidence, he is thought to be a distant cousin to Gladys Saunders, the young woman Len Waters had met while at home on leave. Saunders' history was similar to Waters': he left school after Grade 8 and worked in a sawmill and then in a timber-cutting business with his father and brother, Harry. Saunders joined the army in April 1940, was soon promoted to sergeant, and served in North Africa with the 2/7th Battalion before joining the failed defence of Greece and Crete in early 1941. By August 1942, Saunders was back in Australia. Eight months later he was sent to New Guinea, but he went with a heavy heart: Harry had been killed in action at Gona, Papua, in November 1942, while serving with the 2/14th Battalion AIF.

After his natural leadership caught the eye of commanders, Saunders was sent to Officer Training School. On 25 November 1944 he was the first Aboriginal soldier to graduate as a commissioned officer in the Second AIF. An officer on the selection committee commented to the panel after Saunders had left

Don Waters put together a ring-barking team to work on farms after he moved to Nindigully. Taken at Box Flat, the photo shows Don, standing on the left. Son George is seated on the left, and son Jim is seated on the right of the group of three. (AIATSIS)

Grace Waters and son Barney Waters, then thirteen, at Nindigully. (AIATSIS)

Grace and Don Waters. (Kevin Waters)

Len Waters' brother, Jim, on the right, with Nugget Wightman and Cecil Wightman, at Nindigully in the 1930s. (AIATSIS)

Nindigully school in the 1920s, shortly before Len Waters attended. (State Library of Queensland)

Len Waters on his enlistment in the RAAF in August 1942, aged eighteen. (NAA: A9301, 78144)

Len Waters being presented with his coveted wings on graduation day. (Gladys Waters)

Len Waters (second from left, rear) and fellow 2 OTU graduates. (Gladys Waters)

Above: Hand-colouring of photos was meant to heighten realism, but this photo of Len Waters absurdly denied his Kamilaroi heritage in portraying him as light-skinned. On the back, he wrote a message of appreciation to his mother, Grace, for among other things, 'teaching me right from wrong'. (Gladys Waters)

Above: Len Waters at the time he joined 78 Squadron RAAF. (Gladys Waters)

Above: The flying suit that Len Waters wore was effective but cumbersome. (Gladys Waters)

Left: Len's sister, Florence, on the left, with her cousins Mavis McIntosh, Doris Craigie and Ron McIntosh. Ron was another of the extended family to serve, albeit it briefly, as a signalman in the CMF. (AIATSIS)

A friendly training session for Len Waters (right foreground) with Ken Salter. The crowd are all 78 Squadron ground staff: (left to right) 'Twitchy' Lewis, Lenny Jackson, Stan Keady, Ken Holt, Jack Price, 'Curley' Kim and Jimmy Byrne. Towels and boots seem to be the dress code of the day. (Gordon Clarke)

Len Waters, standing third right, with 78 Squadron mates Max Davey, Mike White and Jack Eagle. Frank Smith is seated. (Gordon Clarke)

US Army perimeter guards on Noemfoor Island with three pilots from 78 Squadron. Peter Finch is third from left (in the dark shirt), followed by Jim Anderson. Len Waters is middle in the slouch hat. (Gordon Clarke)

Two 78 Squadron Kittyhawks with nose art at at Wama strip Morotai Island: *Watch My Form* on its third aircraft, which is believed to be HU-J, and *Black Magic* at a time when Len Waters was flying it. Note the badly faded name on the cowl due to the ravages of the tropical weather. (Gordon Clarke)

Another publicity photo of 78 Squadron pilots. They are (left to right): Frank Smith, Peter Finch, Kev Dodemaide, Eric Hart (obscured), Lyle Ellers, Fred Jones, Harry Kerr (with lanyard), Dick Sudlow (CO), Ken Boyd, Mike Rose (hat on looking down), Bill Turner, James Lee (at back with hat on), Bill Lock, Len Waters (just head), Mike White, Peter Cook, Alan Beinke (obscured), Bill Henry, Alan Gawith, Jim Anderson and Ted Hurst. (Gordon Clarke)

A line up of mostly 'A' Flight Kittyhawks at the edge of Kamari strip Noemfoor Island. The closest is *Black Magic* HU-E. The nine Kittyhawks all appear to be from 78 Squadron. (Gordon Clarke)

78 Wing picture theatre at Noemfoor Island. The projection hut is on the right, with the salubrious seating being the scattered logs. Note the closeness of the jungle behind the screen. (Gordon Clarke)

Len Waters, standing on the running board of the battered Jeep, with squadron mates. (Jeanette Sims)

Pilot Max Davey flew no. 2 to Len Waters. He regarded Waters as 'one heck of a good pilot and a great mate to have'. (Gladys Waters)

The forged identity card Gladys Waters (nee Saunders) used to get a services job during the war. (Gladys Waters)

This is the photo of Gladys Saunders that Grace Waters sent to her son on Morotai. (Gladys Waters)

When he turned 21 Len Waters' 78 Squadron mates set him up among empty bottles for a photo to mark the occasion. (Gladys Waters)

A 'binge night' for 78 Squadron pilots with CO S/L Dick Sudlow on the right foreground. Len Waters was part of nights like these when the beer flowed and the men formed a tight bond as they tried to put the war to one side for a brief period. (Gordon Clarke)

Pilots and administration staff of 78 Squadron, believed taken in August 1945, possibly after VJ-day. Len Waters is sitting on the right. Dick Sudlow is seated in the second row, fourth from the left, with Lyall Ellers next to him. (Gordon Clarke)

Len and Gladys married after the war. They are pictured here with their first-born child, daughter Lenise, in 1948. (Lenise Schloss)

In 1964 Len Waters (right) was shearing at Pathungra Station, near Mt Isa, when this photo was taken for a magazine article. (Mt Isa Library)

Family time was tough to get on the shearing circuit. Here, Gladys and Len Waters share time at the Winton Show in the early 1960s. (Peter Gorman)

Len and Gladys share a moment with Don Waters (right) in the late 1960s. (Peter Gorman)

In 1992 Len Waters visited the Australian War Memorial in Canberra where he spent time with former RAAF Kittyhawk, *Polly*, rekindling memories of *Black Magic*. (Jeanette Sims)

Len Waters revelled in the opportunity fly with Dick Sims in this Victa Airtourer. (Jeanette Sims)

On Anzac Day 1993, in the International Year of Indigenous Peoples, Len and Oodgeroo Noonuccal (formerly Kath Walker) jointly led the Anzac Day march in Brisbane. (Gladys Waters)

In June 1993, the RAAF took Len Waters on an outback tour of Aboriginal communities. Before he left, he was a guest at the RAAF Base Townsville's Air Show and climbed into a Hornet FA/18 cockpit. (Gladys Waters)

One of the last photos taken of Len Waters, at the Townsville air show. (RAAF)

Len Waters pictured here on his final trip with the RAAF, not long before he died. On his left is the Dakota pilot Flight Lieutenant Bruce Doughton, and on his right is Wing Commander Alex Johnson. He had been brought back into the fold. (RAAF)

Len Waters' brother, Private Donald (Jim) Waters. Jim participated in a malaria experiment before serving with the 2nd/23rd Battalion, 9th Division, in New Guinea, Morotai and Tarakan. (Kevin Waters)

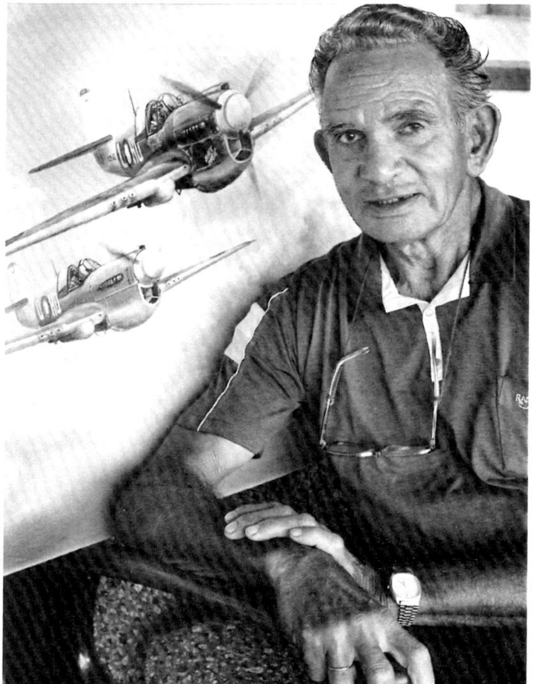

Len Waters pictured in front of a painting of his beloved Kittyhawks. (Jeanette Sims)

the room: 'Here is a bloke able to lead troops. We couldn't care whether he is black, white or brindle. Let's give him a go.' This decision required the approval of General Thomas Blamey, who wrote, 'If the Commanding Officer of the 2/7th Battalion is prepared to accept Sergeant Saunders as an officer, I'm certainly prepared to do the same.'

Reg Saunders struck little racism in the army. Like Len Waters, he had a reputation as a fighter. He knew how to use his fists. 'So I didn't get very much cheek from anybody.' The bar placed on post-war service in Japan angered him. 'Now that the danger is past I feel my race is entitled to equal opportunities with other Australians. We don't want privileges, but opportunities for advancement and fair treatment.' He and Waters both thought they had earned it.

So did Kath Walker, a Noonuccal woman from Stradbroke Island, Queensland. She had been working as a domestic for two shillings and sixpence a week when she joined the Australian Women's Army Service in December 1942 at the age of 22. Two of her brothers were by then prisoners of war in Singapore. While this was a strong motivation, she also knew that joining the army was 'the only way I could learn . . . I would be allowed to learn. It was the only way that Aboriginals could learn extra education at that time.' Immediately she enlisted, she noticed a dramatic difference in the way she was treated. 'In the army, they didn't give a stuff what colour you were. There was a job to be done . . . and all of a sudden the colour line disappeared.' Kath Walker shared the same optimism and growing sense of entitlement as the Waters and Saunders brothers.

Len Waters returned to Brisbane, which had been transformed by the war from a big country town to a metropolis that was now more worldly thanks to the presence of 80,000 American servicemen. He reported to 3 Personnel Depot (3PD) at Sandgate, on the city's outskirts, and was given the choice of either remaining in the RAAF or being discharged. With the war over, the RAAF was in the process of rapidly downsizing and was not encouraging personnel to remain.

The size of the air force had grown rapidly from 3489 officers and airmen in uniform when war began in September 1939 to a peak of 182,000 in August 1944, when Waters was completing his training at Mildura. At war's end, there were 173,622 personnel operating 5585 aircraft, making it—for a short time—one of the five largest air forces in the world, behind the United States, the Soviet Union, Britain and Canada. Waters reluctantly opted for discharge:

> *I think that if they had made a plane available to us every couple of weeks or so, just to throw around the sky and keep our interest keen, I'm sure that I would have stayed in the force. But we became so bored just sitting around playing cards, playing snooker or going to the odd race meeting, that I was quite happy to accept my discharge when it came through.*

Waters could reflect on his service with the RAAF with pride and satisfaction. He had made it to the top echelon of RAAF aircrew as a skilled fighter pilot. Although he had been given the same privileges as his white mates in 78 Squadron, two of them—pilots Peter Finch and Eric Hart—would later assert that he was paid half of what they were getting. While they were doing the same job and saw each other as equals, it would seem that at least some members of the squadron had made the assumption that as an Aborigine, Waters would be paid less. This is not borne out by his service records, which show Waters was on the same pay scale for other aircrew of similar experience and, therefore, received the same remuneration. The question of different pay levels for Aborigines was never discussed at Air Board level, and it was at that level that all pay rates were set.

In the RAAF, however, nobody had a background like Waters. He was unique among fighter pilots. As Ron Guthrie recalled, everybody on Course 44 knew that Waters was Aboriginal. 'You had a goal, it didn't matter what colour or creed you were provided you qualified, you were of the quality and calibre that they wanted. We thought it extra good to have an Aboriginal pilot, somebody with true Australian blood.'

Therein lies the nub of Waters' experience during his years in the RAAF from August 1942 to January 1946: he was that rare thing, an Indigenous Australian who made it into the ranks of fighter pilots at a time when discrimination based on race had created a two-tier society in which Aborigines were not expected to enter the upper level. In civilian society they were held back. Circumstances had given him a unique opportunity to break the mould, and he had grabbed it.

Waters, the self-acknowledged 'coloured boy', had been very conscious of his station in life when he joined the RAAF. But his background was not that of a beaten-down personality, as was the case for other Aboriginal people in pre–World War II Australia. He had been taught through upbringing and the values hammered into him by his parents to hold on to his dignity and to believe that his rights were the same as those of the next man. But to justify his claim on those rights, he had to work for them, as nothing was gained without hard work. Waters took every opportunity on offer.

Being part of the 'elite' was itself heady stuff, and he had been tested at the highest level—flying in war. He was respected as both man and pilot. He had friends in 78 Squadron who came from privileged backgrounds in Sydney and Melbourne, and drank with them in public bars that were out of bounds to other Aboriginal people. 'Two of my best friends came from high-class families in Sydney. I was always accepted as equal to them.' Colour seemed not to be of any consequence. During the war, government and the media had talked up the armed forces as a means of promoting such assimilation.

Mateship in wartime, and the respect they won as individuals, transcended race. For the Waters and Saunders brothers, the process of socialisation in the military broke down racial barriers—something achieved through a mindset of sameness and conformity among service personnel. In this, they were luckier than those serving in specially raised Indigenous units such as the Torres Strait Light Infantry Battalion, formed in 1941 mainly to protect Torres Strait. They patrolled the extensive coastline and searched for crashed enemy and Allied airmen.

Men in some of these units were not formally enlisted, and it took more than 40 years for their services to be recognised.

They earned roughly half the pay of white troops and, unless they served overseas, did not have access to many veterans' benefits after the war. Ultimately, it would take concerted campaigning for anomalies such as back pay to be rectified. And there were the 3000 or more who worked for the military as labourers. A handful joined the United States Army, serving in water transport units.

While Waters was the sole Indigenous fighter pilot, he was not the only Indigenous airman in the South West Pacific Area. Flight Sergeant Arnold Lockyer, an Aboriginal man from Western Australia, was among the last Australians to die in the war. A flight engineer and air gunner in 24 Squadron RAAF, he served in the Northern Territory and then Morotai and Borneo in 1944–45.

Aged 30, Lockyer was a member of the twelve-man crew of a Liberator bomber that was hit by anti-aircraft fire on 27 July 1945 during a photo reconnaissance mission in the Manado area of north-eastern Celebes (Sulawesi). The bomber crashed near Tomohon, but three crew members parachuted to safety and were captured. One was beaten to death the next day, while Lockyer and the other man were interrogated before being chloroformed and buried alive six days after Japan's surrender was announced. Three other members of the Lockyer family served—two overseas in the 2/24th Battalion—and one of them, Private Eric Lockyer, was killed in action at Tarakan in May, 1945. This all happened in Waters' own field of operations.

A few Aboriginal men were decorated for bravery. One was Private Timothy Hughes, a South Australian who served in the 2/10th Battalion. A Rat of Tobruk, he later won the Military

Medal for coolness and bravery under fire while attacking Japanese positions at Buna, Papua. He went on to serve in the New Guinea and Borneo campaigns. A New South Welshman, Trooper Clive Upright, of 2/7th Commando Squadron, was awarded the Military Medal for his actions in attacking the village of Sauri, New Guinea, in May 1945. He had stood up in full view of the enemy to better direct machine-gun fire onto an enemy position.

It was not known at the time, but one other RAAF pilot besides Waters had Aboriginal heritage—Flight Lieutenant David Valentine Paul, who, as a bomber pilot, was the RAAF's first Aboriginal aviator. His great-grandmother, Lucy Fraser, had been an Aboriginal woman from the Northern Tablelands of New South Wales. Known as 'the big fella', Paul grew up on Sydney's North Shore. Like Waters, he left school at the age of fourteen. He worked as a drover and a dry-cleaner but, after the outbreak of war, wanted to join the RAAF. As with Waters, his lack of formal education was a hurdle. To rectify this, he enrolled at a local technical college to obtain the relevant education qualifications before successfully enlisting in the air force in January 1941.

Drafted into the Empire Air Training Scheme and sent to Rhodesia for eight months of training, on graduation he was posted to 454 Squadron RAAF as a pilot. He was soon flying Baltimore bombers over the Aegean Sea. His commanding officer, Wing Commander John Coates, later wrote that he had become one of the squadron's most outstanding pilots.

On 4 December 1943, Paul and his crew failed to return from a reconnaissance operation and were reported as missing.

His family waited for three months before receiving news that his plane had been hit by enemy fighters. Although the aircraft's fuel tank had burst into flames, he had managed to successfully ditch the bomber into the sea. Of the four-man crew, three survived, including Paul. Rescued from the water by two German seaplanes, Paul and the others were sent to a prisoner-of-war camp near Berlin.

While in captivity, Paul was recommended for and was awarded the Distinguished Flying Cross for his 'outstanding leadership, initiative and determination'. He was also awarded the Goldfish Club badge, given to Allied aircrew who survived a ditching at sea with the assistance of a floatation device. At the end of the war, Paul was liberated from the camp and returned to Australia. He joined the New South Wales Police Force, and went on to have a distinguished career. He would continue to serve as a squadron leader in the RAAF Reserve until his death in May 1973.

The general experience for Indigenous service personnel was that although they had been prepared to fight and die for their country, their war service failed to translate into full citizenship rights and recognition—just as had been the case after World War I. Indigenous veterans immediately felt marginalised by conservative ex-service organisations that frequently railed against Indigenous rights. And they could still be denied a drink in pubs and RSL clubs. If they wanted to attend unit reunions or catch up with old mates, that could present a problem. Waters could not imagine that the egalitarianism he had experienced in the war years would not continue. But he was wrong.

PART THREE

BACK TO EARTH

YANAAWUWLY DHAWUN

It's something that gets into your blood and you never lose it. You've just got no idea when you get up there, you're so free, like the birds.

Len Waters

20

A SUITABLE MARRIAGE

Black Magic was no more. In Brisbane, as Waters enjoyed his first festive season free of war in four years, the Kittyhawk that he and Denny Baker had piloted with distinction was still on Tarakan, where it was being stripped of equipment. Then, on or around 26 December 1945, the aircraft was set ablaze. The end of the war had meant the RAAF was left with a huge amount of hardware at bases in the South West Pacific Area. Aircraft that were considered too 'tired' to fly home were burnt after any useful equipment was salvaged.

It was a sad end for a historically important Kittyhawk, one that had taken part in the RAAF's last major air combat in World War II and, under Baker's control, destroyed two Japanese aircraft in the 'Big Do' in June 1945. And then it had been Waters' turn to take over a fighter that seemed serendipitously named for him. Too late for the dogfights, Waters in *Black Magic* had dive-bombed and strafed in the face of lethal ground fire.

As the RAAF rationalised machinery and personnel, Waters met up with old friends from the St George district who were visiting Brisbane as 1945 drew to a close. Among them were the 'Moonie Loonies', a small self-named group that included Darcy Thompson. They were the sons of station owners around St George, and Waters had become friends with them while working on properties shearing and rouseabouting before he enlisted. Darcy, too, had wanted to enlist in the RAAF, but he failed the eye test. He tried the army, but as his brother had joined up, he was obliged to stay on the farm. Because of manpower shortages, farming was decreed a reserved occupation—one that was essential for the production of supplies for the war effort. Darcy thought Waters was a 'terrific fellow', according to his widow, Marguerite Thompson.

Darcy had a wicked sense of humour. Along with the other Moonie Loonies egging each other on, they looked for ways to live up to their sobriquet and, at the same time, to overcome the boredom of station life. Their hijinks were soon notorious in the St George area. To some, they were ratbags and dreadful boys, but to others their antics added a little spice to life in the bush. Either way, their mischief-making was well known. Sometimes they crossed the line with such pranks as putting red dye onto barmaids' underwear as it hung on the clothes line. Tying two cats' tails together and throwing them over a clothes line in the back yard of a hotel was another of their stunts.

According to Waters, some 'carried six guns in holsters on their hips, and some of the things that they did actually seemed to come out of the Wild West but with a real Aussie flavour.' There was the time when one Loonie rushed into a bedroom at night and stuck a revolver in the chest of a sleeping farm worker, asking, 'How would you like to be shot?' The revolver was not loaded, but as the terror-struck worker instantly considered his mortality, a second Loonie stationed outside the window fired another gun into the air. The Loonies thought this hilarious.

Another time they made a false grave on the Moonie Highway, with a tin can for the headstone, and were much amused when an old St George resident, seeing the new mound on the road for the first time, purchased a wreath which she placed on the faux grave. Another night Darcy went to the squatters' annual ball wearing pyjamas, announcing deadpan that it was his 'breeding suit'. As Waters put it, 'There was never a dull moment with them, they didn't show any emotion, and if they considered something had to be done they did it.' While meaning no harm, these were the bored sons of privilege. They had a habit of stashing alcohol at various hiding places on their expansive family properties, to be enjoyed when the opportunity arose. A pig shoot or even checking fences was enough of an excuse to slake a thirst.

Their skylarking could be risky. Still in the RAAF, Waters joined these mates for a drink one night at a Brisbane hotel, which proved just that. Darcy Thompson and his brother had travelled to Brisbane in the lead-up to Christmas 1945. Waiting for his leave to come through, Waters met them at the grand

Bellevue Hotel, the preferred venue for many a Queensland property owner while in Brisbane. As he and the Thompsons settled in the lounge bar for a beer, the brothers noticed that one of their friends had begun playing the piano and was already somewhat intoxicated. 'He was a good boogie-woogie pianist and we had him going, really going. The two brothers kept urging him on and praising his talents as a musician,' Waters remembered. As the night wore on, the piano player confided to them that his greatest ambition was to play the piano in a brothel. Surprised, Waters looked across to Darcy Thompson, who nodded back and said, 'We'll let him realise his ambition.' Waters thought it an excellent idea.

With straight faces, they explained that they had been invited to a house where a woman and her 'four beautiful young daughters' lived. Her husband 'either blew through or was killed at the war', they continued, and being lonely she liked to entertain young men. The tipsy piano player said he would be only too pleased to join them, unaware of the nature of the venue. A taxi took them to Elsie's, a legendary World War II brothel. The entrance had a large green door with a high step, which patrons would step over to enter. It was not a full door, but more like a hole in the wall, the intent of which was to inhibit customers from running out without paying.

Inside, Waters found himself in 'a beautiful big lounge room' in the front of the building. After introductions to the madam and drinks at the bar, Darcy Thompson asked if their friend could play the grand piano in the corner. Given the go-ahead, the piano player immediately made the room come alive.

The scene was quickly imprinted into Waters' memory. 'He started playing "Boogie Woogie Bugle Boy" and the modern stuff at that time, and he really had the place jumping. The girls were all there, beautifully respectably dressed. There were scantily dressed ones among them. They kept disappearing with men who came and went.'

Waters recalled that at the time he 'was very naïve' and had returned from the war still a virgin. This was a night spinning into the realm of the surreal: inhibitions were loosening as the beer flowed, the women wafted and the pianist played on. One of the girls caught Waters' eye:

> *I still had my uniform on and when I went into the room with her, I had my [flight] wings on. She said, 'What squadron did you fly with?' I told her, and she said, do you know a certain officer? I said, 'Yes, I led a flight many times that he flew with. Do you know the man?' She said, 'Yes, as a matter of fact he happens to be my husband.' It almost put me off what I had taken her into the room for.*

Such stories were not uncommon during the war, fuelled by the knowledge that the Americans didn't mind splurging money on women. When Waters and his companion returned to the bar area, he saw that the piano player was 'really under the weather' but, noticing the girls disappearing with different men, he wanted to know if the place was 'as respectable as it seems from the outside', as there seemed to be 'something funny' about it. 'We all burst out laughing. Darcy said, "You've just realised your life's ambition. You've played a piano at a brothel."'

Waters' time in uniform was coming to an end, marked by a promotion from Flight Sergeant to Warrant Officer. On 18 January 1946 he was discharged, walking out of 3PD at Sandgate after nearly three and a half years in the RAAF. He had been awarded the Australian Service Medal, the British War Medal 1939–45, the Pacific Star, the 1939–45 Star, the Dutch War Commemorative Cross 1940–1945, and the Returned from Active Service badge. He stayed around Brisbane for a couple of weeks before heading home to St George on Saturday, 4 February. A friend told him there was a birthday party in town that night at the Balonne Café, commonly known as 'the Greeks', that he might like to attend.

It was for Gladys Saunders, the beautiful, dark-haired teenager he had met the previous year when he took his mother to see the film *Holy Matrimony*. She was turning seventeen, and in 1940s St George, 'the Greeks' on The Terrace was *the* place in town. As a worker at the café later recalled: 'After the pictures, about 100 or 150 happy and excited people would come into the café. It was like a big family here in St George. The pictures promised them Hollywood. The café continued the illusion.' Among those there that night were a few Moonie Loonies. The night buzzed.

Waters had been taken with Gladys after their first meeting, carrying her photo with him while in the islands. She arrived at 8.30 p.m. after finishing work as a housemaid at the nearby Australian Hotel, where she also lived. They were soon reintroduced as the celebrations continued late into the night. Gladys was going out with someone else at the time but, as they talked over a table, she thought Waters was 'nice, a smart-looking guy'. Finally, as the party ended, he offered to walk her back to the hotel, a mere 100 metres away. It was a warm summer night and there was no hurry. When they reached the staff doorway, he pulled her close. He had a question on his mind. As Gladys recalled:

> *He took me home that night, and that night he asked me to marry him. I treated it as a joke. I thought—he's a young bloke, home on leave, thought he was going to be a real smart alec, take me out, thought he was going to be smart. I wasn't ready to be a play toy for the air force. I got that stunned I couldn't believe it. And he said that he had it in his mind when he first saw my photo when he was in the islands, that I was going to be his wife. I said we'd wait and see.*

To her surprise, Waters was back next morning, at 7 o'clock, banging on the door of the hotel staff entrance. When Gladys wanted to know why he was there, he responded that he needed to get her details so that he could make arrangements with the minister for their marriage. Because there was no Church of England in the town, Waters approached the Presbyterian minister. Gladys remained stunned.

> *I mean, I didn't know him! And I thought he was fooling. I honestly didn't think he was fair dinkum. But he was. He used to come up morning, noon and night to the hotel. I was working in the dining room and he was always at one of the dining room windows. When I realised that it was going to be fair dinkum and it was going to be*

> *so soon, I told my boss and my boss hit the roof. She said, 'I can't allow you to get married, you don't know anything about him. It's too soon.'*

That same Sunday night, Waters took Gladys to dinner at 'the Greeks'. They talked about their experiences in life. Waters told her about Margie Jones. Then Gladys explained that she was keen on a soldier with whom she'd been keeping company.

Waters was determined, and determination was central to his character: he had learned early to believe in himself, and to go after what he wanted. This had brought him great rewards. He wore Gladys down in a matter of days. Arrangements were made for a wedding on 16 February—just twelve days after they met at the birthday party. Both families were stunned by the news. As Gladys recalls, 'My Dad had no say in it. My Mum, she objected strongly. She hit the roof. I had to get permission to get married. She wasn't going to sign the paper. In fact, it was the very last day before the wedding, the paper arrived that I could get married.'

Although Grace had introduced them when Len had been on leave in St George in March–April 1945, the idea of the impending nuptials worried her. She had liked Gladys, but now her attitude changed. Just why is not clear. 'Before, I was a real nice girl, but when she found out we were going to get married, I wasn't a real nice girl any longer. I was marrying the snowy-haired boy of the family,' Gladys recalled. Waters was resolute; he wanted to marry Gladys. To avoid a rupture in the family, Don Waters stepped in:

His father came up to the hotel and I was sitting in the office with my boss. He said, 'I'd just like to make myself known to you and accept you into the family and tell you how proud I am to welcome you as my new daughter.' The old man was a lovely person. There's one thing I liked about our families—like my Mum was white, my Dad was dark. His Dad was light-skinned and his Mum was dark. It was a 'suitable' marriage, you know. We were both the same.

Gladys understood. She and Len both had mixed-race backgrounds, and in Australia at the time, this still mattered a lot. It was the key reason for Grace to veto any thoughts of marriage that her son was harbouring for Margie. She was white, and therein lay not just social consequences but potential legal impediments in the racist policies of the day. Although Waters was not registered as Aboriginal, this did not necessarily make him white in the eyes of the Aboriginal Protection Board. According to the law, Aboriginal men marrying white women could lead to prosecution in some jurisdictions. In 1937, the Chief Protector of Aborigines said that people of mixed descent should be absorbed not by the white population but by the 'native community'.

Indigenous families would have been well aware of this official attitude. This ensured that 'blacks stayed black and the whites stayed white'. Queensland deemed 'miscegenation' 'a great moral wrong' in the post-war years. It would not be until 1961 when the Australian Parliament enacted its first Marriage Act, establishing laws for the recognition of unions nationwide, that the power of state Aboriginal Protectors to control whom an

Indigenous person could or could not marry was withdrawn. But in 1946, these views still held sway. Breaking out of these constraints not only challenged Indigenous families but also ran the risk of sanctions.

Assimilation might have been official government policy, but unofficially, the deep influence of past policies of segregation, and the attitudes they engendered, persisted. From this perspective, the looming marriage of Gladys and Len was indeed 'suitable'.

21

BLACKFELLA

Waters was certain he was marrying for love, but Gladys was not so sure. They hardly knew each other, and their backgrounds, despite strong similarities, were also quite different. He had grown up in a tight, loving family that valued education, and the past three years had opened his horizons and tested his mettle.

Gladys's family story reflected the unremitting harshness and racial fluidity of life in the Queensland outback. Her home town of Charleville lay in sparsely settled mulga country, about 400 kilometres north-west of St George. Charleville had a history of frontier racial conflict that was often brutal. In 1945, when Gladys left to work in St George, it was a bustling ten-pub town that had become the service centre to a vast region.

Her childhood had been tough and from time to time traumatic. Her education was sparing. From the age of eleven she worked during school holidays as a domestic on surrounding properties. Her white mother, Gladys McEwan, worked at Charleville's famed Hotel Corones, washing and cooking.

Harry 'Poppa' Corones, a Greek immigrant and fruiterer with a ferocious work ethic, had arrived in Australia in 1907 and two years later moved to Charleville, one of Queensland's wealthiest agricultural communities. Opening the Paris Café, he soon developed a vision for western Queensland. He began building the hotel bearing his name, and by 1924 it was already one of the state's most impressive hotels. It was here, in a huge dining room, that he hosted dinners for aviator Sir Hudson Fysh, as plans were hatched to create Qantas in 1920.

The grand hotel was completed in 1929, just as the economy crashed and the Great Depression began. In the years that followed, Corones would pass on his daughters' cast-off clothes to Gladys and her two sisters. 'My mum was a very tough person, she worked all her life,' Gladys recalled. After school Gladys would go to the hotel to do the ironing, working until after dinner.

Her father, George Maurice Saunders, was Kamilaroi. A proud and clever man, he could turn his hand to anything. A dingo hunter and inland fisherman, he also toured outback New South Wales and Queensland with the famed Colleano's All-Star Circus. Acrobatic skills and tricks fascinated his daughters. A popular man in town, George was never seen outside the house 'unless he was dressed to the nines'. Gladys thought him 'the most spotlessly clean person I've ever come in contact with'.

That was one side of George. But he swung wildly from a loving father when sober to one capable of unpredictable drunken rages. 'When he was sober, you couldn't wish for anyone better, he was a lovely person. But he loved that grog, he used to scare me.' According to Gladys, floggings with a stockwhip marked her childhood. There were times when she felt her life, and the lives of her sisters, were so at risk that she called the police, who would throw George in the lock-up overnight. 'Oh dear, he was violent. When he'd go berserk, he'd go berserk. But I got even a few times.'

Gladys learned early to protect herself—and alcohol remained something that 'made me a very, very, very bitter person'. After a childhood punctuated with physical and mental abuse, she associated alcohol with violence. From those formative years, assertiveness became her modus operandi, giving rise to strongly expressed views. And at seventeen, she was beautiful and alluring to a fighter pilot who had held her photo close while away at war. Perhaps it was this photo that became Waters' proverbial 'rabbit's foot'. Whatever its significance, he was determined to marry her. With the wedding set for 16 February, there was little time to waste.

Gladys was still in a state of disbelief, and except for Don Waters, both families were yet to come to terms with the intended marriage. Waters took it upon himself to organise the event as best he could. It was a time when post-war rationing made coupons necessary to buy anything and everything. With no coupons, a new wedding dress was beyond her. Reluctantly, Gladys settled on a short pale-blue frock made in a hurry by a friend.

On the Saturday of the ceremony, Gladys had the shakes—and second thoughts. She pleaded to be taken back to her hotel room because she had changed her mind, but the day had a momentum that carried her through. They were married in the furnace of a St George summer at the town's Presbyterian church, but no photographs were taken, such was the haste with which the wedding was held. 'It was a nice wedding,' Gladys would recall, but for years after, 'when he got a bit cranky with me, Len would remind me that I had not actually ever said "Yes" to marrying him.'

Marry him she did, and the wedding reception was held at the Waters family home before the newlyweds left to honeymoon at Goondiwindi, 200 kilometres away on the New South Wales border. They stayed at a boarding house and ate at the local Greek café most nights. Waters liked to have a drink at one of the town pubs before dinner, and while Gladys disapproved of any drinking at all, it did give her a chance to have a cigarette—of which Waters strongly disapproved. 'He hated women smoking and he didn't like me smoking, so I couldn't smoke in front of him. So that suited me fine.' A balance of sorts had been found.

In the rush to arrange the wedding, Waters neglected to buy an engagement ring, but Gladys was not too concerned. The money was put to good use in Goondiwindi. 'Well, we had a good time on the money, put it that way. We went out to everything that was on. We enjoyed our life together that way. For three weeks we had a nice time.'

Waters took her to meet the relatives. First stop was New Toomelah reserve, on the banks of the Macintyre River. 'He wanted me to meet all his people, and I'd never been on a mission in my life. The people I met were really lovely. I really admired them. Gee they were clean. Their yards—I noticed that there wasn't a weed or a bit of rubbish or leaf. They swept every day.' New Toomelah had been an Aboriginal reserve since 1937, and was home to Kamilaroi, Wirerai and Bigamul peoples who had been moved there after the closure of Old Toomelah. Behind the well-kept façade and the friendly faces was a history of police surveillance, harassment by managers, and children 'stolen' by welfare. Nevertheless, it was home to many of the extended Waters family. Those who lived there kept the pain hidden.

The honeymoon over, they returned to St George and the reality of work. Waters had reason for confidence: besides proving himself at the highest level in the air force, he had a boxing title under his belt. He knew the self-motivated were rewarded by taking risks, just as he had been. As Australia embarked on post-war development amid burgeoning new optimism, Waters had every reason to think the world was at his feet. He wanted to be part of it. What was there not to be confident about?

Gladys was soon offered her old job at the Australian Hotel, along with the incentive of free board and lodging for them both. Waters had not been in the civilian workforce for three and a half years, but a motor company next to the hotel offered him a job as a mechanic. He saw himself as the sole provider, just as his father had been. Gladys did not agree. 'I put it to Len, and he said, "No wife of mine is going to work,"' she recalled, telling him that it was a good opportunity to save money. They could live on one wage and bank the other. As well, she was taking in washing and ironing from itinerant travellers. 'I finally talked him around to it and we went and stayed at the hotel.'

Accommodation sorted, Waters turned his mind to flying again. Joining the occupation forces in Japan or the commercial airlines in Australia were the only choices for demobbed pilots wanting to keep flying—and he had already been turned down in his belated application to join the BCOF. Remaining a pilot in the RAAF as it rapidly downsized was an ever-decreasing option.

Before he left the RAAF, Ansett Airways began to headhunt pilots interested in a commercial flying career. 'There were fourteen or fifteen of us who went over for the interviews, and there were only three with multi-engine experience and they were taken on immediately after discharge,' Waters recalled. Pilots who had flown with Bomber Command in Europe were given preference over fighter pilots, as they had three advantages: they had piloted multi-engined aircraft, had worked with crew and, most importantly, had experience in night flying on instruments. Likewise, Qantas sought pilots whose skills were suited to the post-war modified Lancaster and Liberator aircraft they primarily used in 1945–47.

Like so many other fighter pilots, Waters did not meet the criteria that commercial airlines had laid down; they could pick and choose from the many now unemployed air force pilots. He remained hopeful. A chance came when a local businessman, Norman Howe, proposed that they set up a regional aerial taxi service in St George. Given the deplorable state of western Queensland roads, an aerial taxi service looked to be a good business proposition. For Howe, a registered bookmaker, it offered the chance to operate at more country race meetings, because the same journey by car would take several days. The idea was that he would buy the plane and Waters would be the pilot, with the business operating on a 50–50 basis.

Howe was willing to pay for Waters to acquire his civilian pilot's licence, and also to purchase an aircraft capable of ferrying up to eight passengers to major towns in outback Queensland. Waters was optimistic, but first he had to get his civilian pilot's licence, the permit for which was under the jurisdiction of the Commonwealth government's Department of Civil Aviation.

Norman Howe said that if he bought the aircraft, would I fly it and start an air taxi service. He said, 'You'd fly it and we'd go half and half.' It was a good idea as far as he was concerned because of the spaces out there—it was 180-odd miles from St George to Cunnamulla, 260 out to Charleville, about 140 to Roma.

The roads weren't that good in those days. It would have helped him with his bookmaking business as well as flying other people around the area and going to stock sales and things like that.

He said, 'If you can get the permit we can start the taxi service and run this business together.' I wouldn't have had any trouble—just a refresher course of about 15 hours, that's all it was. He was prepared to pay for that. I had to secure a permit from Canberra. I applied for it and I didn't even get a reply to my request, so it fell through.

Gladys recalls that her husband applied five times for the required permit from Civil Aviation, giving full details of his service as a RAAF fighter pilot. Importantly, she remembers that in each application he wrote that he was born at Euraba Aborigines' Reserve and had attended Toomelah mission school until he was aged seven. Bureaucrats were left in no doubt he was Aboriginal. However, no records have survived. According to the National Archives of Australia, routine correspondence such as this was largely culled.

Waters was frustrated and disappointed; he had proven himself as a fighter pilot for his country, and he could see no reason why he should not be granted a commercial pilot's licence. It was like 'a kick in the guts', his brother Kevin recalled. According to Gladys, 'Len got down in the dumps. He came to the conclusion that his requests for a licence were refused because he was an Aborigine and, finally, he gave up his quest.' About twelve months later, a similar air taxi service was set up in Cunnamulla by Bobby Goss, an uncle of the future Queensland premier, the late Wayne Goss.

His air force mate Arnie Nunn recalled the dream that Waters talked about on Tarakan as the war drew to a close:

> *We used to sit around talking during periods when nothing was happening—that is, Lenny, me and ground staff and other pilots. We all knew he was an Aborigine and thought it was unfair the way they were treated back home. We all treated Lenny the same as anyone else. We were all fighting a war and he was a good bloke. He was a very good pilot and wanted to keep going after the war. We all encouraged him but he couldn't get past the government authorities. He was hostile about that.*

As this disappointment played out, Waters lost his job as a motor mechanic. Despite being a highly skilled flight mechanic who could put together a Tiger Moth engine blindfolded, he lacked the motor mechanics' trade qualification that he required to join the Australian Workers' Union—all-powerful in the bush. Without his 'ticket', he gave up his job to the only formally qualified motor mechanic in St George—his brother Ranald.

Waters was forced to look elsewhere. He saw an opportunity for a new, up-to-date wool-scouring plant in Longreach, Queensland. This would undoubtedly have been successful, as such a facility to efficiently clean shorn wool in the area was lacking at the time. But this was an era when no bank would lend money to Aborigines. Waters was unable to raise the funds, and his proposal was never realised. By now, Waters was losing faith in the white bureaucracy's willingness to back his proposed business ventures. He concluded it was because of his Aboriginality. This belief was to stay with him and make him increasingly wary of white bureaucracy. He had always been self-reliant; now he became more so.

Gladys was working seven days a week at the hotel and Waters, determined to be the breadwinner, took a job with the shire council, driving a grader on the road between St George and Mungindi. The job meant he was away from St George from Monday to Friday, sleeping in a caravan and returning at weekends. 'She was earning almost as much money as I was. I thought, if I'm going to be the breadwinner, I'm going to have to do something a bit more productive that brings in a bit more money.'

Waters was at a crossroads. Trying to break free of stereotypes imposed by dominant white society had left him feeling defeated. It was expected that Aborigines would be submissive and deferential and not attempt to be equal. Recalling his childhood a generation later, when attitudes remained unchanged, Warren Mundine would comment that as Aborigines, 'we learned to stand back and wait to be asked . . . we learned to keep our heads down and our mouths shut . . . we learned to know our place.'

There seemed no other option for Waters but to go back to the only work he knew and that paid well: shearing and bush work. With a sense of resignation, he told Gladys and his family, 'I guess I'll have to go back to being a blackfella.'

22

FITTING BACK IN

The respect Waters earned in the RAAF was still alive in his mind. Driving the road grader for the Balonne Shire Council was the antithesis of piloting a Kittyhawk. The job was boring and had no future. Such was his thinking one Saturday night as he shared a few beers with his father, Don, and younger brother Barney at a St George pub. Barney and Don were working as shearers, and the talk turned to just how many sheep they were doing each week:

> *I remember Barney had almost shorn 200 sheep one week, but Dad wasn't too far behind him. When walking home they started to talk about it and they decided to have a five-pound wager who would be the first one to shear 200. So I said that I wouldn't mind being in on the bet as well, and they said, 'Oh no, you were only learning when you joined up and it wouldn't be a fair wager.'*

Waters could not know how achievable this was, but the past few years had given him the confidence to back himself. He was able to apply a single-minded focus when he needed to. 'I was a pretty good learner, and couldn't have had a better tutor.' His mentor was 'Baldy' Faulkiner, a champion shearer from the Northern Tablelands of New South Wales in the 1930s.

With £5 to be won, Waters was drawn to the challenge. He joined his father and brother shearing and won the bet. He quickly became the 'gun shearer' in the family. 'Barney never accomplished the deed, and I did it with monotonous regularity. After I got back into the game again, I almost shore 300 a couple of times.' He could shear sheep quickly and efficiently in an industry that was a cornerstone of the Australian economy. Tough as nails, shearers were looked up to and respected.

An early shearing contract was at the Bonus Downs station, south-west of Mitchell, about 320 kilometres from St George. It did not turn out to be one of his most productive jobs. 'There wasn't any "bonus" to be had. It took us just on three months to shear 2000 per man, as we had almost three years' annual rainfall during that time. The sheep were all wethers, that is—castrated rams—and most of them were almost as big as rams.'

However, he was soon at home in the familiar, all-enveloping thump of the machinery of the shearing sheds, with its distinctive smells—and the added challenge to be the ringer. His back bent and body drenched in perspiration, he was quick but careful as he guided the narrow comb over the sheep, making the requisite long blows to remove the fleece in one piece, all the time conscious of not cutting the skin. He mastered the intricate handwork and footwork that tested a shearer's stamina. Unsurprisingly, a study years later would find shearing to be 'the hardest work in the world'—tougher on the body than any other job measured.

After Bonus Downs cut out, shearing at a couple of sheds near St George followed. This was Waters' life now. As he drove over flat, parched paddocks to one corrugated-iron shearing shed after another, he knew that there was no turning back. He took comfort in the familiar smells and sounds of the sheds, the earthiness of lanolin from the fleece that had long seeped into the floorboards, and the steam-driven presses used to compress the bales. This was a timeless environment, one that enveloped him with a lifestyle that had not changed in generations and offered certainty of income—even if there were far easier ways to earn a living. But from this he drew renewed self-esteem—something that had been challenged by the failure to secure his civil aviation pilot licence when it had seemed a mere formality.

But it came at a cost. Working with shearing contractors' teams meant taking on an unforgiving lifestyle. Waters carried his gear in bags he had made from hessian sacks used for baling wool. He understood that the harder he worked at this back-breaking job, the more he was paid. He had a good temperament, a cool head, a big heart and strong arms. This was his life, but it was not his first choice. If those beers at the end of the day were well-earned, they masked disappointment.

Fellow shearer Bill Fisk remembers Waters as 'a good, clean shearer'. They became mates travelling to and from new sheds, long journeys sitting on the back of contractors' flatbed trucks under the searing sun over rough, unsealed roads. There would always be dogs on these trips, jumping over the men, and cartons of beer to while away the time. Every so often the truck would stop, and they'd take turns to get down and open another gate. As none of these gates was ever hinged, it meant 'carrying or dragging'—'C.O.D.', as it was known.

At one of the sheds Fisk remembers Waters yarning about his years in the air force and speaking glowingly yet wistfully of those years in uniform. 'While I was in the air force I was a whitefella,' he told Bill. Now he had to live with the reality that those days were gone, and that to make a decent living was a struggle for Indigenous Australians like him. It had been easier when the nation was at war.

Reconciling this experience and these thoughts weighed increasingly heavily on Waters as the outback shearing sheds became his life. The daily regimen could not have been more different from sitting in a cockpit strafing and bombing.

In less than two years, Waters had gone from front-line fighter pilot to shearer. He had left the wartime world of the RAAF and there was now an inevitable void. Bill Soden, the 78 Squadron flight rigger, understood this when he wrote of a

> *real feeling of loss . . . It is a feeling so many returned men express. It was the combination of mateship, danger and excitement and, overall, the shared experiences and meaningful friendships that made it a 'good war'. I regard the period in the south-west Pacific as the best years of my life.*

Waters shared this sentiment. He had fitted in well and had adjusted to the structure of the RAAF, respecting the discipline and leadership and, above all, the shared camaraderie of 78 Squadron. This had now given way to the mateship of the outback shearing sheds. And mateship had become integral to his life—something from which he drew solace and strength.

With the war over, long-prevailing prejudices in the civilian world began to reappear as the need to pull together, to defend the nation from an enemy, dissipated. The scene was set for a return to the discriminatory policies and attitudes that had operated across Australia pre-war. Equal opportunity went just so far, even in the armed forces which at the end of the war, had reintroduced discriminatory rules requiring men to be of 'substantially European origin' to enlist. It would not be until 1949 that, partly owing to pressure from Indigenous veterans and the Returned and Services League (RSL), that the army finally lifted its colour bar. When the Defence Act was amended in 1951, the RAAF and the navy followed suit.

When the war ended, Queensland Aborigines were required to apply for a certificate of exemption from the provisions of the Aborigines Protection Act in order to be paid award wages in person rather than having part of their wage paid into a trust account. Trust accounts were administered by a police officer acting as the Local Protector of Aborigines. Most returned Indigenous servicemen were granted exemption certificates—or dog tags, as in New South Wales—which caused bitter resentment among other Indigenous people. This served to reinforce the division between 'free' Aborigines and Torres Strait Islanders and those who continued to fall under the Act. Seeds of division were an unintended consequence.

Indigenous servicemen and women had seen their participation in the war effort as an opportunity to earn citizenship and, on return to civilian life, expected equality to continue through their embrace of assimilation in the white world of the military. They were abruptly proved wrong, encountering the same prejudices as other Indigenous Australians who were not part of the war effort. Yet those who were not involved in the war effort now distrusted those who were. As Aboriginal and Torres Strait Islander Commission officer David Huggonson observed in 1994:

> *The psychological impact on many Aboriginal returned service personnel returning to civilian life was horrific . . . In the armed forces they enjoyed equal pay and equal conditions including the right to drink. On return to their home communities they were relegated to less than second-class status.*

Waters was a 'free' Aborigine, and although his brother George was on the New South Wales Exemption Register, the family in St George had never been on the Queensland Exemption Register. Thus, while Len and his family were seen as Aboriginal, they were not caught by the official net and were left in a unique 'grey' area.

His brother Jim was stung by how little had changed. When he returned home to New Toomelah, he saw himself as a 'libertarian' who would be at the forefront of changed race relations through his service. However he soon realised he was once more just a second-class citizen at best. Hardest of all was having to accept that the unofficial but very real segregation that had applied in communities such as nearby Boggabilla before the war still applied.

After serving in the army and then with the occupation force in Japan, Jim looked forward to catching up with white friends from the district who had served with him. But he found old pre-war attitudes had not changed. For a start, hotel bars were segregated, which meant it was difficult to share a beer in a pub with old mates. Community pressure was too great: keeping up these friendships became too difficult, and they were slowly let go.

Jim married Ruby Orcher and remained close to his brother, naming one of his sons Leonard Victor Waters after him. Young Len grew up conscious of the close bond between his father and uncle, and of the significance of carrying the name of his uncle. At the same time, he became very aware of the impact of post-war life on not just white but also Aboriginal friends.

> *Dad couldn't hang around with good friends who were white, he found that very distressing. It really destroyed the spirit of a lot of these returned men. They had put their lives on the line but it did them no favours when they got back. It brought a darkness for them. Dad was very bitter about the army; he had put his life on the line but felt that what he experienced after being discharged was not equal.*

The reappearance of prejudice on such a daily basis was not all that hurt. Soldier settlement blocks that were offered to other returned servicemen in northern New South Wales and elsewhere were not offered to Aboriginal soldiers. 'There was nothing like it for Dad,' Jim's son observed. And there was an additional sense of grievance as Jim saw refugees from war-torn Europe arriving in Australia to be resettled under humanitarian policy.

Jim later told his son that as an Aboriginal man, he had felt increasingly discarded as the migrant ships continued to arrive at Australian ports. His angst was not so much owing to the influx of new Australians but to the government policy that accepted them but ignored the discriminatory lived experience of the nation's original peoples. These new arrivals were being given a chance to determine their futures—something denied to Indigenous Australians. Unsurprisingly, this further underpinned a growing sense of post-war injustice.

And if there was a particular grievance that lingered among the wider Waters clan, it was the knowledge that one of their own who had been a fighter pilot had been blocked from a job as a pilot in the civilian world.

In this Waters was different from his white counterparts. They could slip back into the white civilian world in other capacities, through 'old boy' networks that did not exist for Aboriginal men. He was not alone: Reg Saunders and Kath Walker also experienced similar problems fitting back in. Each knock-back made them question whether assimilation brought equality. In its absence, they had no option but to reluctantly go back to surviving as best they could. Both their marriages fell apart.

After discharge from the army, the only work Saunders could find was in low-wage jobs such as tram conductor, foundry worker and tally clerk. While he got on well with his colleagues, he faced racial abuse from tram passengers. Not one to back down, he often kicked them off the tram. This discrimination extended to the occasional refusal of alcohol in pubs and the ugliness of racial slurs on the streets and football fields. Saunders was not one to be easily cowed and duly defended himself.

Waters confined his fighting to donning boxing gloves to spar with his brothers in the back yard of the St George family home. It was not long before he had something else on his mind—Gladys was about to give birth to their first child. On 24 September 1947, 'a beautiful young girl who we called Lenise May' was born at St George Hospital. The name was a combination of Len's and Gladys's first names. They were infatuated with their baby daughter. 'She was such a doll that it was almost impossible to walk around the shopping centre on Saturday mornings, everyone simply adored her,' Waters would recall.

With Waters back shearing and Lenise born, it was not long before the manager at the Australian Hotel asked Gladys to come back to work again and live there in appropriate accommodation for a young family. She accepted the offer. The arrival of their first child had a profound effect on Waters. Gladys recalls that he decided to open the suitcase in which he kept the bundle of letters that Margie Jones had written to him during the war. While he might have treasured the sentiments in these letters, he knew it was time for them to go. 'After Lenise was born he burnt them.'

23

IN THE RING

Having returned to St George, a sleepy town on the edge of a vast emptiness, Waters knew he was the one who had to re-adapt to the norms of rural Australian society, where being black still carried the burden of discrimination. His family was proud of their Kamilaroi heritage and maintained strong links with extended family at New Toomelah. But, living in an old Queenslander house overlooking the Balonne River, they stood apart from other Murris living in shanties on the outskirts of town. They also stood somewhat apart from their white neighbours. In the process, it seemed they had straddled two worlds—without fully belonging in either.

The Waters family had by now won the town's respect through their success in achieving economic independence and were accepted as part of its social structure. They were model citizens, with a war hero to boot. Waters had returned to this environment and, newly married, quickly fitted back in. The one thing he didn't talk much about was his time in the RAAF. He knew that people just wanted to put the war behind them and get on with their lives.

He had grown up in the past four years and, unlike other returned servicemen, had been shaped but not broken by the war. He had witnessed enemy soldiers dying under *Black Magic*'s murderous strafing fire and bombing raids, but he carried no outward emotional scars from such experiences. He was lean, fit and strong, befitting his nickname, 'Bones'. Rugby league, where he played second row in the forwards, enhanced his image and provided an immediate outlet. He and brothers Kevin, a halfback, and Ranald, a winger, played with the St George rugby league team. They were first graders, while he was mostly in the seconds through lack of consistent opportunity to train with the team.

On one memorable Sunday afternoon, 27 July 1947, five of the Waters brothers played together in the St George B team—Ranald on the wing, Jim and Kevin in the centres, with Len and Barney in the forwards. They defeated Goondiwindi 16–3, with Ranald being singled out by *The Balonne Beacon* for a 'good performance', although the paper lamented it was 'a pity this lad has not more weight'. A year later, in the A-grade final of the 1948 Brassington Cup against Cunnamulla, it was Kevin who threw the cut-out pass that led to the match-winning try in the dying seconds.

One of six brothers, Waters liked to be one of the boys. His experience in the RAAF, and particularly in the islands, reinforced this. Gladys remembered in the early days of marriage that while she worked until 8.30 p.m. each night, 'Len would have his meal as soon as he came home from the garage when he was working there, have his bath, get dressed and go and play pool with the boys. He was always with the boys of a night time until I finished work.' Shearing reinforced this as a lifelong habit. He enjoyed the camaraderie over a beer.

The family contribution to the town's sporting profile was strong—and further underlined by the boxing efforts of Len and younger brother Ranald. Six years his junior Ranald looked up to Len: 'We had the same temperament.' Ranald was not a pretty boxer, indeed more of a 'flat-footed slugger', according to the Brisbane *Courier-Mail.* 'He had a good put-away punch . . . but only useful when he could get in close enough to unleash it,' the paper commented. Gladys Waters long remembered them sparring: Len and Ranald, gloves on, training in the St George back yard as the Outback sun beat down in the late afternoon. Locals came to watch, so good was their reputation. 'It was like a real fight, they were serious about their training. Neither of them took a backward step.'

Sometimes they were on the same bill, as occurred on Saturday night, 27 November 1948. *The Balonne Beacon* noted that under floodlights, in front of the biggest house yet seen during the current series of tournaments in the open-air ring, 'Ranald Waters gave an exhibition of boxing far above the ordinary and had his bout won from early in the first round.' The paper added that 'only . . . the timely arrival of the towel' eleven seconds after the start of the second round saved his opponent from being KO'd. 'Judging on his agility and stamina it will not surprise anyone to see Ranald go to the very top in the fight game. We understand that even now a move is in progress to take him to where he will have this opportunity.'

The report then turned to the bout involving Len Waters and Rodney Harrison, observing that it 'proved to be all that was expected of it and more'.

> *Both men proved their boxing ability and fighting determination to the full, and no praise can be too high for the way they kept at it to the very end of the last round. Waters with his change of style from orthodox to southpaw had Harrison bewildered on several occasions, but apparently was unable to gain enough advantage out of this to either K.O. Harrison or set up an unassailable points lead, for when Harrison came in fast early in the last round, with a punch to Waters' body, that left the latter winded, he made full use of the next thirty seconds to pick up his points leeway, and then for the last part of the round they slugged it out pretty evenly. Referee Joe Hile's decision of a draw could not have been fairer.*

Despite lack of opportunity to train regularly, Waters had lost little of the ability that saw him win the inter-services title during the war, and brother Ranald was showing that boxing skills ran in the family. They kept sparring together in preparation for the opportunity that the paper hinted at. Ranald hoped he could secure an elimination bout that would pave the way for him to challenge for the Queensland lightweight title that the champion Cloncurry Aboriginal boxer Jack Hassen had just relinquished after moving to Sydney in a bid to further his career.

The St George boxing promoter, local businessman Mick Lambert, knew of the Brisbane boxing trainer Jim 'Pop' Jamieson, and contacted him about Ranald's prowess. Pop was interested, and Lambert flew him to Brisbane to meet the trainer. Jamieson duly invited the eighteen-year-old to join his stable of fighters, observing that he was 'a fast, elusive mover', with a particularly long reach. Pop thought he might 'have found a second Jack Hassen'. What also appealed to Pop was that Ranald had a right-hand knock-out punch. One boxing writer described it as 'no maiden's caress' while noting that Ranald did 'most of his damage with his rangy straight lefts and short and long hooks with the same fist'.

Ranald lived with Pop and his wife at inner-city Fortitude Valley, and the trainer found him a job as a mechanic at a nearby garage. There was a gym attached to the house, and he began sparring there daily. But preparation was not just in the ring, as Pop's approach was much more old-fashioned. He believed in honing bush toughness and each weekend sent Ranald to Wynnum to chop wood at a sawmill.

In mid-June 1949, Pop thought Ranald ready. The big night was set for 2 September 1949 at the red-brick Brisbane Stadium. Ranald would challenge Brisbane boxer Brian Brady in the lead-up to challenging for Hassen's vacant Queensland title. Brady had previously trained under Pop but left after an unresolved dispute. Pop was left stewing and resentful and saw the bout as a revenge match. Pop was going to get even, and Ranald was to be his means of revenge. Talk of a £200 side wager between the two camps added spice to the night.

On the morning of the fight, *The Courier-Mail* noted that since he had taken him into his stable, Jamieson had worked on a set plan to tutor 'the coloured lightweight' along lines that would enable him 'to master his old pupil Brady if they ever met. Jamieson fully realises that Brady is a smashing puncher with his right, but he reckons that he has a plan of battle mapped out for Waters.'

Ranald, however, had an uneasy feeling about the approaching fight: he felt he was being rushed, as it was only his fifth fight in the ring, especially as Pop wouldn't allow him to fight his natural fight, which would mean taking the fight up to Brady. On the plus side, Len was going to be in his corner that night as his second. Waters himself had misgivings, thinking that his brother was badly overmatched.

Ranald entered the ring under glaring lights. Five times he was knocked down before fighting back and flooring Brady. But he couldn't finish Brady off when he got back up. In the eighth round, Brady hit him with a sickening blow that sent him to the canvas for the sixth time. Sprawling on the deck dazed, Ranald knew he was finished. Len screamed at his brother to get up as he saw how wobbly Brady was. He knew he was there for the taking. Ranald heard the cry. 'Normally I would have done anything that my big brother asked,' he later recalled. But that night he couldn't find the strength. He groggily mumbled to Len, 'If you want to fight him, get in here, but I'm not getting up.' He took the full count, giving Brady a win by KO. It had been a boxing lesson, despite Ranald's display of 'remarkable stamina and indomitable courage', according to *The Courier-Mail*'s fight report.

Waters thought his brother 'had plenty of skill for such a short career', but in the fight against Brady he 'was starting to cop an unnecessary belting'. The fight lost, Ranald and his brother, along with Gladys and other family members, shrugged off the defeat and, just as they always did on fight nights, took a cab to the Theatre Royal to watch the popular entertainer George Wallace junior. Ranald only had one more fight, for a draw, before returning home to St George, where, as a qualified mechanic, he took a job with the Balonne Shire Council.

Meanwhile, Waters continued his itinerant lifestyle, driven by the shearing circuit, which took him away from St George for weeks at a time. He had no option. In these early years of marriage Gladys often travelled with her husband and baby Lenise. An early job was a fencing and shearing contract at Darcy Thompson's property, Rossmore. There, the Waters erected a large tent for their living quarters not far from the homestead. Darcy's widow, Marguerite, remembers Waters was 'always laughing and smiling, but he never spoke about the war'.

Perhaps what helped to put a smile on his face was that Darcy owned a Tiger Moth. With his devil-may-care attitude, he had no hesitation in letting Waters pilot the aircraft. Thus a pattern was set, one that would be repeated over future years on Outback stations when station owners became aware of the aviation skills of the gun shearer in their sheds.

24

WHEEL OF MISFORTUNE

The dry cough didn't let up. Gladys suspected whooping cough. Her two-year-old's breathing was laboured and her condition continued to deteriorate. Gladys knew Lenise needed hospital care. They were camped in a paddock on a station 100 kilometres from St George, a journey that would take two and a half hours at best. The rough, unsealed roads and the couple of dozen iron gates to be dragged open and lifted closed would slow them up even more. Waters knew he had to move quickly. But he was worried about the risk of being stranded without a spare tyre in the event of an all-too-likely puncture. With no time to lose, he threw a wheel from a nearby station trailer onto the tray of his old Chevrolet ute and headed off, with Gladys nursing Lenise alongside him.

They made it without incident, but on arrival in St George,

Waters was stunned when the police pulled him over. The cockie had rung in, alleging Waters had stolen the wheel. He was arrested and put in the lock-up despite explaining his reason for taking the wheel. Gladys, whose prime concern was the well-being of her daughter, was convinced racism underpinned the cockie's allegation and the attitude of the police, or *gunjies*, as they are commonly known. 'They didn't believe him,' she recalled. The cockie's word held sway with the law over that of a Murri.

Younger brother Kevin was working with them on the same station at the time and remembered how the incident shocked and angered his brother after their hard work for the cockie, who had never questioned their work ethic. Work on the station had been arduous in the heat of that summer in February 1950. 'Len and I were sinking posts. We would go out and cut 40 or 50 posts in the morning and then come back and have a feed. We'd then go and dig post holes with a crowbar and shovel, with Gladys and my wife, Thelma, on the back of the ute dropping the posts in. We were all fit as mallee bulls.'

The cockie was well known as a 'redneck', and Aboriginal workers were under no illusion that it was an 'us and them' situation. Kevin said:

> *Many of the cockies had a lord of the manor attitude, but he was the worst. Despite this, Len thought he had a good relationship with this particular cockie, as he did with many others, such as Darcy Thompson. After what happened that day our hearts dropped to rock bottom. Len and I made the decision to never work there again.*

The incident made the brothers realise that they were, as Warren Mundine has described

> *living a hybrid life between the full restrictions of the law and the freedoms everyone else had . . . but only if we stayed out of trouble, always keeping one eye looking over our shoulders. Most Aboriginal Australians you meet have either lived under this regime or been raised by people who were. And it does affect them.*

Sometimes it was unwise to push Waters. In November 1950, he and Gladys were invited to a wedding in her home town of Charleville, a town Waters had come to dislike. He felt that people like himself were treated as 'outsiders'. He had returned from Charleville to St George on an earlier occasion with two black eyes. He explained to Gladys he had been in a fight after a whitefella had called him a 'black bastard'. As the wedding reception was about to get under way, the groom came up to Waters and said with some condescension, 'I don't object to a blackfella being at my wedding.' Gladys recalled that he didn't quite finish the sentence before Waters punched him hard in the chest. The groom doubled over in pain as Waters took offence at the remark. 'Len wouldn't allow anyone to speak to him like that. He was a very proud man.'

Even though St George was more racially tolerant than many other Outback towns, the borrowed wheel incident typified the sometimes strained post-war relations between police and Aboriginal people. Gladys recalled another incident when Waters, as was normal practice for shearers, went to a

St George hotel to cash his pay cheque and buy her cigarettes. By chance, he ran into one of her uncles, who was drinking at the bar. Drunk, but happy to see Waters, he flung his arms around him exuberantly as a particular police officer walked in. This constable had a reputation among the black community as being quick to arrest whenever he could. Both were arrested and taken to the lock-up, even though Waters had not had a drink. Gladys remembers the experience as yet another humiliation—but one that was a commonplace event for Aborigines in rural Australia.

Waters' misfortune was to have been seen in the company of a drunken Murri relative. His own experience at Moree during the war had alerted him to the capriciousness of police. More accurately, it was often known colloquially as the offence of 'being black in a public place', and encompassed the notorious trifecta charge of offensive language, resist arrest and assault police. It mattered little whether someone was guilty or not of any of these; what mattered in this case was Waters was black and he was there.

Although Aborigines long knew by now that it was pointless to challenge the word of the police, Waters' general respect for the role of police remained. Despite what the family had seen with the actions of police at Toomelah, Don and Grace accepted that, in general, the role of police was crucial to the way communities ran. Imperfect as it was, there had to be the rule of law. Waters grew up learning this principle—something reinforced by his experience in the RAAF.

After the disturbing incidents at St George, the family

moved to Cunnamulla. Attracted by shearing jobs in surrounding stations, they lived in the Gladstone Hotel, where Gladys took a job as a domestic. Handily, her mother lived across the street—something that proved particularly useful after the birth of two more children, Donald and Dianne.

Not long after the move, while working at Noorama station, Waters sheared 200 sheep in a day, becoming the ringer. Gambling each night was common, and Waters had luck on his side. 'I won quite a lot of money and hardly drew from my earnings or wages. We were there about six weeks so I had a quite substantial cheque at cut-out.' Waters thought Cunnamulla the 'best town' in Queensland. As he recalled in a handwritten memoir many years later:

> *In those days there was practically no crime in the town. It was so free and easy that no one closed their doors, day or night, and you could cash your cut-out cheque on Saturday morning, leave your change on the counter of the pub and go and do whatever shopping you needed to do and come back an hour or so after and your change would either be on the counter or under it complete. Today one almost has to take his beer to the toilet with him.*

This was the early 1950s, and the Korean war was also having an impact on rural Australia. With the price of wool at record levels, the economy was booming and there was plenty of work on stations. Kevin Waters recalled how Aboriginal men, alongside white workers, would be gone for lengthy periods earning good wages throughout south-west Queensland. On return to

St George, the cheques would be cashed and, after weeks of hard physical work and no beer, splurged on grog.

When the money ran out, it was back to the bush to repeat the pattern. The risk of arrest for being drunk was never far away, especially for the Aboriginal men living in the so-called 'Hollywood' camp on the far side of the Balonne River. Relations between them and the police were often tense. While not part of that camp, the Waters family still walked a fine line between their Aboriginality and the white community in which they lived.

For the Waters family, the distressing results of interaction with police suddenly became personal. It involved Grace Waters' father, George Bennett. A hero to his people when he returned from World War I, and revered by his grandchildren as a role model, he had become a recluse soon after the war. The post-war years saw his health decline as a result of being gassed on the Western Front.

The Allison family, who owned Delapool station, near Mungindi, took him back on his return because of their appreciation of his war service. They helped him apply for a service personnel pension but his application was declined and referred to the Social Security Department. A year before his death, the payment of an aged pension to George was finally approved. He lived in a hut on the station but rarely moved far from it, apart from the occasional trip to a Mungindi pub, hitching his two horses to a wagonette and making the journey accompanied by his dogs.

On Saturday, 23 September 1950, Bennett made the trip into

Mungindi for a drink at the pub. Later that day, he was arrested for drunkenness and taken to the local police station lock-up. He would not leave the cell alive. Two days later, *The Sydney Morning Herald* reported:

> ABORIGINAL DIES IN PRISON CELL
>
> George Bennett, 67, an Aboriginal, was found dead in a police cell at Mungindi soon after his midday meal yesterday. Bennett was charged with drunkenness and placed in the cell on Saturday. Police said there were no suspicious circumstances. A post-mortem examination will be held.

This was a death in custody. While it was just one of many lonely Aboriginal deaths in police cells somewhere in Australia, the family remembered it with bitterness for generations. Don Waters drove his heartbroken wife to Mungindi to arrange the funeral and burial in the local cemetery.

For George Bennett, war service had brought no entitlements. The discipline of the army, however, had remained with him all his life, and he applied it to his many dogs. In his last years, they were his only real companions. He trained his dogs well, and each would only eat on his command. This proved problematic when Bennett died. His six dogs waited for the command that would never come.

25

STRIKE

When the freak wet of July–August 1954 hit the St George region, Waters was back in the bush, fencing and building stockyards as the rivers rapidly rose and dirt roads turned to impassable quagmires. Six-year-old Lenise was at boarding school, but Waters was on Darcy Thompson's Rossmore property about 100 kilometres from St George, accompanied by Gladys and the two younger children, Donald and Dianne. Waters would reflect later that these were 'some of the happiest days of our marriage. I used to dig the holes and stand the posts and my "dearly beloved" used to help me do the wiring—she could work as good or better than any man.'

Soon Rossmore was isolated, cut off by the flooded Moonie River for six weeks. Neither the mail nor any supplies could get through. As food ran low, the family was forced to eke out meals, many of which Waters cooked from the meagre supplies they still had. 'One particular day I made a damper and handed a slice to Dianne, she looked at the bread and then up to me and said with tears in her eyes, "Daddy, I want budder on it."'

Waters was taken aback. The plaintive request struck a chord. He called out to a local who was working for him at the time, Johnny Bartley, with a proposition. 'I asked him would he be interested in walking into St George with me.' Bartley agreed and they set off, tramping across the sodden paddocks and under ceaseless drizzle. The journey was hazardous.

> *We had to swim the Moonie three times—regarded as one of the most treacherous streams in the west. But we did the trip in and out in two and a half days—a distance of about 130 miles. I must admit we got a taxi back out to the Moonie River, where they had a boat ferrying people over, but then we borrowed pack horses and got the tucker back to our families that way.*
>
> *Actually, John took back a tin of jam, a pound of butter, two loaves of bread and a bottle of rum, half of which he drank on the way back. He was staggering along a hundred yards or so behind me most of the way. I felt like leaving him, but I did appreciate the fact that he accompanied me on the trek into town.*

The flood drowned between 800 and 1000 sheep, Waters recalling that their carcasses were washed up along the boundary fence and his job was to skin the dead sheep, dry the skins and bale them to be sent away to be sold. In the process, he witnessed one of the unexpected hazards that came with the work when one of his team, Pat, who was known as the 'mad Irishman', rolled one of the bodies over to prepare to skin it. 'When he pulled his left hand away, a death adder was hanging from the end of his index finger on his left hand. Now Pat didn't show any fear or alarm, he just pulled out his rifle and shot the end of his finger off. He certainly got rid of the venom, but he had a very sore finger for weeks after.'

*

Another daughter, Gladys Julia-Kaye, was added to the growing family in 1954. Her serious medical condition required a move back to St George to a Housing Commission home. With her life in jeopardy—doctors gave her just twelve months to live—there were frequent trips to the Royal Children's Hospital in Brisbane. This culminated in surgery to repair her congenital heart condition, patent ductus arteriosus, commonly known as 'hole in the heart'. The outcome was successful and was groundbreaking for an eleven-month-old baby in the mid-1950s.

Amid this stressful time, Waters continued to find work, mainly around the St George area. But as the boom from the Korean war faded, the wool industry was facing a crisis after the federal and state industrial courts agreed to a demand by the wool industry to reduce the rates of pay for shearers. Prices had again started to slide, and the graziers argued they could no longer afford to pay a prosperity loading to shearers. The immediate cause was a decision by the Queensland Industrial Court to reduce shearers' pay rates by 10 per cent, the United Graziers' Association having asked for a 15 per cent cut.

Waters believed a strike was imminent—and so did Gladys. Given the ages of the children, she worried that there would be little money coming in, so began selling bits and pieces of furniture. Just before Christmas 1955 they decided to move back to Cunnamulla with their children, this time to live in a four-square-metre canvas tent on the town's camping ground.

The money from the sale of the furniture would be used to buy the necessities for the duration of the looming strike. Several other shearing families also came to live there in either tents or caravans. Conditions were basic. While there was no rent to be paid, there was also no running water and no power. They had to make do with kerosene lamps.

When money ran short, survival meant quietly breaking the law and sheep duffing to put food on the family table. Waters and a mate would borrow a ute and drive out of town to an isolated paddock where they would kill a couple of sheep, the meat from which Gladys would corn.

In January 1956 the strike erupted. Suspicion and paranoia were rife in a dispute that quickly descended into violence in many shearing towns as 'old raters' were pitted against the scab labour of 'new raters'. Philosophically, Waters was a strong unionist. He was a member of the Australian Workers' Union who, like his father, always voted Labor in state and federal elections. He took a strong stand in defence of the 'old raters'. He was scathing about other local shearers who were prepared to accept the new regime. 'Most of the shearers in

St George were very weak regarding conditions in the industry. I didn't want to subject my family to the trauma of clashes of the militant men of the industry and the weak scabby bastards.'

Clearly, Waters could not countenance being drawn into doing scab labour. His father had imbued in him the lessons of hard, honest work in return for fair pay. The family ethos was egalitarian. From the time he left school as a teenager to join his father in the bush, Waters had learned the fundamental importance and interdependence of working in teams. The RAAF served to reinforce this, and his life had depended on it. Underpinning these attitudes was his own Indigenous culture and communalism. Waters had witnessed from a young age the need for a community to stand together. Union membership was a natural step.

In country towns—with Cunnamulla one of the focal points—union representatives made a practice of checking new arrivals as they arrived by train or bus. As one union organiser put it, his main activity was approaching strangers to find out what they were doing and looking at their hands for telltale knuckles. Shearers always grew big knuckles by pressing their hands into the skin of the sheep to make it taut for easier shearing. Scabs, suspected of being brought in by the dominant shearing contractor, Grazcos, were quickly run out of town. He continued:

> *At that time the struggle was becoming hot in Queensland as Grazcos was concentrating all their scab labour in that state and Cunnamulla became known as the hangman's town. The Cunnamulla committee*

boys used to go down the track to meet the trains at various sidings and drag the scabs off and burn their swags. One of the local pubs was blackballed and picketed for harbouring scabs; big patches of black paint were painted all over the pub. Violence against scabs was commonplace and they were given police protection.

In Cunnamulla, the union rep would pay the shearers at the Tattersalls Hotel on Friday nights at the rate of £7 for married shearers. With such little money coming in, Gladys had to keep a tight rein on costs. The family's needs were simple: they just needed money for food, which she cooked over a wood stove—and she quickly earned a reputation for being able to make a meal out of almost anything. This was satisfactory to begin with, but as the strike wore on, nerves frayed, not least as the men gambled at night in a big shed, Waters often among them.

Waters found momentary diversion in an exhibition fight when the Roy Bell boxing troupe came to Cunnamulla for the annual show. His opponent was Jack Hassen, the Charleville boxer who a few years earlier had vacated the Queensland lightweight title Ranald Waters had hoped to win. Hassen's career had been tragically cut short after a fight in September, 1949. Trailing on points in the eleventh round, Hassen battered his opponent, Archie Kemp, to a standstill in a corner before turning to the referee to stop the punishment. But the referee told him to box on. Kemp collapsed and was carried from the ring on a stretcher. He did not regain consciousness and died of a cerebral haemorrhage. Hassen tried to go on, but his heart was no longer in boxing and he retired in 1951.

While the Hassen–Waters fight was billed as a light spar in an exhibition bout at the Cunnamulla Show, it was nonetheless a highlight. Gladys watched them enter the tent ring and then the bell rang. 'It was lovely watching Len spar, beautiful. Then all of a sudden he hit Jack a little bit hard, and I thought, "For Christ's sake, you'll have to get the undertakers." I said, "He's gone."' Everyone knew of Hassen's great punching power, and Gladys feared he would unleash this on her husband in retaliation. Waters knew he had overstepped the mark and acted quickly to make amends. Gladys recalled what followed: 'Len put his arms around Jack and was apologising to him—that's the only thing that saved him.'

With the festering mood of the strike in Cunnamulla, Waters felt a clean break was needed. He decided to take the family to Brisbane. In mid-August 1956 he was allocated a Housing Commission home in the new post-war satellite suburb of Inala, about 20 kilometres south-west of Brisbane. The rent was £2/15 a week and the Waters became one of the first Murri families to move into the suburb, an early post–World War II social housing estate. The suburb had a lot going for it: not only did it mean 'place of peace' in the local Yugambeh language, but the new houses being constructed were mostly designed by post-war modernist architects Robin Boyd, Roy Grounds and Harry Seidler. However, Inala quickly gained a reputation for being one of the roughest suburbs in Brisbane.

Nonetheless, a new home had been beyond the Waters' wildest dreams. They would eventually buy it for £7000 with a war-service loan. Importantly, the repayments were low. Waters had another motivation:

To give our family a chance for a better life we decided to move to the city because in those days there were no high schools west of Toowoomba and Warwick. They were the closest high schools. The squatters and business people in the west could send their kids down to be educated but the working class just could not do that. So we decided to move to the city to give our kids a secondary education.

The move also gave Gladys the opportunity to work. And work she did. She took in ironing, cleaned houses and in time cleaned the local police station, which included making meals for prisoners in the lock-up. The strike ended in October 1956 with a major victory for the shearers when the arbitration system awarded them an increase in their pay rate per 100 sheep shorn. Meanwhile, Waters was travelling vast distances with a shearing contractor, shearing at sheds between Winton in central western Queensland, and Deniliquin, in the New South Wales Riverina. Meanwhile, another daughter, Maxine, was born in 1957.

The readjustment from the bush to the city was harder than expected. Living in the city had definite benefits, but the move to Brisbane's outer suburbs meant being at least 500 kilometres away from extended family still in St George and the support they could provide. 'Moving away from the cultural support of my grandparents, aunts and uncles, and numerous cousins, initially was devastating. However, the bonding between the Murri families and myself at Inala helped greatly,' Lenise remembered.

Waters was constantly away shearing, leaving his family in a suburb beset by growing ethnic tensions between Murris and displaced migrants from post-war Europe. Adding to the tensions were a lack of services and youth support organisations, amid episodes of street violence. The crime rate soon became higher than average. Waters acknowledged the problems and stress this caused to his family:

> *I was away up to 10 months of the year. They would only see me in the middle of the year and a couple of weeks before Christmas and I'd be gone again in the middle of January. It was hard on my wife because she had to be mother and father to the kids while I was away.*

Amid this emerging hardship and family strains, Waters began to think about rejoining the RAAF. He wanted a permanent job with a steady income. He knew of World War II pilots who were re-enlisting as the Malayan Emergency intensified. At the time, the RAAF was preparing to take control of the Butterworth Air Base in Malaya to station a fighter and bomber wing under the build-up of the Commonwealth Strategic Reserve.

In June 1957, the Department of Air considered Waters' application as an ex-airman for re-enlistment in an unspecified mustering. He underwent a medical examination, and was classified as Class 1. The office of the director of personnel services considered that he was 'suitable on type for re-enlistment in the mustering of his choice, subject of course to vacancies and ability to pass trade tests.'

The term 'on type' suggests Waters was seeking to rejoin as aircrew. By 1957 the RAAF was only employing officers as pilots. 'Trade test' in the RAAF was a once common term that is now no longer used. It applied to non-commissioned ranks mainly and referred to the proficiency test they had to pass in order to progress through the ranks in their trade, mustering or category.

The term was used across the board, from the traditional mechanical trades to clerks, medics and equipment or stores workers. Anyone re-entering the RAAF would be trade tested against the standard for the rank-category they were applying for. But it is not clear from the files what position Waters was seeking, whether pilot or flight fitter, though it seems more likely that he was hoping to be a pilot.

By this time, the RAAF's front-line fighters were Sabre jets, and Waters probably would not have been considered suitable as a jet pilot. Gladys would later recall that Waters wanted to re-enlist to 'better himself'. Nothing came of the application. Perhaps Waters had a change of mind and just withdrew, disinclined to go back to ground staff and work as an aircraft mechanic. But he told her the RAAF didn't want him. 'It hurt him,' she recalled.

That was not the end of the hurt. In 1960 he applied for a job with the Queensland Office of the Director of Native Affairs. As Gladys put it: 'He was refused the job with no explanation why. He never complained to me about his treatment and that he'd failed to get a good secure job.'

Not only had his hopes of a renewed flying career now been dashed for the second time, but he had been turned down by the very department—albeit one then controlled by often unsympathetic white bureaucrats—that was supposed to champion the interests of Aboriginal people. The office was notoriously racist, a reputation that would worsen over the years. It opposed payment of award wages to Indigenous workers, was implicated in the removal of Aboriginal children from their parents, and oversaw the destruction of Indigenous communities. Independent federal MP and former Queensland Aboriginal Affairs Minister Bob Katter called it an 'evil regime'.

Waters' beliefs would have ensured conflict with the office's harsh and oppressive policies. But disillusionment over these job failures settled on him and he began to feel shame.

26

THE LONER

Waters was a crooner, be it in the shearers' huts after a day in the sheds or at family get-togethers. He rather saw himself as a Bing Crosby or Perry Como, according to his bemused brother Kevin. In early 1961 he put his talent to good use by helping to raise funds for the Inala Brigadettes marching girls team. Lenise, by now thirteen, was a Brigadette, and she and the team were to represent Queensland at the Australian titles to be held in Tasmania that year.

Waters was happy to oblige by not just being master of ceremonies at these fundraisers but also singing, nattily dressed in a tuxedo and bow tie. Daughter Dianne recalled that when he took to the dance floor with Gladys, the sight was mesmerising. With Gladys dressed in a dress of Chantilly lace, her head held high, often with eyes closed, they would float around the floor. 'He was a stunning dancer, just like Fred Astaire,' Dianne remembered. Waters often tried to win a laugh on such nights by crouching down low during the dance, with Gladys unaware of and perplexed by the chuckling.

This was the height of the marching girls' era, when every weekend, thousands of girls in every state of Australia donned jaunty caps, short skirts, and high white boots to march through the streets at football matches, carnivals and fetes. When the competition was held, the Brigadettes defeated 41 other teams to take the 1961 junior Australian title.

On their return to Brisbane Airport, a press photographer lined them up with their grand 'wedding cake' trophy for a photo for the next morning's *Courier-Mail*. Before the photo was taken, the coach took Lenise aside and applied white powdery make-up to lighten her face so she would not appear different from the other girls. 'I was the only girl this happened to, it was so degrading,' she recalled. She was too embarrassed to tell even her parents. The impact of this denial of her colour rankled more over time.

Waters the crooner entered his own singing competition. A year later he took to the stage when the 4KQ Suburban and Country Talent Quest was broadcast live from Inala. Interviewed about his line of work before he sang, Waters replied modestly, 'General labouring—I go out west and do a bit of shearing, that sort of thing.' He was act number five, and launched into a rendition of *When You Were Sweet Sixteen*. This had particular significance because he had met Gladys when she was that age. That night, he came second—to Gladys's sister.

As their seventeenth wedding anniversary approached in February 1963, and yet again he was away, Waters felt moved to mark it a different way, writing Gladys a verse both of love and remorse. He called it 'Seventeen Hard Summers'. This was not just a recommitment to the marriage but also an acknowledgement of his failings. He had known, he wrote, as soon as he saw her photo during wartime, that she was the one he wanted to marry.

How the months dragged on till the end came and I arrived back home
I realised before very long that I would never again want to roam.
But you seemed at first quite indifferent. 'Got another bloke,' so you said.
Till I love stricken and worried was
Almost out of my head.
But I noticed when'er I was passing, you
Mostly seemed to be looking
And before very long we, a church for our
Wedding were booking.
That was seventeen years come this summer
The sixteenth of February the date
Since the day that we walked from that
Small church,
And you became my precious life's mate.

But the years had been difficult as they struggled to make a home and raise a family.

We haven't had so many good times, there's
Been worry and trouble and strife.
But through hardships and our few pleasures
I thank God for you my sweet wife.
I know that you chide and you scold me
And sometimes get under my skin
But I realise only too fully, without you
The strife I'd be in.
Yes it's been Seventeen Hard Summers and
Ends most times hard to meet
But, tucked in are a few precious moments, that
To me still are very sweet.

Once again, he would not be home to mark their anniversary, but, he implored:

Think of me as I will be of you,
And who knows one of these days dear, we
May make all our wishing come true.

The verse suggests life had become an unrelenting struggle—with not so many good times, and with growing 'worry and trouble', but with just a glimmer of hope. It was an insight into a marriage and family life that, as Waters approached 40, were under great strain. The constant separations for months at a time were taking their toll as he followed shearing jobs in the Outback. There was little scope for communication with home, with phones often dependent on insecure and unreliable party lines. He and Gladys were forced into living increasingly separate lives. He later recalled of these years:

> *I am very much aware of all the really pleasant things I have missed through my being away from my family during their developing years. My son Don once told me, 'Dad you felt you had to go away for your work, but you just don't realise how much you were missed at home.'*
>
> *I do know that it had to be really hard on Gladys being mother and father to the kids for at least 10 months of the year especially in a place like Inala during the mid-1950s and into the sixties, as that suburb had a really bad reputation in those years.*

Waters' contribution while away shearing was to wire money to the local post office before midday each Saturday. If it didn't arrive, there was an immediate impact on Gladys, and so too, the whole family, adding to the stress of making ends meet. With the children becoming teenagers, she could be a tough disciplinarian. Family relationships fractured, in some cases irreparably.

Yet, Waters knew that the only work left to him was shearing if he was to earn enough money for the family. It was what he did best. As he recalled: 'I used to go up north of Longreach around Winton and Julia Creek where the sheep don't grow nearly as much wool, and for years, I shore over 1000 sheep a week and on more than one occasion over 1250.' The further north he went the less wool the sheep carried. They were known simply as 'white mice'.

Waters had been one of five shearers working for a contractor on Pathungra Station, 160 kilometres south of Mt Isa, earning £8/6/3 per 100 sheep and doing 200 a day. Shearers were paid £6 for messing, with the grazier providing accommodation, while the contractor paid his wages and provided transport and everything necessary for the team. It was a time of drought in a harsh landscape, and this had forced sheep numbers down from 15,000 to 9000. It had been five years since decent rain and a good season. Kangaroos competed with sheep for the scarce feed, and packs of wild dogs were killing lambs by the hundreds. The heat was unrelenting.

A magazine article published at the time noted Waters' presence in the Pathungra shearing shed, near Boulia, and described the merciless landscape in which he and the other shearers worked:

> *Heading north across trackless paddocks seemingly bare of grass, we drove towards the range of hills, a continuation of the Selwyn range, which dominated the northern skyline. The southerly end of the range has been eroded by rain and wind over the years until now it mainly consists of round, smooth sandstone hills that look like white plum puddings. Wherever we looked, there were signs of the drought. The dry, red soil lay loose on the ground without even the usual clumps of spinifex to prevent it from being whipped up by the wind. The hot afternoon sun made the ground shimmer, and heat waves distorted the outlines of the hills.*

With heads down and backs bent in the shed, the five shearers 'worked ceaselessly to boost their tally of fleeces', pulling wethers from the pen and separating the fleece from the body with swift, sure strokes of the cutters. In what appeared to be a matter of seconds, the dazed animals were released to join their 'naked-looking relatives' in the pen. The fleeces were then gathered and taken to the sorting table, where they were classed and the broken pieces picked out. Classing finished, the fleeces and smaller lots of wool were put into the appropriate bins before going to the wool presser and being mechanically compressed into a bale for carting to Brisbane. Each fleece that Waters cut weighed around 2.7 kilograms, and up to 33 of these went into making up a bale weighing around 136 kilograms. By the time shearing finished, the team would have filled about 260 bales.

Waters was hundreds of miles from home and up to his neck in 'sheep shit and grease', but the money from shearing was better than labouring in and around St George or Brisbane. Shearing by now had become something more than just a job. It had to be, because a day's shearing has been likened to burning the same amount of energy as running a marathon. Waters understood this, just as he knew the intense anticipation that accompanied the approaching end of each day's shift. Given the extreme physical exertion required day after day, year after year it was an exquisite moment when the last sheep was shorn and he could sit down and gulp half a gallon of water. This was intensely satisfying, and life felt pretty good.

One of Waters' fellow shearers from this time, Peter Gorman, remembers often going outside and sitting on a bale of wool, yarning with him, at the end of a day's work. 'He was a bit of a loner, but once he got to know you, you were his mate. He was a pretty caring sort of fellow with a good sense of humour and he could tell a good story.' Gorman recalled an occasion when he and Waters were shearing out around Hughenden in western Queensland when they got into his car with some stubbies and drove the long trip over a red dirt road to the shed. It was hot, and Waters wound down the rear windows. In his rear-vision mirror, Gorman could see red dust being drawn into the back of the car. Waters had fallen asleep, unaware of the dust settling on him. Arriving at the shed, Gorman, with a wry smile, suggested to Waters that he could do with a shower. Waters was taken aback until he saw his reflection in a mirror, expostulating, 'I look like a bloody Red Indian!'

Gorman felt close to Waters, and these were the relationships that sustained him away from home. To the other shearers in the sheds, Waters must have been something of an enigma: the gun shearer could be found reading anything from Carter Brown to Shakespeare. The first Gorman knew of Waters' air force exploits was when he was invited to his Inala home one afternoon. 'I walked in and saw a photo of him in his RAAF uniform, and then the boxing trophy he had won on Morotai. We had been in lots of sheds together, but he just never mentioned anything about it.'

In all these years of shearing, Waters was always loath to talk about his wartime experience, rarely mentioning it. Contractor Bert Lowrey, for whom he worked in the New England district in the 1960s and early '70s, recalled Waters as a modest man who kept quiet about his career as a fighter pilot. 'He never told me or any of his workmates that he'd been in the RAAF, let alone been a fighter pilot.'

But Lowrey remembered an occasion when Waters' technical knowledge of aviation surfaced at an unexpected moment. The date was 21 July 1969 and history was being made. Lowrey was as much at a loss as the others to comprehend what was happening:

> *We were at a shearing shed called Borgara, on the other side of Walgett, when Neil Armstrong landed on the moon. There was a team of 25 shearers listening to the wireless at about 7 o'clock in the morning when the news came through. One of the shearers wondered out loud how they did it. Well, out of the blue Len explained it to us. Very much in layman's terms, but being a pilot he knew what they were doing.*

This was a spine-tingling moment around the world. But here, in a shearing shed in Outback New South Wales, it is not difficult to visualise Waters using his hands to help explain the physics of space travel to this incredulous group as they drank their early morning cup of tea.

It had been 25 years since Waters put his aviation handbooks away. There would have been a level of wistfulness in the excitement of the moment.

27

THE SATURDAY RITUAL

They were a gun shearing team known as the 'Flying Eight'. The team travelled from as far afield as Winton in central western Queensland, down through the New England region and Mildura in New South Wales to Ceduna and Naracoorte in South Australia. No one could shear faster with these narrow combs than Waters and his seven mates. And they held him in high regard. Not only was he quick, but his long blows were also neat. Waters' rule was never to kneel on the sheep's stomach; that only caused distress.

This was emblematic of Waters' integrity—something that his mates recognised. Kevin Webster was one of them, and knew Waters well. 'A good shearer, a good bloke, straight up and down, the sort of bloke you were proud to knock around with. He was not a skite or big noter. I sheared in quite a few sheds with Lenny and I never heard him say a bad word about anybody.' So much so that his daughter, Dianne, who had begun travelling with them as a cook, married one of the team, Ron Stedman, on her father's recommendation.

Waters fitted comfortably into the mateship of the shearing sheds. He accepted that even the cook's constant diet of mutton was part of this lifestyle. Indeed, he epitomised the camaraderie and humour that typified the Outback ethos of the Australian legend. Such was the pattern of his life, week in, week out, only interrupted by weekends when a lift to town on the back of a contractor's flatbed truck provided some respite. Hotels were always the magnet for Saturdays spent forgetting the back-breaking ordeal of the week. Beers were drunk and bets were made. He loved to punt.

Waters was at home in this environment, where gambling on horse racing flourished in pubs throughout Australia. Although it was illegal, police turned a blind eye to SP bookies who operated in pubs, whether city or country. Waters took punting seriously, always studying the form guide in the *Truth* newspaper before placing his bets with the local SP bookie.

Fights at pubs on Saturdays were not uncommon, often sparked by competing claims or a personal grievance. Waters' shearing mate Bill Fisk recalled: 'I knew he could fight, he had a couple of bare-knuckle fights at the back of the pub at Winton.' Such fights were never the result of racial abuse, however. 'No one ever called Lenny a blackfella. You were either a worker or a shirker, whether you were black, white or brindle. He was no slouch, he was a good shearer and everyone knew it.'

Waters' son, Don, was introduced to this culture when, at the age of about fifteen, he joined his father on shearing jobs: 'My first job was out there with him in the sheds near Toobea in the mid-'60s. I saw him in a couple of fights—he could handle himself all right.' On one occasion, Waters came to the defence of a fellow shearer at a pub. As Don described it: 'This big black bloke put him on the floor and started to give it to him. The old man was only about twelve stone [76 kg]. But the publican ordered them to take it outside. As soon as they squared up again the old man got him with one and he went from standing up to sitting on the ground. The old man did not start it, but he finished it.' On another occasion Waters came to his son's defence while they were at sheds near Goondiwindi. As Don recalls:

> *This bloke was having a go at me and wanted to fight when we were all out behind the tank stand. Everybody was cleaning themselves up before going into town to cut loose. The old man gave me his toothbrush and towel, and said to this bloke, 'Do you want to fight?' And with that he just went whack. The bloke went down. I asked why he had come to my defence and he said, 'You might have to fight for me one day.'*

The Saturday drinking culture was the norm for shearers and other itinerant workers in the post-war years. They were away from home for months on end, without the usual domestic responsibilities. They had no backyard lawns to mow, cars to wash or kids to take to sport. There was little to restrain them from spending the day sinking schooners leaning against a long bar. Waters had enjoyed male company all his life; he had six brothers, worked in a bush team from the age of fourteen, and joined the male preserve of RAAF fighter pilots. As Gladys was quick to point out, he liked to be one of the boys. Shearing meant that, like it or not, life was on the road.

Personified by the prose of Lawson and Paterson, there has long been a romanticism attached to the tradition of the bushman and the shearer—'the vision of the hard, simple, satisfying life of the bush as the essence of being Australian'. The myth of the bush was seductive. The credo of mateship went with it. The strong commitment to mutual support, cohesion and egalitarianism was reaffirmed by Saturdays in the pub. There was a powerful tradition of 'work and burst'—the drunken blowout in town 'at the end and on the proceeds of a hard spell of work in the bush'.

Waters understood the pull of this life in which alcohol was an integral part. Virtually everyone took part in the Saturday ritual of binge drinking. One story that Waters thought symptomatic of this involved one of the shearers who had been with him at Pathungra station, 'Bull' Thompson. He respected Bull and thought him a 'real character'. Come one Saturday morning after a week shearing, one of the younger boys who was to drink with him that day was slow getting ready. 'Bull' thought him 'a bit of a lair'. After more than an hour he had lost patience, and urged his companion to hurry up as it was getting perilously close to 10 a.m. and opening time. His drinking mate asked him why it was so important to be at the pub so early, as it would be open for twelve hours. Bull responded, 'Yes, but if you go to the movies, you don't want to get there after the curtain rises, do you?' There seemed to be little else to do but drink and drink, with no one offering caution.

Like a soldier's return from war into a functioning household, Waters' return home after months away was often very different from any eager anticipation around it. Gladys ran a tight ship, with each of the children having their designated chores. Waters' presence inevitably changed dynamics in the family, both positively and negatively. Gladys was used to being in control, while Waters was used to not having to answer to anyone. Life in a shearers' hut was in complete contrast to that of a family home. Marital strain was inevitable. Over the years Waters found it increasingly difficult not to drink while home from the shearing circuit, but Gladys loathed the grog as a result of her father's heavy drinking. Sparks began to fly.

28

GRIEF

With a late-night knock on the door came the news Waters had dreaded. The police officer on the doorstep told him that his mother had not survived a heart attack at St George two days earlier. It was June 1964, and Waters was home at Inala. It was a time before more sophisticated communications, when a home phone was still a luxury. Contacting the police to pass on an important message was common practice.

The news left Waters understandably grief-stricken. He had to get to St George, but as Gladys recalled, 'We did not have a brass razoo.' Waters walked to the nearest public phone to tell his mate Ted Weldon, a Wiradjuri man, about his predicament. In an act of sharing not uncommon in Aboriginal communities, Weldon wasted no time; he filled his car and drove to the Waters' home, giving them his car to drive to St George for the funeral.

Bundling their children into the car, Len and Gladys drove through rain all night. It was a long, hard journey, much of it over unsealed roads. They did not arrive until mid-morning. Just 63, Grace was held in high regard by Aboriginal and non-Aboriginal alike. That afternoon, St George came to a standstill—shops closed, and the line of cars stretched from the church to the cemetery and kept on coming. In the church, the congregation sang the hymn 'Amazing Grace'. It became the family theme song, to be sung at family gatherings thereafter.

For the Waters children, Grace had been the keeper of Kamilaroi cultural knowledge and stories passed down from their ancestors, especially through her mother, Granny Craigie. Grace was, as her granddaughter, Lenise, remembered, 'the rock that cemented our family values, our cultural and spiritual ways. She was able to integrate her Aboriginality with Christianity and this had a domino effect on her children and grandchildren.' Grace had been a bridge between two cultures. Now suddenly there was a void.

This was a time when the certainties underpinning Waters' optimism faltered. Grace had been his inspiration and role model: she read voraciously and imprinted on him the value of education, and he had learned from her commitment to self-improvement. Education was critical to opening up the way forward for her family. Waters understood this, and from this he had achieved unique status as a fighter pilot, literally and metaphorically flying high, only to be dragged back to earth by forces beyond his control. He was a gun shearer, but his life now seemed set on a path of unfulfilled promise and little recognition.

More pain followed eight years later. At dusk on 16 June 1972, his father, Don, stepped off a kerb onto a road in Toowoomba and was struck by a car. He died ten days later. Again, St George came to a standstill for the funeral of a respected figure in the town. Waters made the sombre trip home for his father's funeral.

Waters himself was not long out of hospital after a car accident in Brisbane just six weeks earlier. He had been driving towards Indooroopilly when a refrigerated truck smashed into his Ford Fairlane at an intersection. He was spun around on the road and dragged under the rear of the truck. The car was wrecked. Waters was taken to Princess Alexandra Hospital.

Gladys recalled: 'The police came at midnight. They said, "Get to the hospital as quick as you can, he's lost a bucket of blood already from the head."' Waters was treated for extensive head injuries, had a steel plate inserted into his skull, and was off work for several weeks. When he thought he had recovered, he returned to shearing. There were no apparent after-effects at this time.

Adding to the family sorrow was the death of Len's younger sister D'Nella Rose after she fell down stairs at a Winton hotel in 1973. D'Nella had lived a hard life: she had contracted polio as a child, and as an adult she was a victim of alcohol-fuelled domestic violence. The forcible removal of her children that followed left her inconsolable. This was a story that sent shockwaves through the wider Waters clan—yet they were powerless to prevent an unfolding tragedy. In the 1950s, when D'Nella married a Scotsman, it was not unusual for children of mixed-race marriages to come under the eye of welfare.

Waters' daughter Lenise wrote of the trauma around the taking of D'Nella's children:

> *When the welfare came for the children they were manhandled the way they were put in the vehicle. This was common practice when children were taken. The mother started wailing with this horrible pitch. The children were screaming for their mother. She ran after the car until she lost sight of the car and lost her voice. The children continued to cry out for their mother.*
>
> *The mother didn't understand why her children were not given to any of her family. Her immediate family lived in the same town as she did. The Aboriginal cultural way was to look after extended family members if the family wasn't coping . . . The parents became lost souls.*

The following year, on 16 September 1974, Waters' brother Jim died after years of ill-health. The family attributed his death to the after-effects of his involvement in the trials of anti-malarial drugs during World War II. Jim's funeral was a typical gathering of the extended family. Waters drove with his family from Brisbane, while brothers Kevin and Ranald travelled with their families from St George.

Kevin and Ranald's drive was not without incident, serving further to remind them that discrimination was still potent in the bush. They left St George at 5 a.m. on the day of the funeral and, after crossing the border, stopped to eat in the prosperous town of Narrabri. This country was the heart of what was once the Kamilaroi nation. 'We pulled up about 8 a.m. for breakfast at a café, but when we went inside we were refused service. We went down the street and got service at another café,' Kevin recalled.

It had been a long time since Kevin and his wife Thelma had experienced blunt refusal of service in a cafe based on their colour. The last time had been 1951 in Moree, when it was still 'a very separated town'. It was galling that such racism was still alive more than 20 years later. Going to a family funeral made the rejection harder. 'We had never experienced that in St George—in fact, never struck it in Queensland.'

The grief continued. In January 1976, the family was again in mourning. George Waters, the eldest of Don and Grace's sons, drowned when he slipped and fell while trying to cross the Mehi River at Moree. The death hit Waters hard: he had first worked with George as a teenager on leaving school, and during the war they had been thrown into a cell overnight in the Moree lock-up because of the town's racist laws. Few things seemed to be going right.

But at least his children were doing well, establishing careers through the education he had been denied and so desperately wanted them to have. Lenise was in education, Don had gone into business management, Julia in banking and the public service, Kim in cultural heritage, and Maxine in the Queensland Police rising to the rank of inspector. Waters was proud that they were showing the benefits of the move to the city. It was the one bright light of his life.

29

BLEAK TIMES

As the 1970s unfolded, Waters' health worsened. He began to experience dizzy spells, attributed to the head injury he sustained in his earlier car accident. As well, shearing had taken a toll on his knees. 'They wore my knees out gripping them,' he would recall of the technique required to hold sheep. He had had knee replacement surgery in 1966, which allowed his shearing career to continue for a time. He would later amuse himself watching people's reactions after he invited them to tap his knees. 'Here, bang my knees. Hear that? I've got stainless-steel ones now,' he would say.

Despite the knee replacements, he was struggling on his legs. Boisterous rams butting his steel knees in the sheds only ensured further wear and tear. He reluctantly gave shearing away, comforting himself with the knowledge that he would have shorn more than a million sheep over the years. Down on his luck and unsettled, he struggled with itinerant work, sometimes as a shearers' cook, much as his father had done. Waters took work in the cotton fields around Moree, removing stones before the cotton-picking machinery could drive onto the field. There were jobs as a labourer in the building and construction industry, at a car wrecking yard, and later at a Brisbane abattoir in the slaughter room. A job working a concrete pump followed, then another driving the equipment truck to building sites in Brisbane.

A good friend of Gladys's, who ran a business at Inala, wanted to retire and offered the lease to her, along with an adjoining store. She and her husband offered to help the Waters with finance. The Waters were enthusiastic: Gladys would run one, and Len would turn his skill as a shearers' cook to advantage and open a café in the other. But the owner of the premises, himself a migrant who had done well with property, would not give his approval. 'You are not selling it to that blackfella, I am not having a blackfella in my shops,' he bluntly told the leaseholders. They pointed out that Waters 'had fought for this country for people like you to come and live here.' The owner was unmoved. Gladys also rang him, hoping to change his mind, all to no avail. 'Len was very upset,' she said. The fighter pilot turned gun shearer had fallen to the lowest point of his life. And his health was now precarious, as he himself recognised. 'I continued working normally until towards the end of October 1976, when I started having blackouts, including five or six times while driving a truck,' he recalled. During 1977, Waters was hospitalised on four occasions. Exhaustive tests and a brain scan revealed considerable scarring caused by the injury from the car accident on the right side of his brain. This had led to focal epilepsy, the cause of his blackouts. He was prescribed anticonvulsant, anti-anxiety and antidepressant medication, as well as aspirin daily. Despite this cocktail, severe headaches continued.

The impact of the accident was not just devastating for his health, but also for the way he viewed himself. In January 1977, he was granted a service pension of $2.85 a fortnight. This was a pittance that he viewed as an insult. No longer was he the breadwinner, and the idea of Gladys being the main earner for the family was difficult to accept. He sought solace in alcohol, but found time to lay out the depth of his despondency. And his fears.

> *After working for over forty years and always priding myself for always being able to work alongside, and generally in front of most, I am now invalided and find myself a 'kept' man. I've very seldom been idle previously, but now, sometimes I have to wake my wife after she has turned the alarm off because she is completely exhausted trying to keep working to make ends meet.*
>
> *I become very disgruntled through having to sit at home and of course the one person who I owe so much to is the one who cops most of my anger and abuse. The situation has caused me to become very morose, and I am very concerned that I could do something drastic, that I would regret, if this situation is allowed to continue for much longer.*

Waters knew he was on the edge of a dark place, somewhere he had never been before, and feared his own reactions. He had always been able to look to the future with confidence. Now it was different; there was little in his life he had control over. He could no longer call on the perseverance and determination that had been such features of his life. He was suddenly disconnected from basic psychological needs: a feeling of belonging and of being valued, a sense that he was good at something. The RAAF and shearing had given him that; being unemployed left him in free fall. Not working robbed him of the last vestiges of his self-esteem. He was caught in an existential crisis.

He had grown up at a time when few women worked. This had been the case in his own family, where his father had been the sole breadwinner and his mother had kept house. Gladys, on the other hand, had worked from the age of eleven. Work gave her a sense of independence. Now he wanted her to give up work because if she did so, it would allow him to claim a larger pension.

Being at home while she continued to work hit him hard. 'What's a man to do? What will people think of me, sitting home here with his wife going out to work?' he told Gladys. She was working as a cleaner at the local police station and was determined to continue 'because I was getting really good money'. And she didn't know how not to work. But with her husband 'really down in the dumps', she borrowed $11,000 from the police credit union and paid off debts in his name. She hoped that easing the burden of debt would provide some relief at home, however temporary.

Waters had sought compensation for his injuries, but the truck driver's insurance company went into liquidation.

Legislation had to be amended to allow him to make a claim against the Nominal Defendant. Faced with delays in the Queensland Parliament, Waters wrote to the office of Premier Joh Bjelke-Petersen, bringing his personal situation to the premier's attention and appealing for the amendments to be instituted. The changes were duly passed.

Waters was awarded $86,000 compensation for the car accident. This was a windfall. One of his first acts was to buy a car for Gladys and pay off the outstanding credit union loan. For the first time they were debt free, and Gladys was ecstatic. 'You don't know that feeling when you don't owe a cent to a soul.' Waters used the proceeds to buy two small rural holdings, the first a 40-hectare property at Weambilla, near Chinchilla, 300 kilometres west of Brisbane, on which he built a weekender.

His grandsons Maurice and Kerwin spent time with him at the farm. 'We had a tin shack with a dirt floor and goannas scurrying through,' Maurice remembered. Waters' stepson, Geoffrey, who Gladys had given birth to before meeting him, also spent time at Chinchilla. By now, they had something in common—Geoffrey had done two tours of duty in Vietnam with 105th Battery Royal Australian Artillery. They both understood the horror and trauma of war.

Later, Waters bought a six-hectare property near Laidley, outside Brisbane, where he built a two-bedroom house. He named the farm Glenmaur—a combination of Gladys, Len and grandson Maurice. This was his hobby farm, with a citrus orchard and ducks, turkeys, chickens and goats. Maurice fondly remembered these times, when he would soak up knowledge from his grandfather. 'He read encyclopaedias while we were out there, and he would also take me out country and talk to me about traditional culture and massacres he had been told about,' Maurice said.

Also sharing these times at Laidley was his son, Don, who remembers that his father was 'pretty cluey, pretty handy with his hands. He was always building or making things. He was never idle.' He also remembers his father philosophising about beer he drank. 'He said, "If beer tasted any good, you'd be able to buy beer-flavoured chocolates and lollies. But it doesn't, so therefore people must drink it for another reason."' There was more than an admission here. Waters could binge drink not because he liked the taste but because he could forget.

Another grandson, Marcus, remembered an occasion when Waters walked into the kitchen at Inala when he was in high school. Waters noticed his grandson's demeanour and asked if there was anything wrong. Marcus explained that over the next couple of weeks he was to sit his senior exams—and that this was the most important time of his life. Waters would have none of it. 'The most important time of your life? You're seventeen, you haven't even made love to a woman yet, held a child in your arms as it falls asleep or worked for a living—and the next few weeks are the most important few weeks of your life?' Marcus was irritated by the way his grandfather would always simplify what he saw as ancient wisdom into a kind of loose parable:

I tried to explain to my grandfather that he didn't fully understand, but of course he did—it was I who didn't understand. My grandfather patiently let me finish and then he continued. 'It's like this, Marcus, the white man forces you to think about so many things which just aren't that important, so much so that you forget what really is important!'

Now Pop didn't mean white man as in all white men, Pop was no racist. What Pop meant was that he was discussing the way most non-Indigenous people he had met throughout his life had acted, and had believed in a certain way.

Pop could see in my reaction that he wasn't getting through—I just wasn't getting it. That's when he said it, words of wisdom that I will remember for the rest of my life: 'Understanding gravity doesn't make an apple taste any nicer—it still falls from the bloody tree . . . '

I didn't know fully at the time what it was my grandfather had just said to me, but I knew it was profound.

Marcus would in time see these comments as a reflection of 'grace and experience which brings knowledge and consequence through wisdom'. While youth blurred perception, the seed was planted whereby he would come to embrace and be sustained by his Kamilaroi roots. Another who spent time with Waters during these years was his niece Lorenda Hill, who lived at Inala with her mother, Gladys's sister.

As cracks in his relationship with Gladys deepened, Waters would often take his swag over to his sister-in-law's house and stay there. It was during these stays that Waters would talk with Lorenda about Aboriginal culture, wanting her to understand its richness and importance. 'He would tell me all different Dreamtime stories. I was fascinated, we would sit up and talk for hours. He would carve and paint emu eggs and carve boomerangs. He taught me to throw a boomerang out at St George and Cunnamulla.'

Waters' connection to his Kamilaroi culture had experienced a revival since Chinchilla, where he had started carving emu eggs. He had learned the art of carving the eggs as a child at Toomelah mission, watching his uncle, Walter Binge, and another elder, Harry Lang, using mussel shells to incise designs. The shells quickly blunted or broke and they began to use the cutters from worn out shearing hand pieces.

In later years, he recounted how another Kamilaroi elder, Frank Woods, spent his days hunched over an emu egg. Painstakingly, the old man would inscribe the shell's three primary layers. The aim of Kalti Paarti, or emu-egg carving, was to use the colours of each layer to the best advantage to create scenes on the shell's surface. The end result of Woods' work enthralled the young Waters. 'He really fascinated me, the way he used to do his work. He did arts and crafts of all sorts, but the way he did his eggs was something unreal. He used to break wine bottles just to clear the mottled part of the egg off first and then he would get the old black mussel shells and do the carving with that.'

He found some income stability through the sale of his handicrafts. Besides taking orders, he would sell the eggs he carved at major events, such as Brisbane's Expo '88, setting up a table and chair outside the venue. When asked later if he felt uncomfortable selling his eggs to Japanese tourists, he was quick to say, 'Their money is as good as anyone else's.'

Waters put his handyman and carpentry skills to good use with furniture making and building renovations at his Inala home, but where he derived his greatest pleasure was from making toys for his growing number of grandchildren. On the front lawn he built an aeroplane that sat atop an old car coil spring and in which young children could sit and dream of flight themselves. His granddaughter, Stacey Giles, remembers a dolls house that he made for her that had rooms and a hinged tin roof that lifted open. It was delivered to St George on a truck in time for Christmas. 'Pop worked through the night to get it to me on time.' A year later, five-year-old Stacey had dreams of becoming a shearer and announced that all she wanted was a shearer's handpiece that had to be green. Waters duly made her an authentic narrow tooth Lister.

Waters spent more and more time at the farm. But it seemed as if his life was falling apart; he was in danger of losing himself amid so many uncertainties. His drinking began to build up a long list of traffic offences, as well as drunk-and-disorderly charges. As Gladys put it, 'We were fighting a lot over his drinking. I used to say to Lennie, "For Christ's sake don't end up like the rest of the Aborigines." I've got this thing—I don't like to see an Aboriginal person drunk. I don't care about anybody else. It's just something I don't like to see.'

But see it she must. Another incident hit the family hard. Grace's brother Joe Craigie was dead. As Waters explained, Joe was living in Lismore at a 'halfway house, drying out', when he was bashed after cashing his pension cheque 'and was done in for it'. Everyone was fond of Uncle Joe, and for him to meet such a violent end was a shock. But it was a warning, and to Gladys it just proved a point. These were bleak times.

30

ICARUS

The telephone rang, and Len idly picked it up. 'Could I speak to Mr Waters?' the caller inquired. Len replied that unfortunately Mr Waters had been buried several years ago. The caller extended his sympathy but wanted to know to whom he was talking. 'This is one of his sons, Len.' It was September 1986 and the caller, Dr Robert Hall, was relieved. 'You're the one I want to speak to. I don't know whether you realise it or not, but you have to be the only Aboriginal who flew an aircraft during the war.'

Taken aback, Waters laughed, adding, 'You have to be joking.' No, Hall told him, it was true. 'I've done the research, and you're the only one. There are only about three others who were aircrew. I'll be up in Brisbane tomorrow. Is it all right if I come out and have a yarn to you?' 'No worries,' said

Waters. Next day, Hall sat down with Waters in the kitchen of the Waters' Inala home and told him he was researching a book he planned to call *Black Diggers*, the story of Aborigines and Torres Strait Islanders in World War II. There would be a chapter about him in the book.

Hall spent the afternoon recording Waters' memories and marvelling at how he had achieved his ambition to fly. Waters was left stunned. 'I had no idea whatsoever that I was the only one to do it, until Bob Hall told me.' He had never seen himself as unique, and certainly never as any kind of hero. 'I just did what I wanted to do, which was a lifelong ambition.'

This was the first time that Waters had ever been given reason to reflect not only on what he had accomplished at a personal level during the war but how this stood in the pantheon of Aboriginal achievement. From training in Tiger Moths to flying Kittyhawks, he had always just seen himself as one of the boys.

There had been some minor recognition of his achievement in an article in the Toowoomba *Chronicle* in December 1981, as part of a series by a local historian dealing with the Indigenous contribution to Australian war efforts. The article noted that Waters, 'despite his race and his lack of formal education', had been able to 'break the barrier and become a fighter pilot in the RAAF'.

But it took Hall's research as part of a thesis for his military history doctorate to establish that Waters had been the only Aboriginal fighter pilot. His phone call marked a turning point for Waters. The anonymity that seemed to have enveloped him for all these years began to lift. When *Black Diggers* was published in 1989, there was Waters in *Black Magic* on the front cover. Finally, a degree of public recognition was beginning to emerge—and with it, the stirrings of awareness that Indigenous Australians had contributed to the nation's war effort. It was no longer just the admirable Reg Saunders; now, others like Waters were filling in the picture.

This belated recognition began to lift his spirits. He made a trip to Canberra to visit his daughter Lenise. While there, she organised a meeting that had been a long time coming: Reg Saunders was living in the national capital. This was a meeting of two of the highest-ranking Indigenous servicemen from World War II. Each had long known of the other, and the chance to meet was something they both wanted. They met at a suburban club and, over a few beers, spent an afternoon talking and getting to know each other. They had much in common: from wartime experiences to post-war discrimination. Saunders apparently observed that it was unfair that Waters had not been commissioned as an officer. Waters thought Saunders was 'a gentleman's gentleman'.

They would both later appear on an SBS program about Aborigines who fought for Australia. During the interview, Waters agreed with Saunders' explanation of why Aborigines had wanted to fight a white man's war:

> *Aborigines are also Australians so any war that was fought would have to involve Aborigines because had Hitler and his mob taken over this country, we would have been dirt, we would have been worse off under him than under George III or IV or whoever it was. The*

other thing was that the Aborigines have been fighting for a long time for this country. My people fought a war for many years. They were decimated from about 40,000 people to about 5000. And that's men, women and children. We really suffered. And we were prepared to fight for our country and Australia is still our country, doesn't matter who else is here.

Around this time, a friend of Waters at Laidley organised a short-term job for him as the caretaker of a property in Goroke, in Victoria's Wimmera. After hearing of his arrival in the district, his old 78 Squadron mate Max Davey, living at nearby Nhill, sought him out. It had been 43 years since they had seen each other at Tarakan airstrip, on 18 August 1945. In a story about the reunion of old comrades, *The Wimmera Mail-Times* noted that Waters was Australia's only Aboriginal fighter pilot. Davey was lavish in his praise:

Len was one heck of a good pilot and a great mate to have. He was a very popular member of the squadron. Mates were crucial back then. With little experience of your own, they were who you learnt the job—and survival—from. You weren't on your own up there, mates had to look after you, you were part of a team, you covered each other as you dived in. We had lots of bad times, but the good times more than made up for it. We wouldn't have missed it for quids, would we?

'No way,' Waters said in wholehearted agreement. 'It was the worst day's work I ever did getting out of [the RAAF].'

It would seem that Waters had long reflected on his decision to quit the RAAF at war's end. This one comment to a country newspaper revealed a deep regret. The story about the reunion of two old comrades added that although the memories were still vibrant, even they found it hard to believe they had done so much so young. 'I have to laugh when I say to the children to be careful on the roads,' Davey said.

What was implicit from this chance meeting was the re-affirmation of the bonds forged in war. A photo of Waters and Davey on Morotai Island, young, shirtless and grinning, seemingly without a care in the world, accompanied the story. In a brief period during war, a tight connection had been forged—one so timeless that it was effortlessly picked up in Horsham decades later as if it were yesterday. Another photo reflected this ease as they laughed together while they thumbed through a book on Kittyhawks—and remembered.

The trip saw Waters take to the air once more in a Tiger Moth, the property owner having two of the aircraft. 'We flew just about every morning and afternoon. It's something that gets into your blood and you never lose it. You've just got no idea when you get up there, you're so free, like the birds. I could never change my ideas on that.'

Memorable as the trip to Goroke was, it was anything but a holiday for Waters. His life was becoming unstable. He and Gladys had not long separated as simmering tensions came to a head. They sold the house at Inala, their family home for the previous 33 years. She blamed his head injury and the interaction of grog and the medication he had been taking following the accident. His mood became unpredictable and argumentative.

There were now times when this was not the Len the family had known and loved. For others outside the family but who knew him well, he nonetheless remained the gentleman that he had always seemed, always greeting them politely and genuinely.

Gladys moved to Cunnamulla, where she had family. Waters was rootless. As Peter Gorman remembered, 'Being the shearer you get the wanderlust. And Len had it.' And so the moves began: to his sister Flo's home in Toowoomba, to his brother Kevin's home in St George, then the decision to move to Cunnamulla. There, he moved into the home of Gladys's stepsister Lorraine, and took a job as a shearers' cook at Kahmoo station. But there was trouble—not of Waters' making—and the job was lost. Before long, he had taken a unit in the same retirement village as Gladys. It seemed that although they could no longer live under the same roof, there was, like a moth to a flame, a connection they could not entirely break.

And it was there he stayed, and where Sydney high school teacher Jeanette Sims found him. She came from a comfortable background in the leafy Sydney suburb of Killara. A social conscience had prompted her interest in the nation's treatment of its first inhabitants. She also had an interest in aviation, as her husband, Dick, had been a pilot with 22 (City of Sydney) Squadron RAAF during the 1950s.

In July 1992, as part of university research on Aboriginal employment during World War II, she read *Black Diggers*. She was astonished to read about Waters—who was 'not only a pilot, but a fighter pilot!' She also knew 'that Aboriginal children during the thirties and forties had very few educational opportunities available to them. 'I knew that a very high degree of mathematical skill was required, among other aptitude skills. And so to find that an Aboriginal fighter pilot had been in active service during the Second World War was unbelievable.'

She tracked Waters down at Cunnamulla and wrote him a letter. Her husband had access to a reconditioned Harvard, the naval version of the Wirraway, in which he had trained, and they offered to take him flying. When Waters responded that he would be thrilled to accept the offer, Jeanette drove from Muswellbrook, where Dick managed a timber mill, to Cunnamulla to pick him up in late November 1992. Waters was waiting for her when she limped into town early one evening, her car bearing evidence of damage after hitting a kangaroo on the isolated road from St George. Waters showed her an emu egg he was carving for her. 'It was beautifully done, the RAAF coat of arms. He was using a very sharp penknife,' she recalled.

Next morning, he introduced her to Gladys and then took her to the Trappers Inn, a run-down colonial-era pub where Aborigines gathered for a drink. 'We went inside and I was introduced to Neredah Wraight, the very affable publican. She told me how Len was always neatly dressed, always a gentleman. I could see that she enjoyed looking after him. She told me that he sculpted the billiard queues for the hotel.' Neredah managed the welfare cheques that the Aborigines lived on, while outside the pub her husband had a taxi to drive them home.

They left Cunnamulla and passed through Nindigully, where Waters was reminded of his school days and the chance for a bursary in Brisbane that he had passed up to go to work in the bush with his father. His life unfolded as they drove over the narrow roads, through scrubby plains and past the familiar locations of his childhood on the way to Sydney and the Sims' art deco home.

Poor weather at Nowra prevented use of the Harvard; instead, Dick Sims took Waters to Camden Airport to fly a two-seater, dual-control Victa Airtourer. Waters would have been aware of the symmetry: he was returning to the birthplace of 78 Squadron to once again feel the exhilaration of flight. The Victa was a far cry from *Black Magic*, having a top speed of just over 140 mph, or less than half that of the Kittyhawk. In the Victa's favour was reliability, once having created a record for circumnavigating the globe in 1969. Sweet handling, they were well suited to basic aerobatics. This was in Sims' mind that day as he climbed into the pilot's seat, with co-pilot Waters alongside.

Once airborne, Sims performed various aerobatic manoeuvres and asked Waters if he would like to be shown a loop. Time and again Waters had put Kittyhawks through such aerobatic manoeuvres during wartime training exercises and had no doubt that he still possessed the skills he had learned all those years ago. 'Dick,' he said, 'you don't need to show me, I can manage.' Giving him the controls, Sims said, 'OK, you fly the plane.' Sims had flown many hours in the Airtourer and wondered how Waters would handle the aircraft, knowing there was no room for error as they flew over fields 3000 feet below them. As he recalled, Waters did not hesitate to begin the aerobatics:

> *He pushed the nose down gently and the aircraft picked up speed. He pulled the stick back, back, back and was pointing upwards at about 125 knots. He kept the Victa in a perfect vertical plane. We went over the top upside down and he kept the wings level with the horizon as he prepared to complete the loop. We came down and hit disturbed air where we had started and felt the bump, which meant he had done a perfect loop. He did three such loops in a row. Not many pilots can guarantee to do a loop and hit the bump perfectly. I told Len it was really excellent flying. It was a great achievement. He had been trained well and had not forgotten a thing.*

Waters climbed out of the plane with a wide grin. 'It was a great fly,' he told Sims. That evening, the Simses invited a few ex-RAAF personnel and their wives for dinner. They were all keen to hear Waters' memories of *Black Magic*, listening intently to the modest old fighter pilot as his wartime stories unfolded: not least the 37mm shell that lodged perilously behind his head. Those present that night could relate to his experience. One of them, Henry Main, ex-76 Squadron, was a wireless air gunner who was shot down in a Vultee Vengeance dive-bomber in New Guinea, while another, Ray Seaver ex-77 Squadron, had flown Meteor jet fighters in Korea. Another guest, Ian Mackellar, had joined the air force in 1945 and remembered Waters that night as a 'quiet, charming bloke, a very gentle sort of person who did not promote himself in any way whatsoever.' He saw in Waters' life a 'reflection of how Australians have treated Aborigines generally. Sadly, he was not appreciated after the war.' As the wine flowed late into the night around the mahogany dining table, Waters drank only orange juice. Indeed, he stayed away from alcohol for the entire ten exhausting days in Sydney.

While staying at the Simses', Waters read about the life of Aboriginal station hand Jimmie Barker, the son of a German pastoral worker and a Murawari woman. Born in 1900, Jimmie grew up in the Brewarrina region of north-west New South Wales and at the age of twelve had been compulsorily moved with his mother and brother to a government reserve. Denied educational opportunities in the segregated school system, Jimmie taught himself to read and developed a keen interest in the engineering technology used on grazing properties. In the book *The Two Worlds of Jimmie Barker, The Life of an Australian Aboriginal 1900–1972*, Jimmie would later write: 'I still feel that some part of me is closely linked with my heritage. I might have modern views in many ways, but there is another line of thought that draws me backwards. I feel that I am living between two worlds, and I am not even a full blood.'

Jimmie saw the impact of alcohol on Aborigines early on when he worked with men on remote stations for several months without a break. 'I noticed how they descended on the town and were completely drunk until they returned to their outlying stations . . . A situation arose where dark men were being arrested in the town whether they had been drinking or not.' To Jimmie, constant discrimination and a feeling of injustice spurred many non-drinkers to grog. Waters read the book avidly, telling Jeanette he identified with many of the incidents and conclusions. Like Jimmie Barker, Waters was a man caught between two worlds.

There had been time during his stay in Sydney, and again on the 2000-kilometre round trip to Cunnamulla, to mull over his life and the lessons he had drawn from it. He was proud of his academic achievements, from the time his Nindigully teacher had identified him as a gifted student and given him extra tuition through to his outstanding achievement in pilot training. He felt he 'belonged' in the white world but had been forced to live 'as an outcast' from it. The knowledge of this eroded his sense of self and place.

As she listened, Jeanette was struck by an image of Icarus soaring too close to the sun, only for the rays to melt the wax in his wings and tumble out of the sky into the sea. While Icarus drowned, Waters had been brought down not by his vanity but the 'limitations imposed on him by the dominant white society'. She quickly sensed that Waters 'could have been great, he could have been a success, if only he had been allowed into that other world'.

The problem was, Waters had tasted that 'other world' for four years. His disjointed life since would have been one that Jimmie Barker understood.

31

FLASH BLACK

If Waters was born on the margins, then a stroke of luck came with it—through his parents' worldview, he was never in doubt about the essence of his identity. He had a strong sense of self and of this he was certain, right from childhood. Yet if he was 'the wrong colour for the whites', then paradoxically he was too 'white' for some in the Aboriginal community—and 'too smart' for his own good. This was how he explained himself to Jeanette Sims. Thus, he frequently found himself in disputes.

His daughter Kim Orchard wrote about times when family members and other Aborigines called him a 'flash black' who was 'big-noting himself':

> *Dad continued to strive for bigger and better things at the expense of his relationship with his family. The air force had taught him that he could*

achieve the best but did not show him how he could cope appropriately with the repercussions, especially from an Aboriginal point of view. So many times I heard Dad say that he was a 'human being' first and as a result of that expected people to treat him as an equal.

Equality and acceptance were elusive. Many returned Indigenous soldiers did not just feel unwanted by their own communities because they had fought a 'white man's war', but they also faced white exclusion. Waters understood this, not least through the experience of his brother Jimmy. They were both proud of their service. From the first Anzac Day commemoration he attended in St George in 1946, Waters took pride in pinning on his medals and marching. Afterwards, he always joined his mates for the traditional afternoon game of two-up at the St George RSL club.

Waters was welcome there—unlike at the Cunnamulla RSL, where Aboriginal servicemen were barred. As Gladys recalls, the discrimination rankled:

When we went to Cunnamulla in 1946 and 1950, and again while we were there during the shearers' strike, Len was not allowed into the club because he was an Aborigine. It was only in the late 1980s after it was becoming known that he was the only Aboriginal fighter pilot that he was welcome. After they let Len in, they had to let all Aboriginal ex-servicemen in.

The Cunnamulla RSL club was not alone with its colour bar; it was a widespread practice that had long left a bitter taste among Aboriginal war veterans across Australia. They could take a bullet but not share a beer. In these lands where Waters was born, raised and worked, the story of Mick Flick brought Anzac Day and racism into sharp focus. Mick, who, like his family, was known to the Waters family, was the World War I veteran whose children had been barred from Collarenebri public school after he returned from the war.

He was sixteen when he enlisted, and he had assumed that on return he would have the same rights as white veterans. As his daughter Isabel Flick recalled, he found that 'he was not such a respected soldier as the white man'. Like many Aboriginal returned servicemen, he was effectively blocked from being granted soldier-settlement land.

For years he marched with mixed feelings on Anzac Day, accompanying a white mate with whom he had served. But he would not go with him afterwards to the RSL, even though it was open to all on that one day. For the rest of the year, no Aborigines, not even returned servicemen, were allowed into the club. Mick refused to take part in the RSL's one-day-of-the-year desegregation. Instead, he chose to spend the afternoon with an old Aboriginal comrade and others in the camps on the local reserve.

After his white friend's death in the mid-1950s, Mick was reluctant to take any part in the next Anzac Day. But when his children pressed him to continue the tradition, he donned his uniform and medals and went to the march with his family watching. This was not to be an ordinary march, however. As historian Professor Heather Goodall has described it:

They couldn't find him at first, but then they saw him, a solitary figure, approaching the march from the opposite direction. Grim-faced, erect and looking fixedly ahead, Mick Flick strode through the ranks of the white soldiers who had denied his children land and education. The parade faltered, out of step and confused, but Mick marched beyond it, on to the camps on the reserve, to share his remembrance meal with the people he felt understood his service and sacrifice.

Mick Flick had made his point, but change was slow in coming. In the meantime, Australian servicemen, including Aboriginal servicemen, fought in the Korean war and then the Vietnam war. Waters, while critical of the way the Americans relegated Australia to a secondary role in his area of operations in the South West Pacific Area during World War II, always believed that it was right for Australia to fight in that war. But it ended there; he was critical of the nation's involvement in Korea and Vietnam. He expanded on his thoughts in an interview:

We should never have been in either one of them, it's just that the Yanks dragged us in. These days, it's not just that you swear allegiance to the Crown, you've got to be a good buddy to the Yanks, because they're using our country for bases—they're endangering us. Like Vietnam. I have a stepson, he was like me, he went away a flag-waver for doing his little bit, but when he came back, he mightn't have been red, but he was pink, when he saw what went on there. When I see the way we've been used today . . . it's no longer for your king or queen of the country, is it?

Anzac Day 1993 was to be different for Indigenous servicemen, Waters among them. It was the International Year of Indigenous Peoples, and it meant there was a renewed focus on Indigenous military service. This led to a decision that black Anzacs would be invited to lead that year's Brisbane Anzac Day march. And so it happened that Waters and Oodgeroo Noonuccal (the poet Kath Walker) joined a contingent of Indigenous returned service personnel to do something that was never offered to Mick Flick—to lead the march.

There were about 50 Aboriginal veterans, children with their fathers, mothers, grandmothers and grandfathers, carrying a full-length Aboriginal-designed banner. Along with Oodgeroo and Waters was the widow of Captain Reg Saunders, who had died three years earlier. Photos of the occasion show a sense of pride in their step. Waters felt honoured. His achievements as a fighter pilot as well as an Aborigine were finally being recognised in the nation's most time-honoured way, on its unofficial national day.

Shortly before that Anzac Day, Waters' pride in being a black Digger emerged in a media interview. He didn't begrudge fighting a white man's war, he was fighting for his country. What he did begrudge, however, were the stirrers, both black and white. Laying out his thoughts, he contended:

> *Each man makes his own destiny, not the stirrers and politicians. Too many people—both black and white—have a chip on their shoulders. They should stop moaning and get on with life . . . Black or white, it is each person's own attitude to life that decides their destiny. Not whingeing and moaning and scoring political points.*

Although he was a strong Labor supporter who believed in the principle of egalitarianism and helping people down on their luck, he had been taught from childhood to fend for himself.

He strongly supported the 1967 referendum that was to allow the inclusion of Aboriginal Australians in the census and to empower Federal Parliament to legislate specifically for them, and is known to have joined at least one land rights march in Brisbane during the long years of the repressive Bjelke-Petersen government. When Peter Gorman asked him about it, Waters replied that he wanted to support the protesters. However, at a personal level he was critical of the impact of Aboriginal welfare policy. He believed in subsequent years that 'far too much assistance had been given to Aboriginal people, that it had taken away their need to get out there and do their own thing.'

His approach to life was the very opposite of what he saw as learned helplessness, where a community felt it had no control over decisions affecting it. He had worked hard to provide for his family and had taken all the knocks dealt to him. His firm belief was that education was the only way for Aboriginal advancement.

But his views on welfare did not endear him to Aboriginal activists, whom he accused of 'sitting on their bums and accepting handouts'. They in turn saw him as a white lackey. This was a no-win situation where he was caught in a netherworld, not sure where he fitted in. Drinking gave him a short-term reprieve, but it was no long-term solution.

32

FREE FALL

Waters caught the bus back to Cunnamulla after the Anzac Day march, still buoyed by the experience. He was soon catching up with his mates at the pub, talking about the day, under Neredah Wraight's watchful eye at the Trappers Inn. This had long been his refuge, and there was a rhythm to the ritual of ordering a cold schooner in the late afternoon or evening. It gave him comfort. Life's problems dissipated with each drink and were put to one side for a while. Then all he had to do after closing time was walk a few blocks home under the softly diffused street lighting in the cool of yet another Outback night. It was easy, a routine he had known for so many years that it was second nature.

Three weeks after the Anzac Day march, this daily routine finally caught up with Waters. He needed detoxification for alcohol addiction and was admitted to Cunnamulla hospital.

For someone with his long history of drinking, including many binges, withdrawing from alcohol would have been agonising. But it was necessary. Already, his medical record showed a history of falls. On admission, he was confused and had been blacking out all day.

He had much on his mind during this time for which he needed to be ready. In view of his increasing public profile, the RAAF had approached him with a special tour as part of the RAAF's contribution to the Year of the World's Indigenous Peoples. The planned tour in a World War II Dakota was to include Cooktown, Lockhart River, Bamaga and Horn Island to enable Aboriginal people to meet one of their own high achievers. The air force saw in Waters a chance to interest Indigenous youth in enlisting in the RAAF.

But as his time in hospital dragged on, his sense of frustration started to spin out of control. The medical record shows he talked 'nonstop about flying his planes'. He still needed medical care but was keen to be discharged to prepare for and take part in the approaching tour. Overwhelmed with anxiety, he confronted both the medical superintendent and the matron. In his determination to leave, he started pushing in an unseemly physical confrontation with staff.

He walked out of the hospital, returning to his pensioner unit where, on 28 May 1993, he wrote a statement that he sent to the local newspaper, *The Western Sun*. In the letter, published twelve days later, he talked of 'characters who got under my skin', and admitted that he had a problem with alcohol. He went on:

After being in hospital for almost a week, I knew that I was fit to be discharged as I have a completely full card of activity ahead of me that has really been put behind schedule because of a very traumatic period that I have had to endure over the last 12 months.

I realise that my concern has not been fully appreciated . . . I tried to impress on the minds of the two most prominent people that I appealed to yesterday, that I was quite capable of caring for myself and getting my act back on stage. I thought that psychologically they would understand, but their reaction was completely opposite to my wishes . . . one of them has suggested that I could apply to be admitted to the old-people lodge at the hospital, that is when I decided to take things into my own hands and walk out of the hospital; I may live to regret my actions, but I gravely doubt that.

It was insinuated that I would not be able to control my alcoholic problem, now that is something that I have proved in the past. I spent Xmas and New Year with 'my' family from St George and Toowoomba. They can and will verify that I had one 7oz beer on Christmas Eve and one New Year's Eve night.

. . . I actually heard the two people (who opposed my discharge last week) mention Blue Nursing Service. Now I realise fully they do a very valuable service, but I can swear without any shadow of doubt that I myself am quite capable of caring for myself for quite some time yet. I actually feel so insulted by the behaviour of the two people that I appealed to recently.

. . . This was the closest I have ever come to begging in my life, and to receive the kick in the face the way I was recently has made me more [determined] than ever to prove that I am still capable of caring for and proving myself in any company . . . I have walked on

both sides of the fence and for a worthwhile wager, I would have a go at the top of the fence.

Determinedly, Leonard Waters.

Waters was a proud man. Valid or not, he saw the assumption of the medical professionals as demeaning. He felt insulted and humiliated by their undoubted well-intentioned recommendations. Perhaps this was one humiliation too many, and he was not going to acquiesce, yet again, in the face of authority. This time he had something hugely significant to look forward to and he was not going to miss it. The 'full card of activity' that lay in front of him involved not only the RAAF tour around Outback Queensland to begin on 12 June, but also 78 Squadron's 50th anniversary in July.

These were central pillars of his life, a golden time when childhood dreams took flight, when, despite the horror of war, there was a certainty of role and an equality of race. Nothing was going to hold him back from the opportunity to once more embrace this rare and heady world that it had been his privilege to enter, albeit briefly, 50 years earlier. Out of hospital, he was soon making light of the incident, according to his medical records.

Three days after the letter was published, Waters travelled from Cunnamulla to RAAF Base Amberley to begin his Outback trip. It had been five decades since he had been in a Dakota, the workhorse that took him to and from the war. Airmen speak with reverence about the Dakota, an aircraft that stirs nostalgic memories for so many. And this particular Dakota had a history of service in the war. When Prime Minister John Curtin died at The Lodge in Canberra in July 1945, it was this plane that had flown his body back to Perth for burial. Now, it was to fly Waters around Outback Queensland for a rare Indigenous tour.

First stop was Townsville, where he was the VIP guest at the RAAF Base Townsville's Air Show. There were 30,000 spectators there that day to watch F/A-18 Hornets in action, together with the Caribou cargo aircraft, the Hawker Siddeley HS 748 and the 'venerable Dakota'. Waters was enthralled by the chance to climb into a Hornet cockpit and soak up the feeling and the contrast between his beloved *Black Magic* and this modern-day combat jet, designed as both a fighter and an attack aircraft.

The contrast between the Kittyhawk, with its single-engine piston power and basic pilot controls, and the twin-engine supersonic, all-weather Hornet was stark. But Waters was in his element. The experience was all too brief. After he climbed out of the jet, the local paper reported:

> *Len Waters stood aloof from the crowd . . . his eyes searching the horizon. Four pinpricks in the sky soon became screaming F/A-18 jets and then, just as quickly, they were gone. Mr Waters nodded his head in appreciation. 'Wow, that is something else,' he said. 'Yes, things have changed since I was in the air force.'*

Wing Commander Ken Llewelyn was in charge of the tour and recalled that the Dakota and crew, plus the 'irrepressible

Len Waters', starred at the air show. He was involved in an Australian War Memorial project at the time to record interviews with RAAF World War II veterans and leapt at the chance to take Waters on the Outback tour. It did not take long before he realised he was dealing with someone special. Over the next five days, before leaving each morning, he talked with Waters about his life and career.

He saw Waters as 'fit and very alert' and noted that he rarely slept during the transit flights, preferring to read books or carve intricate designs on emu eggs. According to Llewelyn's report of the trip, Waters 'was a staunch believer of the ethic of hard work'. He took every opportunity to assist young Aborigines and talk to them about his own life if he thought it would help them. The highlight for Waters was taking the controls from the co-pilot's seat. He was being brought back into the fold.

Llewelyn quickly warmed to Waters, finding him an intelligent, engaging individual:

> *An Aborigine who had left school at 14, worked as a shearer, joined the air force as a mechanic and then was accepted for pilot training was indeed remarkable. And then to be selected to fly the P-40 Kittyhawk fighter was an amazing feat. Len was not only smart, but very disciplined and determined to make the grade.*
>
> *He could easily have become embittered with his 'racist' treatment by the bureaucracy after the war, especially his efforts to set-up a regional airline. He had little choice but return to shearing. I regard Len as a hero.*

These were heady times for Waters. No sooner had he returned from this RAAF tour than he had to prepare for the momentous event of the 50th anniversary of the formation of 78 Squadron. The reunion of squadron veterans was to be held at Camden, south-west of Sydney, where the unit was formed on 20 July 1943. He travelled to Sydney and joined the celebrations at Camden on 17 and 18 July 1993.

He was among the veterans who marched through the town, with the high point being the lunch that followed. Frank Smith and Bob Crawford were there. Crawford, who had not seen Waters since leaving Tarakan in 1945, greeted him warmly, as did all his old mates. Crawford recalled: 'It was a wonderful show. The greatest surprise in my life was to meet Len again and see how well he had weathered in 50-odd years. He had just finished a tour going around Australia, talking to the lads. He was so well and fit and in good spirits. He was very popular in the squadron.'

What had been reignited for these veterans was the tight bond of war service, when each time they took to the skies the threat of death flew with them. These men trusted each other with their lives. To be greeted with such warmth 50 years later, to reminisce about old times and old losses, to laugh about each other's foibles and shared times of partying around stashes of beer and jungle juice, reached deep into each man's psyche. Only those who had been through those times could know this depth of emotional connection.

Invigorated by the reunion with his old mates, where he only drank orange juice, Waters returned to Cunnamulla in high spirits. He told Gladys about the occasion, causing her to comment later that being with his air force mates had 'done a lot for him'. While he 'turned to drink' when stressed, he was able to avoid it when the circumstances demanded. But old habits die hard, and he was in free fall.

33

ALONE

In the chill August night, Waters lay in the wet grass. Through his haze, he could see his home, just across the road. As the fog enveloped him, getting there was the challenge. It had been a long evening, as there was not much to do in Cunnamulla at night except drink. Waters had begun drinking at the Trappers Inn, just a short walk from his pensioner unit. His drinking mates were two other Aborigines whose reputation as troublemakers was such that Neredah Wraight became increasingly concerned as the night wore on. She knew Waters' health was fragile; everyone in town knew he had been in hospital just three months earlier for detoxification. His letter to *The Western Sun* only ensured that if he got on the grog, then alarm bells would ring. And he was now on the grog.

Neredah asked Waters to leave to go home and take his two

mates with him. He was never a troublesome drinker and he did so, leaving with his mates and heading off to the Warrego Hotel, a pub up the road with high stools and a bar of galvanised iron. They settled in and continued drinking for several more hours. Finally, Waters accidentally knocked over a glass of beer and put his head on the counter. Intoxicated, he could easily have fallen asleep at the bar, but something told him it would be better to leave. 'Sorry,' he said. He got up and walked out into the night.

Normally, Neredah's husband Arthur took care of transport for Waters when he'd had a few drinks, driving him home without charge when the night finished. But Waters had not finished the night at the Trappers Inn, and the publican at the Warrego didn't think to ring Arthur. Waters set off on foot for home but, disoriented, he started walking in the wrong direction. Realising his mistake, he turned around and stumbled back along the unsealed Louise Street footpath towards the Warrego River and home.

Shortly after, at about 10.30 p.m., he fell over in front of a house in Louise Street, just across the road from his unit. By chance, the occupant noticed a figure on the grass outside. He did not recognise who it was, assuming it was just someone who had been 'down at the river drinking alcohol and had come up onto the grass to sleep it off'. This was a common practice, and the residents didn't think too much more about it. But he did make one last check about forty minutes later, just before going to bed:

I looked out my front door and could see that the same male person was now leaning over my front fence, facing towards my house with

> *his head down as if he was very tired. This gentleman did not appear to be in any difficulty at the time so I closed my door and retired for the night.*

That night, the temperature in Cunnamulla dropped to 7°C, but it wasn't necessarily the cool of the night that was problematic for Waters; it was first negotiating an embankment and then crossing the road to home. The distance was not far, just a few metres, but it was nonetheless a challenge on this night.

Waters did not make it home. It seems he tried but probably lost his balance and fell down the embankment, close to the edge of the road. There he lay, face down, all night. At 6.40 a.m. on 24 August, another resident of Louise Street saw Waters lying at the bottom of the embankment. Having known Waters for 20 years, he immediately recognised who it was. 'Len was lying outside my neighbour's home at 5 Louise Street. I then called out to him, as I thought he had just fallen and hurt himself. When I received no reply I walked over to Len and shook him and I then took his pulse and I realised then that he wasn't breathing.'

A doctor was called and, after examining Waters, declared him dead. He had died where he lay, on the edge of the road, in the early hours of the morning. Gladys's sister, who lived in the same complex of units, heard the news first and phoned her in Brisbane, where she was staying at the time. One by one, their children were informed.

The following day a post-mortem examination was performed. The cause of death was found to be 'pneumonia due to aspiration of gastric acid due to alcohol intoxication'. In effect, Waters died as a result of choking while drunk. The time of death was put at shortly after midnight on the 24th. Although rumours have persisted about the possibility of foul play, there was no evidence to support this. Poignantly, Waters died on the 51st anniversary of his enlistment in the RAAF. A life that had begun with such promise had ended alone.

The vicissitudes of Water's life were beyond public understanding at the time. 'Aboriginal fighter pilot' was how the media described him in reports of his death. But that's not all that he was. Those close to him knew the hardships and disappointments he had endured. His family and friends needed no prompting to know the hurt he felt at the failure of federal aviation authorities to respond to his repeated applications for a civil aviation licence. They implicitly understood that this was how it was, that disappointment was the norm when dealing with white bureaucracy. To them, it was yet another example of Aborigines being kept on the outside looking in.

Yet such a man could not be allowed to go to a pauper's grave. He was the first, and the only known, Indigenous RAAF fighter pilot. Whatever his frailties, he deserved much more than that. The St George RSL recognised this and organised the return of his body to St George for burial in the same cemetery as his parents.

The RAAF was determined that Waters should not be forgotten. He was a hero, after all, someone with a unique achievement to his name. His death could not go unmarked. Old comrades from 78 Squadron, Bob Crawford, Geoff Cutler and Frank Smith among them, were invited to join a C-130 Hercules flight to St George.

On 28 August 1993, a large crowd gathered at the town's Anglican church for a funeral that brought St George to a halt. Family members, former comrades, an RAAF detail, and townspeople who knew him as just a shearer and ordinary bloke, gathered to farewell Waters with military honours. Wing Commander Alex Johnston, who had flown with Waters in the Dakota on his final flight, spoke of their all too brief friendship but, more importantly, of the impact that Waters had had on RAAF personnel. His daughters Lenise and Kim delivered eulogies of a loving father and a good mate. His distraught son, Don, joined them to speak of a father they revered. And then the congregation sang 'Amazing Grace'. Fittingly, a bouquet of blue orchids draped the coffin.

The cortege made a slow procession through the main street to the cemetery on the other side of town. There, with drizzle falling, one of Waters' grandsons led the procession to the graveside. As the bugler's Last Post concluded and the straps under Waters' coffin were unfurled, nine RAAF F/A-18 Hornets rent the skies above. The fighters were on their way to an exercise in northern Australia, and arrangements were made to alter their flightpath to fly over St George. The scream of the jets masked the haunting sounds of weeping as one of the Hornets abruptly pulled away and climbed steeply as the rest continued in level flight, signifying a rare 'missing man' personal tribute by the RAAF. This was much more than a simple fly-past; it was a statement that acknowledged Waters' achievement in becoming the nation's sole Aboriginal fighter pilot and reaffirmed that he would be missed.

The mourners adjourned to the St George RSL for a wake where Crawford, Cutler and Smith recounted stories about their mate. He was not just a champion boxer but also a skilled pilot and, most importantly, someone they respected. For three years in the RAAF the Aboriginal boy from Boomi and Nindigully had mixed with scions of white establishment families. He was just one of the boys. Those bonds formed in war brought about a rarity in Australian society, especially at that time in Australia's history when the status of Aborigines was one of outsiders in their own country.

34

TWO WORLDS

Just a few months before Waters died, Prime Minister Paul Keating spoke at a park in Redfern, Sydney. It was December 1992, and Keating was marking the start of the Year of the World's Indigenous Peoples. Although controversial, his address was quickly to be regarded as one of the great prime ministerial speeches.

For the first time, a prime minister gave due weight to the role of Aborigines in Australian history, conceding that while Australia had built a prosperous and remarkably harmonious multicultural society, it was the Aborigines 'to whom the most injustice has been done'. The starting point, Keating said, might be to recognise that the problem started with non-Aboriginal Australians:

> *It begins, I think, with that act of recognition. Recognition that it was we who did the dispossessing. We took the traditional lands and smashed the traditional way of life. We brought the diseases, the alcohol. We committed the murders. We took the children from their mothers. We practised discrimination and exclusion. It was our ignorance and our prejudice. And our failure to imagine these things being done to us.*

The past, Keating said, lived on in inequality, racism, injustice and 'fractured identity'. He noted that where Aboriginal Australians had been included in the life of modern Australia, they had made remarkable contributions. 'They are there in the wars. They are there in the Australian legend.'

While Keating spoke from the heart that day, his aim was not just to induce white guilt but to encourage the nation to learn the lessons of the Indigenous experience over the previous 200 years. His tone struck a chord not just with the Aboriginal audience present but, over time, with the wider community.

At no stage in his speech did Keating refer to any one individual by name. If he had, Len Waters could easily have been that person, as he fitted the criteria Keating set out. But Keating also realised there was a double-edged sword that sometimes applied to Indigenous Australians who successfully entered the mainstream. He once remarked to Noel Pearson: 'The problem with your mob is you're like crabs in a bucket. If one of you starts climbing out and gets his claws on the rim, about to pull himself over the top to freedom, the other mob will be pulling him back down into the bucket. You all end up cooked.'

Pearson thought Keating 'dead right':

> *I see this every day among the people with whom I work, whom I love and whose futures I work to try to improve. People striving to climb to a better life who are thwarted. People who do not think it right that anyone should climb to a better life. People who have hope but not the courage; the desire but not the will. And I don't blame them for their sense of debilitation.*

Waters fitted the metaphor—he was one such 'crab' on the rim of the bucket. He paid a high price for daring to dream. Having made it as a fighter pilot, his fall was all the greater. And with it came a 'fractured identity'. He spoke of the educational opportunities he had had and how this was unusual for his people at that time. Because of this, he persuaded himself that he could pass easily between the two worlds if he wanted to.

But he couldn't. His background as an Indigenous Australian meant that he had come from a race dismissed as the lowest on earth. As Noel Pearson put it, 'No people rated lower on the ruling scales of human worth.' In colonial times and, indeed, well into the 20th century, 'their deaths elicited the least level of moral reproval.'

This was what 'being a blackfella again' meant. This was not a throwaway line; Waters used it deliberately in conversations with family and shearing mates over the post-war years, with a grudging acceptance that equality and opportunity had passed him by. It would haunt him for the rest of his life. Accepting it involved bitter acknowledgement of the gross wrongs that had been done to his race since 1788 and trying, somehow, to survive the tortuous twists and turns to keep one's dignity. Yet Waters knew that there was no monocultural past to which Indigenous Australians could return; while he kept his Kamilaroi roots, he knew the future was bicultural.

Dr Ian Lilley, Professor in Aboriginal and Torres Strait Islander Studies at the University of Queensland, never met Waters, but within a year of his death became involved in a pension appeal mounted on behalf of Gladys after the Department of Veterans' Affairs rejected her initial application for a war widow's pension. Lilley, who had been a soldier in the army reserve and is a member of a military family, was in no doubt that while servicemen in general could have difficulty adjusting to civilian life after active service, it was all the harder for Aborigines. 'Waters would have had additional problems not suffered by Europeans,' he contended. Noting that Waters had said in his letter to *The Western Sun* that he had 'walked on both sides of the fence', Lilley went on:

> *It must have been extraordinarily dispiriting for him after the war to confront again the institutionalised discrimination and opportunistic racism which were characteristic of the times, especially in the places where he worked. He clearly believed he had left such things behind him when he joined the RAAF, where reportedly he suffered no discrimination.*
>
> *Waters' situation after demobilisation would have been doubly difficult with regard to discrimination because the strongly egalitarian tendencies of Aboriginal society and the complex Aboriginal concept*

of 'shame' work against individuals who stand out from the group. Being regarded as 'flash' in this way is not positive and would have resulted in some sort of social sanctions from his extended family and other members of the Aboriginal community.

Lilley hypothesised that Waters' reluctance to discuss his worries with family members stemmed from a combination of his own pride, which was evident in his letter to the Cunnamulla paper, and the shame he felt. Despite his achievements, Waters was suffering difficulties like those faced by other Aboriginal people. Ironically, these achievements put a distance between him and the Aboriginal community.

Wing Commander Ken Llewelyn, who accompanied Waters on his final tour with the RAAF just weeks before he died, sensed 'anger, disillusionment, frustration and trauma resulting from his inability to build an appropriate post-war career'. Llewelyn continued in his comments in support of a war widow's pension for Gladys: 'He emphasised he wished to continue his career as a pilot. When he reverted to his travels as a shearer it would have come at a great cost to his ego.'

In support of Gladys's appeal, the local federal MHR and Minister for Resources, David Beddall, wrote to the Minister for Veterans' Affairs, Con Sciacca. He noted that Waters had 'suffered from recurring bouts of malaria, had epilepsy and two kneecaps replaced' after the war, and that because of his 'ill health and drinking problems, Mrs Waters went to work and supported the couple's five children on income received from her position as a cleaner'. Waters' sole financial contribution to the family was his meagre pension. Importantly, Beddall further commented: 'Due to his inability to cope with bureaucracy, at no stage did he make the effort to apply for any entitlement to Disability Pension, although this was recommended by his treating medical practitioners.'

Knock-backs from government bureaucracy over the years had had a cumulative effect, resulting in avoidance. Foremost among these was the departmental silence that prevented him pursuing a civil pilot's licence immediately post-war. It is impossible to know whether bureaucratic racism was the reason for this; however, the circumstantial evidence supports such a conclusion. Waters was to live with that belief all his life.

As his life drew to a close, Waters admitted that it had been a mistake to leave the RAAF so soon after war's end. His squadron mates dispersed, many going on to jobs with prospects arranged through 'old boy' networks not available to him. So it was back to the shearing sheds. Not only was this a psychological let-down, it was the worst possible culture that someone vulnerable to alcohol could have entered. Shearing and binge drinking were synonymous, and for Waters, having been already introduced to the practice during the war, this was dangerous territory, especially for someone carrying the wound of a knock-back he had not expected to a post-war aviation career. The weight of this never lifted.

After he died a drawing was found folded up in his dressing-gown pocket. It was a sketch of a male figure with his arms outstretched and tie flying back, walking along a railway line towards the heavy timber buffer, which was at the edge of a cliff. Underneath Waters had written, 'End of line go thie . . .'

Cunnamulla lies at the end of the Western Line, which starts at Toowoomba and runs for more than 800 kilometres through the major towns of Dalby, Roma and Charleville. Thus it was, indeed, the end of the line for Waters, but the words go further than just this literal meaning—they imply a mixture of resignation and bitterness. And a likelihood that he believed his life was coming to an end.

So many dreams, so many hopes, brought back to earth with a heavy thud. Waters' marriage to Gladys reflected the harshness of post-war rural Australia. Just maintaining the basic necessities of life in times of economic austerity became a constant struggle. Their relationship was tempestuous and, in the end, one of dashed expectations. Too much grog drove them apart.

Four years after Waters' death, Gladys felt moved to write some reflective words about their years together. 'Many have uttered bitter words about our relationship, but they were not privy to whispers of love and devotion or aware of our determination to live our lives our way.' There had been hard times, good times and some 'very splendid ones' woven into their five decades together.

Waters long struggled to make sense of a life that in 1946 had held so much promise. In the end, the man who had asserted that he had 'walked on both sides of the fence' instead was left stranded midway, caught between two worlds.

Epilogue

IF ONLY HE HAD KNOWN

Honours flowed for Waters after his death, ensuring a unique legacy, albeit belated. A commemorative stamp, an aerogram, parks and streets named after him, including at Inala, where he had lived for so many years. When the Leonard Victor Waters Memorial Park was officially opened at Boggabilla in October 1996, the mayor of Moree Plains Shire spoke of how Waters and his brother Jim were role models for all Australians. His hope was for reconciliation, and 'that we go into the new millennium as one community'. A RAAF F-111C flypast broke the quiet as it ripped through the sky above before disappearing beyond the trees and across the Macintyre River to the east.

Among the mourners who had attended Waters' funeral was Brett West, a Yamatji man and former jackeroo from Western Australia. At the time he was posted to 77 Squadron RAAF and was asked to represent the air force at the funeral. West did not know a great deal about Waters but the experience of attending the service and speaking to the Waters family affected him deeply. The penny dropped—Waters' story, he believed, could be the inspiration for Aboriginal kids to join the air force. 'I realised how much this bloke meant. From that moment I was determined to make the link for Indigenous kids, the link between them and the military. It's always pleased me that Indigenous kids are in awe of his story when I tell them about him.'

In February 2009, a smoking ceremony and memorial service in honour of Waters was held at the Boggabilla memorial. Gladys spoke during the service of Waters' love of flying, after which the family hymn 'Amazing Grace' was sung. There was another nod to Waters: the president of the Moree RSL sub-branch delivered the Ode; perhaps this was atonement for what had befallen Waters at Moree during World War II. The service was a prelude to another later that day at Toomelah, where a memorial was unveiled not just to Waters but to all those local Indigenous men who fought for Australia, from the Boer war to the present.

*

The RAAF dedicated an F/A-18A Hornet to Waters, painted in the colours of the Worimi people of the New South Wales central coast, the home of RAAF Base Williamtown. On the fighter were stencilled Waters' name and the image of a wedge-tailed eagle, the bird of prey that had so fascinated him as it circled over the plains of his childhood country. A streak of dotted lines on the fuselage tracks the eagle's flight with a sense of speed that mirrors the Hornet itself. The curved circles around the tail image and cockpit reflect a camping place, where clans people gather to rest, share stories and pass knowledge down from generation to generation. At the unveiling, the Chief of Air Force, Air Marshal Geoff Brown, AO, said Waters had been a pioneer and leader in every sense of the word. 'I hope that if he was here today, he would be honoured by the artwork that has been chosen.'

Gladys presented the Australian War Memorial with Waters' flying helmet, medals, escape map, pilot's logbook, wings and earphones. In 2016 the AWM staged an exhibition, 'For Country for Nation', that recognised the contribution of Indigenous Australians to all wars in which the nation had been involved. Waters was an integral part of this exhibition.

It has been mooted that the new Sydney airport at Badgery's Creek be named in honour of Waters. Other names have been proffered but he has long been the sentimental favourite . . . If only he had known.

In St George, a plaque on a sandstone plinth overlooking the Balonne River reaffirms Waters' memory in a more down-to-earth way. It stands on a grassy bank alongside an identical memorial commemorating another RAAF hero from the St George district, Squadron Leader John Jackson, who was educated, ironically, at Brisbane Grammar School—the same school that was so nearly Waters'. Jackson ran the family grazing property at St George, bought his own aeroplane, and joined the RAAF Reserve before World War II saw him called up. He went on to fly in both the Middle East and the South West Pacific Area, where he led 75 Squadron RAAF. An ace,

Jackson was credited with shooting down eight enemy aircraft in his Kittyhawk before he himself was shot down over Port Moresby on 28 April 1942.

Jackson and Waters came from vastly different backgrounds, one from wealth and the other from Aboriginal rural poverty, yet both were driven by the same desire to fly. Less than a metre apart, their monuments are angled towards each other as if in mutual respect. Gaining equality in life was Waters' elusive dream; gaining that equality within the non-Indigenous community has been the same elusive goal of Aborigines and Torres Strait Islanders for two centuries.

In the words of Stan Grant, 'As a nation, we struggle to reconcile ourselves to our past and our place.' Fundamental to the Australian story for the past century has been the Anzac legend, on which so much of the nation's perception of itself has been built.

Whether subconscious or not, it became a story that excluded Indigenous Australians—so much so that former Queensland premier Joh Bjelke-Petersen could assert that Aboriginal people could not receive land rights, because they did not defend this country. This was uttered by a politician who neither flew a fighter plane nor served in World War II. Bjelke-Petersen struck no difficulty in obtaining his own civilian pilot's licence.

With his front-line service in the RAAF, Waters challenges and loosens the 'white' stranglehold on the Anzac legend. Although he was able to make a crack in this 'black ceiling', the same barrier became impenetrable once the war ended. Waters had glimpsed the future only to have it denied him. That was his tragedy—and also Australia's.

ACKNOWLEDGEMENTS

Gaining a modicum of understanding of what it means to be an Indigenous Australian has been a key experience in writing this book for me, as well as my fellow researcher and wife, Sue. It has been a personal journey of discovery.

I was concerned to elicit as true a picture of Len Waters as was possible 25 years after his death. For this I am indebted to his family, for it is only with the fullest picture of the man, warts and all, that it is possible to place him in the context of an Indigenous man in 20th century post-war Australia.

Family anecdotes help enormously in building a picture to understand such a personality as Len Waters. A life that had begun with such extraordinary promise instead became a metaphor for the experience of Aborigines in post-war Australia. Through his trials and tribulations, his family lived with the consequences of his failure to fully realise the dream that seemed tantalisingly close.

I am especially indebted to Len Waters' wife, Gladys, for her preparedness to share memories of life with Len and a host of files, including letters, photos and memoirs, covering their lives. This must have been difficult at times, but like me, Gladys wanted as true a depiction of the man as possible.

Len's younger brother, Kevin, has been wonderfully helpful and generous in sharing knowledge of the early years of the Waters family, along with the post-war years. I thank him for his willingness to share this with me.

Len's eldest daughter, Lenise Schloss, too, has been particularly generous in sharing personal reminiscences, memorabilia of her father and knowledge of Kamilaroi culture. She has been extremely patient with unending questions. Thanks also go to her son, Dr Marcus Waters, who shared childhood memories of his grandfather.

Thanks also go to Len Waters' daughter, Di Konowec, his granddaughter, Stacey Giles, his sister, Beatrice Du Pre Chamier, his daughter, Julia Waters, son Don Waters, grandson Maurice Waters and niece Lorenda Hill.

I am grateful to both Dr Robert Hall and RAAF Wing Commander Ken Llewellyn who, in many hours of interviews with Len Waters, both gave his story an invaluable authenticity. Hearing his voice describe events was fundamental in gaining insight, particularly into his time in the RAAF.

Gordon Clarke deserves special mention. His forensic knowledge of 78 Squadron RAAF personnel, aircraft and role in the

South West Pacific Area during World War II was invaluable. His book, *This Smuttee Squadron*, was a well-used reference to better understand the squadron and its operations. His editing of the relevant chapters of *The Missing Man* was insightful and meticulous.

Thanks also go to RAAF historian, Martin James of the RAAF's Air Power Development Centre, at Fairbairn in Canberra, who was always ready to help with questions regarding Len Waters' RAAF years. And also to Squadron Leader Gary Oakley for his help with gathering information.

Indigenous writers who have blazed trails and inspired my own thinking and knowledge are Stan Grant, Noel Pearson, Warren Mundine and James Miller. I extend my gratitude to them for their scholarship.

Len's late daughter, Kim, wrote her own short biography of her father in the early 1990s. This provided important insights and corroboration, and helped with the timeline of his life.

Thanks go to Moree Indigenous historian, Noeline Briggs-Smith, who generously shared research that enabled me to build a picture of discrimination in Moree up to and including the war years. Des Crump was generous with his time and I thank him for providing the Kamilaroi section titles. And thanks to Barney McGrady in Mungindi for his help and local knowledge, along with Peter Thompson and his contribution to research in the area.

I thank Professor Ian Lilley for reading the manuscript. Likewise, Professor Heather Goodall who was generous with her advice that helped in resolving historical and cultural questions.

Jeanette and Richard Sims deserve a special mention. Jeanette's perceptive account of her interaction with Len a few months before he died provided a poignant insight into his life and reminisces at that time. And thanks to Richard for his memories of the wonderful flight he had with Len.

Others I want to thank are Len's shearing mates, Bill Fisk, Peter Gorman and Kevin Webster, whose recollections enabled me to build a picture of his long years on the post-war shearing circuit. Thanks also to boxing historian Bob Webster for his help.

Thanks go to ex-RAAF pilots from Len's era, Squadron Leader Leigh 'Laddie' Hindley and Squadron leader Ron Guthrie. Leading Aircraftman (LAC) John Wheatley kindly shared his memories of Len Waters and 78 Squadron, as did LAC Arnie Nunn. Warrant Officer Brett West also helped with his recollection of Len Waters' funeral.

Patty Huston kindly shared her memories of life on Balagna station, while Robyn Fuhrmeister, Marguerite Thompson, Blanche McNelly, Vida Hardy, 'Megs' Morris, Bob Warboys and Robert Buchan also provided background on St George. So too did Bill Dendle with the history of Sun Pictures, and Val Bucholtz with her recollections of life in Cunnamulla around the time that Len Waters died.

Once again, my thanks go to the team at Allen & Unwin—Rebecca Kaiser and Siobhan Cantrill, and to editor Liz Keenan for her usual forensic eye.

NOTES

Throughout this book I have drawn on interviews conducted with Len Waters by Dr Robert Hall in September 1986 and November 1991, and by Wing Commander Ken Llewelyn in June 1993. Where Len Waters' comments cover the same territory I have judiciously drawn from both sources to best tell the story.

All chapters bear the results of the many interviews that were conducted with members of the Waters family to gather detailed accounts of Len Waters' life. The interviews were conducted with his widow Gladys Waters, his brother Kevin Waters, his sister Beatrice Vera Du Pres Charmier, his daughters Lenise Schloss, Dianne Russell, Julia Waters, his son Donald, and grandchildren Marcus Waters, Maurice Waters and Stacey Giles. Bill Saunders, Gladys' second cousin, also contributed his recollections.

I have also referenced Len Waters' RAAF logbook, and his own hand-written autobiography, as well as the short biography, *My Father the Flyer*, by his daughter, the late Kim Orchard.

Information about Len Waters' RAAF career was sourced from his service file held by the National Archives of Australia: NAA file, Series no. A9301, Control symbol 78144.

Other sources are referenced in the following chapters.

1 Worlds apart

See Heather Goodall thesis, *A History of Aboriginal Communities in New South Wales, 1909–1939*, University of Sydney, 1982; p 137, regarding risk of removal of children.

See James Miller, *Koori: A Will to Win*, pp 167, 170, regarding risk of removal.

The quote from Florence Weatherall (nee Waters) was drawn from Derek Royal's article, 'Black magic', pp 60–63, *The Australian Way*, November 1996.

See Leigh Edmonds, 'How Australians were made airminded,' *Continuum: Australian Journal of Media & Culture*, Vol. 7, No. 1, 1993.

See *The Balonne Beacon*, 7 July, 1932 regarding Smithy's visit to St George.

The 'ganinala malga malga' reference was drawn from *Half-Caste, Out-Cast. An ethnographic analysis of the processes underlying adaptation among Aboriginal people in rural town, south-west Queensland*, p 124, PhD thesis by Anne-Katrin Eckermann, University of Queensland, 1977.

For background on Kamilaroi culture, see: Dr Robert Fuller, *The Conversation*, 'How ancient Aboriginal star maps have shaped Australia's highway network,' 7 April 2016; and http://www.everyculture.com/Oceania/Kamilaroi.html#ixzz4Qsiich7H

2 Dependency

For the Mick Flick story, see Heather Goodall, 'Not Such A Respected Soldier: the Impact of WWI on Aborigines in NSW,' *Teaching History*, 4 December 1987, pp 3–6.

See Aborigines Protection Board annual report 1933 for the reference to the perceived abilities of Aboriginal children.

The Sydney Mail report on Euraba reserve was published on 21 January 1914.

See *The Shoalhaven Telegraph*, 31 October 1917 for the report on the Bomaderry Aboriginal Children's Home.

See W.E.H. Stanner, *The Boyer Lectures 1968: After the Dreaming*, pp 14, 15 regarding protection and segregation.

3 Dispossession

For background on Aborigines and World War I, see Professor Mick Dodson and Siobhan McDonnell, 'Why did they serve?' *Wartime*, Issue 76, Spring 2016, pp 10–16; also: https://www.awm.gov.au/about/our-work/projects/indigenous-service

The Richmond River Herald and Northern Districts Advertiser, 2 September 1919 carried the account of the welcome home to Euraba.

See *The North Western Courier*, Narrabri, 20 August 1925 regarding the 'black swamp'.

See Ruth Fink, 'The Caste Barrier—an Obstacle to the Assimilation of Part-Aborigines in north-west New South Wales,' *Oceania*, Vol. XXVIII, 1957–58, p 109, for the destructive role of reserve managers.

Regarding the impact of protection laws, see Noel Pearson, Gough Whitlam eulogy: http://www.reconciliationsa.org.au/news/reconciliation/read-noel-pearsons-eulogy-for-the-late-former-prime-minister-gough-whitlam

Madeline McGrady was quoted in Human Rights Australia, 'Toomelah: Report on the problems and needs of Aborigines living on the New South Wales–Queensland border,' June 1988: https://www.humanrights.gov.au/our-work/aboriginal-and-torres-strait-islander-social-justice/publications/toomelah-report-1988

See James Miller, *Koori: A Will to Win*, p 163 regarding the contention that Aboriginal people would die out.

Regarding expansion by squatters, see: espace.library.uq.edu.au

For a history of pastoralism in Queensland, see Dr Geoff Ginn, 'Queensland Historical Atlas: Pastoralism 1860s–1915': http://www.qhatlas.com.au/pastoralism-1860s-1915

See Dr Rosalind Kidd, *Discovering Whiteness*, 2002 regarding theft and fraud of earnings.

See Jeanie Bell, 'The persistence of Aboriginal kinship and marriage rules in Australia: Adapting traditional ways into modern practices,' *The Journal of the European Association for Studies of Australia*, Vol. 4 No. 1, 2013, regarding the breakdown of the kinship and marriage rules.

Warren Mundine, *In Black and White*, p 38, provides background to the role of moiety and skin group.

4 Skin

For Kamilaroi background, see Michelle Carpenter, *Kamilaroi—a Nation's Identity*, Macquarie University: https://kamilaroianationsidentity.weebly.com

Regarding Boobera Lagoon, background came from Carl McGrady, Aboriginal Education Assistant, Boggabilla.

The first Commonwealth/State conference on 'Native Welfare', 1937 considered the new policy of assimilation.

Noel Pearson has referred to the untrammelled powers of managers; also, see the Australian Human Rights Commission's *Toomelah Report*: https://www.humanrights.gov.au/our-work/aboriginal-and-torres-strait-islander-social-justice/publications/toomelah-report-1988

The Ruby Waters interview is held by Australian Institute of Aboriginal and Torres Strait Islanders (AIATSIS), permission was given to the author by her son, Len.

5 Choice

Althea Wolfe and Bruce Wolfe were interviewed in 2017 regarding their father Jim's views of Len Waters' scholastic ability.

Regarding the Waters family and exemption certificates, see Queensland Exemption Register 1908–1936: http://www.cifhs.com/qldrecords/exem1908_1936.html and 1936–41: http://www.cifhs.com/qldrecords/exem1936_1941.html

The reference to boxing gloves was drawn from *ATSIC News*, Winter 1994.

Moree Council minutes dealing with the artesian baths were dated 18 August 1930 and were provided by Noeline Briggs-Smith, together with other material relating to discriminatory practices in the town.

The Sydney Morning Herald, 17 September 1932 reported the Moree corroboree.

The North Western Courier, 16 August 1934 published the 'Abos to the Rescue' story.

See Len Waters remarks to his mother, AWM2016.399.2

6 Standing apart

See Rae Norris, *The More Things Change: Continuity in Australian Indigenous Employment Disadvantage 1788–1967*, PhD thesis Griffith University, 2006; see pp 179–80, for background to Aboriginal wages in Queensland.

Bob Webster, Brisbane boxing historian, provided background on tent boxing.

Personal interview with Vida Hardy.

For background on differences between Aborigines living on reserves and missions and those who did not, see Maria Lane, 'Two Indigenous Populations? Two Diverging Paradigms?', 12 March 2007, www.FirstSources.info

For Stan Grant's description of his grandfather's generation, see 'The Australian Dream: Blood, History and Becoming Stan Grant,' *Quarterly Essay*, Issue 64, 2016, p 40.

Professor Mick Dodson and Siobhan McDonnell, *Wartime*, Issue 76, Spring 2016, p 13, refer to the Military Board memorandum.

Prime Minister R.G. Menzies, *Empire Air Force: Australia Plays Her Part*, made the statement and broadcast on 11 October 1939.

For background to the operation of the Empire Air Training Scheme, see J.M. McCarthy, 'The Defence of Australia and the Empire Air Training Scheme: 1939–1942,' *Australian Journal of Politics & History*, 20, No. 3, December 1974, pp 326–34.

For the RAAF's strength, see Chris Clark and Sanu Kainikara, eds, 'Empire Air Training Scheme: raise, train and sustain during World War II,' *Pathfinder*, Vol. 4, 2010.

The Balonne Beacon, 11 December 1941 published the enrolment requirement.

7 Different doors

Reference to the new aptitude intelligence was made in *The Morning Bulletin*, Rockhampton, 24 June 1941.

John Curtin speech to America was made on 14 March 1942: Curtin Library: http://john.curtin.edu.au/audio/00434.html

See Professor Mick Dodson and Siobhan McDonnell, *Wartime*, Issue 76, Spring 2016, on why enlisting in the services was attractive to Indigenous Australians, p 15.

The Morning Bulletin, Rockhampton, 18 July 1942 carried Frank Forde's comments.

The Pittsworth Sentinel, 16 May 1942 referred to the RAAF recruitment drive.

Len Waters' comments can be found in his NAA file, Series no. A9301, Control symbol 78144, document 129.

8 The erk

Len Waters' exam results can be found in NAA file, Series no. A9301, Control symbol 78144.

For MacArthur's comments about the air force being the key to victory, see 'The Limited Offensive,' p 20, the Official History of WWII, *Australia in the War of 1939–1945. Series 3—Air.*

Len Waters' views on where airmen came from were recorded in a later conversation with Max Davey reported in *The Wimmera Mail-Times*, 17 August 1988.

Prime Minister R.G. Menzies wrote to the Minister for the Air, James Fairbairn, on 10 November 1939 arguing for the abandonment of rigid educational qualifications; quoted John McCarthy, *A Last Call of Empire*, p 37.

See Robert Hall's book, *Fighters from the Fringe*, pp 159–60, for Len Waters' quote about his study habits.

9 Solo

For the description of drill sergeants, see Arthur Sandell, *Dicing with Death: An Airman's Account of His Training and Operations Against Japan,* p 21.

John McCarthy, *A last call of Empire: Australian aircrew, Britain and the Empire Air Training Scheme*, pp 39, 144 note 45, refers to the obsession with becoming a pilot.

For Len Waters' marks and observations on his progress as a pilot, see his NAA file, Series no. A9301, Control symbol 78144.

Dick Sudlow described his own first solo flight in, *Flying with Lady Luck*, p 9.

10 Utopia

For a description of life at 5 Service Flying Training School Uranquinty, see Leigh 'Laddie' Hindley, p 9, *The Joys and Dangers of an Aviation Pilot*, Air Power Development Centre, Canberra, 2013.

Dick Sudlow refers to the tension between ground staff and trainee pilots in *Flying with Lady Luck,* pp 15, 16.

Len Waters' progress as a trainee pilot was drawn from his NAA file, Series no. A9301, Control symbol 78144.

Ron Guthrie's recollections came in a personal interview.

For the 'Personal Characteristics Assessments Rating Scale', *Directorate of Training Pamphlet,* AWM082249, 155.28 A938p.

The Daily Advertiser, Wagga Wagga, published its views on 'British stock' on 4 July 1944, the same day that Waters graduated.

See John McCarthy, *A Last Call of Empire: Australian aircrew, Britain and the Empire Air Training Scheme*, p 40, for reference to the popular theory of what made pilot material.

Tom Wolfe's book, *The Right Stuff*, discusses the attributes that go towards making a fighter pilot.

11 The thrill of it

See Kristen Alexander, *Clive Caldwell Air Ace*, pp 30, 157, 158 for background to Clive Caldwell's attitudes and views.

See Dick Sudlow, *Flying with Lady Luck*, p 48 for his recollections of being an instructor at Mildura.

See Waters' NAA file, Series no. A9301, Control symbol 78144 for his marks at Mildura and the assessment of his performance and attitude.

12 Misadventure in Moree

Len Waters' comment about his father being regarded as the 'whitest Aborigine' was made to Jeanette Sims.

Personal communications with Indigenous historian Noelene Briggs-Smith, regarding history of discrimination in Moree.

Heather Goodall, 'Not Such a Respected Soldier: The Impact of World War I on Aborigines in New South Wales,' *Teaching History*, 4 December 1987, pp 3–6 provides background to prevailing attitudes in rural areas.

Regarding the threat of removal of children by police, see Dr Christine Jennett, 'Policing and Indigenous Peoples in Australia,' paper presented at the *History of Crime, Policing and Punishment Conference* convened by the Australian Institute of Criminology in conjunction with Charles Sturt University, held in Canberra, 9–10 December 1999.

For the issue of citizenship rights, see James Miller, *Koori: A Will to Win*, p 176, re Joe Lawson, MLA, New South Wales Parliamentary Debates, 4 May 1943, Vol. CLXX, p 2839.

The instruction to Queensland police not to take notes is cited by Jo Kamira, former manager of the Australian Federal Police, ATSI Unit, ACT, 'Indigenous Participation in Policing—From Native Police to

Now in Policing—Has Anything Changed?', paper presented at the *History of Crime, Policing and Punishment Conference* convened by the Australian Institute of Criminology in conjunction with Charles Sturt University, held in Canberra, 9–10 December 1999.

The hand-coloured portrait of Len Waters is located at AWM2016.399.2

13 Bad show

The description of Japanese soldiers was drawn from K.M. Horler's *Tropical Tour*, p 43, unpublished memoir, Office of Air Force History.

See Hindley, Leigh 'Laddie', *The Joys and Dangers of an Aviation Pilot*, pp 30, 31 for details of equipment pilots carried for survival on the ground.

The Bill Soden quote was drawn from his manuscript, W.J. Soden, *An account of a boy's life on King Island 1935–41*, AWM, MSS1432, p 59.

Dick Sudlow's account of his arrival on Noemfoor is detailed in *Flying with Lady Luck*, pp 59, 60.

The shadow shooting reference is drawn from Gordon Clarke, *This Smuttee Squadron: The History of 78 Squadron RAAF During and Post* WW2, self-published, Brisbane, 2012, p 226.

For the death of Stan Hattersley, see his NAA file, Series no. A705, Control symbol 166/17/667. See also, Gordon Clarke, *This Smuttee Squadron: The History of 78 Squadron RAAF During and Post* WW2, p 227.

Re Grace to Margie Jones, this account of events is based on separate interviews with Gladys Waters and Lenise Schloss.

14 Here today, gone to Morotai

The description of daily life on Noemfoor was drawn from Leigh Hindley, *The Joys and Dangers of an Aviation Pilot,* p 27, and James Harding, *It Had 2 B.U. The Life Story of 80 Squadron RAAF*, p 118.

Dick Sudlow's account of the move to Morotai was drawn from *Flying with Lady Luck*, pp 62, 63.

Lyall Ellers described the 'Aussie revenge' in a conversation with Gordon Clarke, September 2017.

The account of film night behaviour was drawn from K.M. Horler, *Tropical Tour*, unpublished memoir, Office of Air Force History, Fairbairn, Canberra, while Gordon Clarke also added to this with the story of the shot at the screen.

15 Fighting fit

Wings, 20 March 1945; Sapper C.H. Cecil, *The Sporting Globe*, 22 September 1945.

Liam Kane, 'Shared amenities and troops' relations,' unpublished draft chapter of PhD thesis, UNSW, dealing with relations between Australian and American troops in the South West Pacific Area.

John 'Curley' Wheatley, personal interview, April 2017, re Waters' boxing ability.

Details of Waters' flights in *Black Magic* referred to in this chapter were sourced from his logbook. See AWM PR00308. His account of the 37mm shell was sourced from comments in interviews more than 40 years after the event. His views on *Black Magic* were sourced from a personal interview with Arnie Nunn, December 2017.

I have also utilised Gordon Clarke's detailed accounts of the operations of 78 Squadron in his book, *This Smuttee Squadron: The History of 78 Squadron RAAF During and Post* WW2. I also drew on the book for background to the Geoff Atherton story, which was further augmented by information from pacificvictoryroll.com

This Smuttee Squadron and James Harding's *It Had 2 B.U. The Life Story of 80 Squadron RAAF*, provided background to the operations of 78 Wing.

16 Wind-down

See Dick Sudlow, *Flying with Lady Luck*, p 67, re frustration in the ranks.

The signal from Air Vice-Marshal Bostock is quoted in the Official History of WWII, *Australia in the War of 1939–1945. Series 3—Air*, p 445.

See Mark Johnson, *Whispering Death: Australian Airmen in the Pacific War*, p 408, re 'Morotai Mutiny'.

Re flying on Anzac Day, see Gordon Clarke, *This Smuttee Squadron*, p 302.

17 One of the boys

The reference to good fighters in the 93rd Infantry Division was quoted by Buddy Thomson in the cover notes for his record, *Who fought for him, The story of Len Waters*, Outback Records, Kingaroy, Queensland.

Bob Crawford's remarks about the fight were made in a radio interview.

Dick Sims' comments about the fight were made to Kevin Waters, 28 August 1993, as recalled by Kevin Waters.

See *Wings*, 20 March 1945; copies held by Office of Air Force History, Fairbairn, Canberra.

See Dick Sudlow, *Flying with Lady Luck,* p 61.

Personal interview with Len Waters' nephew, Len Waters, re his father, Jim Waters, October 2017.

Gordon Clarke, *This Smuttee Squadron,* p 299 re Morotai and Tarakan movements.

78 Squadron Operations Record Book, May 1945. NAA file, Series no. A9186, Control symbol 107.

For Cutler quote, see Derek Royal, 'Black Magic,' *The Australian Way*, November 1996.

18 Coming of age

For file of F.O. Jones, see NAA file, Series no. A9300, Item barcode 5257910.

Re Lyall Ellers, information via email from Gordon Clarke, October 2017.

78 Squadron Operations Record Book, June 1945, NAA file, Series no. A9186, Control symbol 107.

Statement, Frank Smith to Jack Macqueen; records of Gladys Waters, privately held.

Personal interview with Len Waters' nephew, Len Waters, October 2017.

Re Dyaks, see Official History of WWII, *Australia in the War of 1939–1945*, 'Air War Against Japan,' 1943–1945, p 490; also Gordon Clarke, *This Smuttee Squadron,* p 329.

Dick Sudlow, *Flying with Lady Luck*, p 72, dive-bombing accuracy.

Gordon Clarke, *This Smuttee Squadron,* re Sudlow and losing pilots, p 336.

See Waters logbook re Sandakan; also see Clarke, p 327.

See Official History of WWII, *Australia in the War of 1939–1945*, 'Air War Against Japan,' p 489 re Tabanio.

See Len Waters' autobiography re Balikpapan.

See Len Waters' logbook, re being weathered out, AWM PR00308.

Re crash of two P-40s, and Ted Quinn, see James Harding, *It Had 2 B.U.*, pp 175, 176.

Re the Japanese surrender, see Official History of WWII, *Australia in the War of 1939–1945*, 'Air War Against Japan,' p 490.

For James Harding quote, see *It Had 2 B.U.*, p 176.

See Dick Sudlow, *Flying with Lady Luck,* p 72, re celebrations.

See 78 Squadron Operations Record Book, June 1945, NAA file, Series no. A9186, Control symbol 107, for Sudlow rating.

19 True Australian Blood

Re Len Waters' sports skills, Gordon Clarke interview with Lyall Ellers, September 2017.

Personal interview with Ron Guthrie, September 2017: http://www.austradesecure.com/radschool/Vol22/page9.htm

For background to the Guthrie story, see Frank Alley, Radschool Association Magazine, Vol. 22.

Re Reg Saunders, see Harry Gordon, *The Embarrassing Australian*, pp 135–6.

Information regarding Len Waters' pay was drawn from material provided by Martin James, Directorate of History, RAAF, Fairbairn.

Background regarding Indigenous Australians at war was drawn from the John Moremon article, 'A brief history of Indigenous Australians at War':

https://www.dva.gov.au/i-am/aboriginal-andor-torres-strait-islander/indigenous-australians-war

For information on David Valentine Paul, see: https://www.awm.gov.au/sites/default/files/David_Paul.pdf

20 A suitable marriage

Gordon Clarke, 'Will the Real "Black Magic" Stand Up,' *Flightpath*, Vol. 16 no. 4, May–June 2005, pp 23–29.

Re the Greeks café in St George, see *Greek Cafés and Milk Bars of Australia*, Effy Alexakis and Leonard Janiszewski.

See Katherine Ellinghaus, 'Controlling interracial marriage in Australia,' *Aboriginal History Journal*, Vol. 27, 2003, p 199.

Also, see Sophie Verass, 'Illegal Love: Is this NT couple Australia's Richard and Mildred Loving?' 7 April 2017: http://www.sbs.com.au/nitv/article/2017/04/07/illegal-love-nt-couple-australias-richard-and-mildred-loving

21 Blackfella

For background to the Hotel Corones, Charleville, see *The Courier-Mail*, 24 October 2017.

At my request, the National Archives of Australia undertook a search of Department of Civil Aviation files for letters written by Len Waters in 1946–47. However, the boxes ran out before they reached 'W' for Waters. NAA explained that sometimes they only received records in part and not in whole and it would appear this was the case with the particular series that may have held such letters. This represented a 'dead end,' according to the NAA in a note to me on 12 July 2017. A further search indicated that the series had been heavily culled, with surviving records primarily of a policy focus. Thus, correspondence such as Waters' at that time was viewed as routine and not filed permanently.

Arnie Nunn's remarks were made in a personal interview, 15 December 2017.

The reference to the wool scourer plant was sourced from Tony Matthews' book, *True Blue Queenslanders: Heroes, Heroines and Battlers*, p 41; also see Warren Mundine for background to the difficulty faced by Aborigines in securing bank loans: *Warren Mundine in Black & White*, p 58, and p 8 about learning to stand back.

22 Fitting back in

Bill Fisk's remarks were made in personal interviews during 2017.

See W.J. Soden, *An account of a boy's life on King Island 1935–41*, pp 94, 95 for his comments on the feeling of post-war loss.

David Huggonson's 14 July 1994 letter is held in Gladys Waters' private files.

The views of Len Waters' nephew, Len Waters, were made during personal interviews in October 2017.

23 In the ring

The St George Rugby League club program for the match gave details of the Waters brothers playing together, while *The Balonne Beacon* report of the match appeared on 31 July 1947.

Ranald Waters comments about temperament were sourced from the *ATSIC News*, special edition, Winter 1994.

See Wayne Smith, *The Courier-Mail*, 30 May 1994 for the description of Ranald's style.

See *The Balonne Beacon*, 2 December 1948, for the account of Len Waters' boxing bout against Rodney Harrison.

Jamieson's view that Ranald may have been another Jack Hassen were in *The Balonne Beacon*, 27 January 1949.

See *The Courier-Mail*, 2 September 1949 for Ranald's punching style.

See *The Sunday Mail*, 10 July 1949 for Ranald's training regime.

The Courier-Mail, 2, 3 September 1949 carried the story on the background to the fight, and Ranald's defeat.

24 Wheel of misfortune

See Warren Mundine, *In Black & White*, p 7 for his views on hybrid life.

The story about the 'black bastard' comment is contained in notes compiled by Jack Macqueen and held in Gladys Waters' private files.

She provided further detail in a letter on 24 August 1994, and in a personal interview in November 2017.

The Sydney Morning Herald story about George Bennett's death was published on 25 September 1950.

25 Strike

To this day Dianne is always offered 'budder' by the wider Waters clan.

For background to the 1956 shearers' strike, see Kosmas Tsokhas, *ABC Bush Telegraph*, 20 September 2006.

Neil Byron's account of the 1956 strike is at: http://asslh.org.au/hummer/vol-3-no-5/unbroken-commitment/

See Waters' NAA file and document dated 11 June 1957, regarding his attempt to rejoin the RAAF, Series no. A9301, Control symbol 78144.

Martin James, RAAF historian, Fairbairn, provided background on Waters' application.

Gladys Waters' comments are contained in correspondence with Jack Macqueen, which she holds.

Bob Katter's comments about the Queensland Office of Native Affairs were published by *The Australian*, 2 November 2010.

26 The loner

'Seventeen Hard Summers' is held by Gladys Waters.

Mimag, November 1962, Vol. 15, No. 10 is held by Gladys Waters.

Peter Gorman was personally interviewed in November 2017.

Bert Lowrey's account of Waters' explanation of the moon landing was quoted by journalist Joel Gould, *The Northern Daily Leader*. Undated copy of article held by Gladys Waters.

27 The Saturday ritual

Dianne Russell described the activities of the 'Flying Eight' in a personal interview in March 2018, along with the reference to her marriage.

Kevin Webster's recollections came in a personal interview in March 2018.

Bill Fisk's comments were given in a personal interview in 24 September 2017.

For background to 'work and burst', see Robin Room, 'The dialectic of drinking in Australian life: from the Rum Corps to the wine column,' *Australian Drug and Alcohol Review*, 1988.

28 Grief

Information drawn from correspondence held by Gladys Waters, and interviews with her, Lenise Schloss and Kevin Waters was used for this chapter.

29 Bleak times

Len Waters' comments about shearing and his stainless steel knees were reported in *The Courier-Mail*, 18 November 1992.

The comments by Marcus Waters about his grandfather were drawn from his thesis, *Contemporary Urban Indigenous 'Dreamings': Interaction, Engagement and Creative Practice*, Griffith University, May 2012.

Lorenda Hill was interviewed in March 2017.

Stacey Giles was interviewed in March 2018.

Former federal minister David Beddall referred to the charges Waters had accumulated in a letter held by Gladys Waters in support of her pension application.

Len Waters wrote about the death of Joe Craigie in a letter to Lenise Schloss in December 1987.

30 Icarus

Bob Armstrong, 'Aborigines at War: Service rules were confusing,' *The Chronicle*, Toowoomba, 2 December 1981.

SBS, *Frontline*, 1988.

See *The Wimmera Mail-Times*, 17 August 1988, for the meeting with Max Davey.

Peter Gorman was interviewed in November 2017.

Jeanette Sims provided background material to her dealings with Len Waters.

For Jimmie Barker's 'two worlds' quote, see *The Two Worlds of Jimmie Barker, The Life of an Australian Aboriginal 1900–1972,* as told to Janet Mathews, Australian Institute of Aboriginal Studies, Canberra, 1977, p 181.

Jeanette Sims remarks about 'the dominant white society' were drawn from a letter to the War Veterans' Review Board, 28 July 1994.

31 Flash black

The 'wrong colour' reference was drawn from Jeanette Sims, letter to the War Veterans' Review Board, 28 July 1994.

The Mick Flick story was sourced from Heather Goodall's 'Not Such a Respected Soldier: the Impact of WWI on Aborigines in NSW,' *Teaching History*, 4 December 1987, pp 3–6.

SBS, *Frontline*, 1988.

See *The Courier-Mail*, 18 November 1992, for Waters' thoughts on destiny.

Waters' views on welfare assistance to Aborigines were drawn from conversations he had with Wing Commander Ken Llewelyn and Jeanette Sims. These views were contained in letters to Jack Macqueen, held by Gladys Waters.

32 Free fall

Waters' medical record, dated 28 May 1993, is held by Gladys Waters.

The article in *The Western Sun* was published on 9 June 1993.

The Townsville Bulletin, 15 June 1993 reported the air show at RAAF Base Townsville, and discussed further in a personal interview in December 2017.

Ken Llewelyn's report of the trip in the Dakota with Waters was published in the *RAAF News*, August 1993 edition.

33 Alone

Qld police witness statement, Jamie Noel Sawtell, 19 November 1993, copy held by Gladys Waters.

Qld police witness statement, Gordon Crawford, 14 October 1993, copy held by Gladys Waters.

34 Two worlds

For Paul Keating's speech for the International Year of the World's Indigenous Peoples, 10 December 1992, see: https://antar.org.au/sites/default/files/paul_keating_speech_transcript.pdf

For Noel Pearson's 'crabs in a bucket' comments, see *The Australian*, 6 August 2011.

Also, see Noel Pearson and Shireen Morris, eds, *A Rightful Place: A Road Map to Recognition*, p 53.

Dr Ian Lilley's letter to Jack Macqueen was dated 23 August 1994.

Wing Commander Ken Llewelyn's letter to Jack Macqueen was dated 17 August 1994.

The David Beddall letter to Con Sciacca, in support of the claim, is held by Gladys Waters.

Gladys Waters verse, privately held.

Epilogue

Brett West was interviewed in December 2017.

For the Stan Grant quote, see, 'A Makarrata Declaration: A Declaration of our Country,' in the Pearson and Morris book, *A Rightful Place: A Road Map to Recognition*, p 139.

The reference to the Bjelke-Petersen quote was drawn from Kim Orchard's biography, *My Father the Flyer*. It was also raised in the SBS program, *Frontline*, with Len Waters, Reg Saunders and Oodgeroo Noonuccal.

BIBLIOGRAPHY

Books, memoirs and theses

Alexakis, Effy, and Janiszewski, Leonard, *Greek Cafés and Milk Bars of Australia*, Halstead Press, Braddon, ACT, 2016.

Alexander, Kristen, *Clive Caldwell Air Ace*, Allen & Unwin, Sydney, 2006.

Clarke, Gordon, *This Smuttee Squadron: The History of 78 Squadron RAAF During and Post* WW2, self-published, Brisbane, 2012.

Elder, Bruce, *Blood on the Wattle, Massacres and Maltreatment of Aboriginal Australians since 1788*, New Holland Publishers, Sydney, 1998.

Goodall, Heather, *A History of Aboriginal Communities in New South Wales, 1909–1939*, University of Sydney, 1982.

Gordon, Harry, *The Embarrassing Australian: The Story of an Aboriginal Warrior*, Lansdowne Press, Melbourne, 1962.

Grant, Stan, *Talking To My Country*, HarperCollins, Sydney, 2016.

Hall, Robert, *The Black Diggers: Aborigines and Torres Strait Islanders in the Second World War*, Allen & Unwin, Sydney, 1989.

—— *Fighters from the Fringe*, Aboriginal Studies Press, Canberra, 1995.

Harding, James, *It Had 2 B.U. The Life Story of 80 Squadron RAAF*, Chandos, Melbourne, 1966.

Hindley, Leigh 'Laddie', *The Joys and Dangers of an Aviation Pilot*, the Air Power Development Centre, Canberra, 2013.

Horler, K.M., *Tropical Tour,* unpublished memoir, Office of Air Force History, Fairbairn, Canberra.

Johnson, Mark, *Whispering Death: Australian Airmen in the Pacific War*, Allen & Unwin, Sydney, 2011.

Mathews, Janet, *The Two Worlds of Jimmie Barker, The Life of an Australian Aboriginal 1900–1972*, as told to Janet Mathews, Australian Institute of Aboriginal Studies, Canberra, 1977.

Matthews, Tony, *True Blue Queenslanders: Heroes, Heroines and Battlers*, Central Queensland University Press, Rockhampton, 2001.

McCarthy, J.M., *A Last Call of Empire: Australian aircrew, Britain and the Empire Air Training Scheme*, Australian War Memorial, Canberra, 1988.

Miller, James, *Koori: A Will to Win,* Angus & Robertson, Sydney, 1986.

Mundine, Warren, *In Black & White: Race, Politics and Changing Australia*, Pantera Press, Sydney, 2017.

Odgers, George, *Australia in the War of 1939–1945. Series 3—Air,* Australian War Memorial, Canberra.

O'Loughlin, Michael, with Main, Jim, *Micky O: Determination. Hard Work. And a Little Bit of Magic.* HarperCollins, Sydney, 2012.

Orchard, Kim, *My Father the Flyer*, self-published.

Pearson, Noel and Morris, Shireen, eds, *A Rightful Place: A Road Map to Recognition*, Black Inc., Melbourne, 2017.

Sandell, Arthur, *Dicing with Death: An Airman's Account of His Training and Operations Against Japan,* Aerospace Centre, Fairbairn ACT, 2001.

Stanner, W.E.H., *The Boyer Lectures 1968: After the Dreaming*, The Australian Broadcasting Commission, Sydney, 1969.

Sudlow, Dick, *Flying with Lady Luck*, Richard Paget Sudlow, Ulladulla, 1999.

Waters, Marcus, *Contemporary Urban Indigenous 'Dreamings': Interaction, Engagement and Creative Practice*, Griffith University, Brisbane, May 2012.

Wolfe, Tom, *The Right Stuff*, Farrer, Straus and Giroux, USA, 1979.

Journals, papers and unpublished memoirs

Bell, Jeanie, 'The persistence of Aboriginal kinship and marriage rules in Australia: Adapting traditional ways into modern practices,' *The Journal of the European Association for Studies of Australia,* Vol. 4, No. 1, 2013.

Directorate of Training Pamphlet, RAAF Headquarters, Melbourne, 'Personal Characteristics Assessments Rating Scale,' AWM082249, 155.28 A938p.

Eckermann, Anne-Katrin, *Half-Caste, Out-Cast. An ethnographic analysis of the processes underlying adaptation among Aboriginal people in rural town, south-west Queensland*, PhD thesis, University of Queensland, Brisbane, 1977.

Edmonds, Leigh, 'How Australians were made airminded,' *Continuum: Australian Journal of Media & Culture*, Vol. 7, No. 1, 1993.

Ellinghaus, Katherine, 'Controlling interracial marriage in Australia,' *Aboriginal History Journal*, Vol. 27, 2003.

Fuller, Robert, 'How ancient Aboriginal star maps have shaped Australia's highway network,' *The Conversation*, 7 April 2016.

Fuller, Robert, Norris, Ray and Trudgett, Michelle, 'The Astronomy of the Kamilaroi People and their Neighbours,' https://arxiv.org/pdf/1311.0076.pdf

Goodall, Heather, 'Not Such a Respected Soldier: The Impact of World War I on Aborigines in New South Wales,' *Teaching History*, 4 December 1987.

Grant, Stan, 'The Australian Dream: Blood, History and Becoming Stan Grant,' *Quarterly Essay,* Issue 64, 2016.

Hall, Robert, 'Black Magic: Leonard Waters—World War II fighter pilot,' *Aboriginal History*, Vol. 16, 1992.

Human Rights Commission Australia, 'Toomelah: Report on the problems and needs of Aborigines living on the New South Wales–Queensland border,' June 1988: https://www.humanrights.gov.au/our-work/aboriginal-and-torres-strait-islander-social-justice/publications/toomelah-report-1988

Jennett, Dr Christine, 'Policing and Indigenous Peoples in Australia,' paper presented at the History of Crime, Policing and Punishment Conference convened by the Australian Institute of Criminology in conjunction with Charles Sturt University, held in Canberra, 9–10 December 1999.

Kamira, Jo, former Manager of the Australian Federal Police, ATSI Unit, ACT, 'Indigenous Participation in Policing—From Native Police To Now—Has Anything Changed?', paper presented at the History of

Crime, Policing and Punishment Conference convened by the Australian Institute of Criminology in conjunction with Charles Sturt University, held in Canberra, 9–10 December 1999.

Kane, Liam, *Shared amenities and troops' relations*, unpublished PhD thesis, University of New South Wales.

Lane, Maria, 'Two Indigenous Populations? Two Diverging Paradigms?' 12 March 2007, www.FirstSources.info

McCarthy, John, *A last call of Empire: Australian aircrew, Britain and the Empire Air Training Scheme*, Australian War Memorial, Canberra, 1988.

—— 'The Defence of Australia and the Empire Air Training Scheme: 1939–1942,' *Australian Journal of Politics & History*, Vol. 20, No. 3, December 1974, pp 326–34.

National Archives of Australia, 'Leonard Victor Waters file,' Series no. A9301, Control symbol 78144.

Norris, Rae, *The More Things Change: Continuity in Australian Indigenous Employment Disadvantage 1788–1967*, PhD thesis, Griffith University, Brisbane, 2006.

Room, Robin, 'The dialectic of drinking in Australian life: from the Rum Corps to the wine column,' *Australian Drug and Alcohol Review*, 1988, Vol. 7, pp 413–37.

Royal, Derek, 'Black magic,' *The Australian Way*, November, 1996.

Soden, W.J., 'An account of a boy's life on King Island 1935–41', AWM, MSS1432.

Newspapers and magazines

ATSIC News, Winter 1994.

The Australian, 2 November 2010, 6 August 2011.

The Balonne Beacon, 7 July 1932, 11 December 1941, 31 July 1947, 2 December 1948, 27 January 1949.

The Chronicle, Toowoomba, article by Bob Armstrong, 2 December 1981.

The Conversation, Professor John Maynard, 'Capturing the lived history of the Aborigines Protection Board while we still can', 4 September 2015.

The Courier-Mail, 2 September 1949, 3 September 1949, 18 November 1992, 30 May 1994, 24 October 2017.

The Daily Advertiser, Wagga Wagga, 4 July 1944.

The Moree North-West Champion, January–July 1932.
The Morning Bulletin, Rockhampton, 24 June 1941, 18 July 1942.
The North Western Courier, Narrabri, 20 August 1925, 16 August 1934.
The Pittsworth Sentinel, 16 May 1942.
RAAF News, August 1993.
The Richmond River Herald and Northern Districts Advertiser, 2 September 1919, p 2.
SBS: 'Illegal Love: Is this NT couple Australia's Richard and Mildred Loving?' 7 April 2017: http://www.sbs.com.au/nitv/article/2017/04/07/illegal-love-nt-couple-australias-richard-and-mildred-loving
The Shoalhaven Telegraph, 31 October 1917.
The Sporting Globe, article by Sapper C.H. Cecil, 22 September 1945.
The Sunday Mail, 10 July 1949.
The Sydney Mail, 21 January 1914.
The Sydney Morning Herald, 17 September 1932, 25 September 1950.
The Townsville Bulletin, 15 June 1993.
Wartime, Issue 76, Spring 2016.
The Western Sun, Cunnamulla, 9 June 1993.
The Wimmera Mail-Times, 17 August 1988.
Wings, 20 March 1945.

Film, newsreels and audio

Australians at War Film Archive, Robert Crawford, archive 112, UNSW Canberra, 2003: http://australiansatwarfilmarchive.unsw.edu.au
Bill Carty newsreel, Galea Bay attack, 9–10 January 1945, see: https://www.awm.gov.au/collection/C189048
British Pathé, re Air-Minded Aboriginals, 1933, see: https://www.britishpathe.com/video/air-minded-aboriginals/query/aboriginal
John Curtin speech to America, 14 March 1942, Curtin Library: http://john.curtin.edu.au/audio/00434.html
Buddy Thomson, *Who fought for him, The story of Len Waters*, Outback Records, Kingaroy, Queensland.

INDEX

Aboriginal Girls' Training Home (Cootamundra) 5
Aboriginal people *see* Indigenous Australians
aircraft *see by name*
Airspeed Oxford utility monoplane 61
American military
  93rd Division 155
  boxing competitions 133–4, 153–5
  RAAF, and 112, 124–5, 130–1, 152
  racial tensions 155–7
Andrew, Flight Lieutenant Albert 117
Ansett Airways 206
Anzac Day ceremonies 285–8, 290
Atebrin (mepacrine) 106–7
Atherton, Wing Commander Geoff 139–40, 151–2
Australia at war 53–4
  Indigenous military service 19–22, 46, 55, 102–3, 179–87
Australian Aborigines' League 180
Australian Imperial Force (AIF) 53
  Aboriginal soldiers 19–20
Australian War Memorial 313
Australian Women's Army Service 181
Australian Workers Union 209, 237
Avro Anson light bomber 61
Awabakal clan 16, 19

Baker, Flight Lieutenant Denis 'Denny' 110, 113, 125, 136, 191
Balagna station 7, 24, 36, 40, 148
Balikpapan 167–8, 170, 171
Barker, Jimmie 282, 283
Bartley, Johnny 235
Batten, Jean 7
Beddall, David 308–9
Beinke, Flight Sergeant Allan 138
Bellevue Hotel 194–5
Bennett, George 15, 19–22, 232–3
Biak Island 109
Bigambul people 28, 205
Binge, Walter 28, 271
Bird, Charlie Turner 19–21
Bjelke-Petersen, Joh 268, 289, 314
Black Diggers 274, 278
Black, Flight Lieutenant Joe 163
Black Magic xi, 110, 114, 126, 136–8, 142, 169–72, 221, 274, 280, 294
  postwar destruction of 191–2
Blamey, General Sir Thomas 106, 125, 181
Board for the Protection of Aborigines 4, 15, 22, 104, 199
Boggabilla 217, 311
Bomaderry Aboriginal Children's Home 5, 17
Bomberai Peninsula 112
Bonus Downs station 212–13
Boobera Lagoon 28
Boomerang fighter 61, 164
Boonall West 7
Borneo 150, 159, 168, 172, 177, 185
boxing 42–3, 69–70, 71
  military service, during 122–23, 132–4, 153–5
  postwar 219, 221–6, 239–40
  pub fights 255–6
Boyd, Robin 240
Brady, Brian 224–6
Brantian Estate 171–2
British Commonwealth Occupation Force (BCOF) 177, 179, 206
Brown, Air Marshal Geoff 313

Caldwell, Clive 89–91, 93, 152
Carty, Bill 134
Celebes Islands 137–9, 141–3, 185
Chambers, Dr Cyril 'Doc' 141, 157
Charleville 147, 148, 150, 201–2, 229
Chifley, Ben 178
Chinchilla 268, 271

Citizen Military Forces (CMF) 53
Coates, Wing Commander John 186
combat training 85
Commonwealth Aircraft Corporation (CAC) 80
Corones, Harry 'Poppa' 202
Coutts, Ian 10
Craigie, Joe 272
Crawford, Flight Lieutenant Bob 98, 154, 157, 296, 301, 303
Cunnamulla 231, 237–40, 278–9, 290, 298–9, 309
  racial discrimination 285–6
Curnow, Group Captain Tom 86
Curtin, John 54, 294
Cutler, Geoff 160–2, 301, 303
Cutler, Roden 160

Dakota 291, 293–4, 302
Davey, Max 153, 276–7
Delapool station 232
Department of Civil Aviation 207
Depression 6, 8, 33, 38, 43, 202
Desert War 89
Dhinawan the Emu 12
dogfights 92, 95–6, 109–10, 131
Doom Island 117
Douglas C-47 transport 108
Dreaming 12, 270
Dyaks 168

Ellers, Flying Officer Lyall 163, 164–5, 176
Empire Air Training Scheme 46–7, 54, 62–3, 66, 186
emu-egg carving (Kalti Paarti) 270–1, 279, 295
Euraba reserve 16, 17, 20, 22

F/A-18 Hornets xii, 294, 302, 312–13
Faulkiner, 'Baldy' 212
Fields, Gracie 177
fighter pilots xi, 64, 65, 84, 88, 183–4, 252–3, 274, 278–9
  aircraft, relationship to 136
  'Aussie revenge' trick 128
  characteristics 62, 89–91, 114–15, 116
  Japanese, treatment by 110–11, 135
  postwar employment 206
  survival equipment 110–11
Finch, Pilot Officer Peter 138, 157
Fisk, Bill 213–14
Flick, Isabel 286
Flick, Mick 14, 286–7, 288
'Flying Eight' 254
'For Country for Nation' 313
Forde, Frank 55
Fraser, Lucy 186
Fysh, Sir Hudson 202

Galela 124, 126, 131
Garriya (Rainbow Serpent) 28
Gibbes, Bobby 90–1
Giles, Stacey 272
Gladstone Hotel 231
Glenmaur 268–9
Gorman, Peter 251–2, 278, 289
Goroke 276–7
Goss, Bobby 208
Goss, Wayne 208
Grant, Stan 45, 314
Griffith, Flight Lieutenant Johnny 119–21, 173
Grounds, Roy 240
Gunditjmara people 15
gunfire during high-speed combat 93
Guthrie, Squadron Leader Ron 81, 87, 178–9, 183

Hall, Dr Robert 273–4
Halmahera (Maluku) island group 113, 115, 118, 123–4, 126, 129, 130, 135, 137–9, 143
Hann, Flying Officer Laurie 135
Harding, Pilot James 174
Hardy, Vida 9, 44
Harrison, Rodney 223
Harvard 279–280
Hassen, Jack 223, 239–40
Hatetabako 123, 124, 126, 129, 135
Hattersley, Sergeant Stan 116, 117–18, 120
Hill, Lorenda 270–1
Hill, Pilot Officer Roland 171–2
Hindley, Leigh 78
Hinkler, Bert 7, 8
Hiroshima 172
HMAS *Cowra* 131
HMAS *Kapunda* 131
HMAS *Swan* 131
Hot Stuff! 136
Hotel Corones 202
Howe, Norman 206–7
Huggonson, David 216
Hughes, Private Timothy 185–6

Icarus 283
Idore 123
Inala 240–2, 259, 264, 311
Inala Brigadettes 245, 246
Indigenous Australians 45, 65–6, 288, 304–6
  alcohol, and 230, 232–3, 272, 282
  children, removal of 261–2
  cultural identity 23, 25–8
  death in custody 233
  education 14–15, 40
  exemption certificates 101–3, 107, 215–16
  'fractured identity' 306, 307
  land rights 24–5, 314
  military service 19–22, 46, 55, 102–3, 179–87, 215, 275–6, 281, 314
  'miscegenation' 199–200
  moieties 25
  police, relationship with 24, 30, 37, 44, 101–5, 228, 230, 232
  postwar treatment 187, 199–200, 208–10, 215–19, 228–30, 243–4, 281, 285–9
  prewar treatment 16–18, 22–5, 29–30, 33, 36–8, 44, 54–5, 99–105
  recognition of 305, 311–13
  refugees, contrast with treatment of 218
  resettlement of 22, 24–5, 37
  segregation/assimilation 29–30, 101, 199–200, 217
  soldier settlement blocks 217–18
  wages 41–2, 183
  wartime, during 54–5
institutional racism/discrimination 104, 307–8
International Year of Indigenous Peoples 288, 291, 304
Irian Jaya 108

Jackson, Squadron Leader John 313–14
Jamieson, Jim 'Pop' 224–5
Japan 47, 53–4, 87, 174
  Darwin, bombing of 53
  invasion of Australia, fears of xi, 53–6
  military 110
  New Guinea, in 53, 55, 61, 108–9, 142
  prisoners of war, treatment of 110–11, 135
  surrender 174
Johnson, Amy 7
Johnson, Wing Commander Alex 302
Jones, Flying Officer Fred 163–5
Jones, Margie 105–6, 119, 145, 199, 219
Judys 109
'jungle juice' 141, 157–8

Kai Islands 111, 112, 115
Kalti Paarti (emu-egg carving) 270–1, 279, 295
Kamilaroi people 4, 5, 11–12, 15, 21, 202, 205, 270
  aircraft, impact of 10–11
  language and culture 23, 27–8, 36, 71, 220
Kamiri airstrip 112, 116
Kaputhin the Eagle 11
Katter, Bob 244
Keating, Paul 304–5
Kemp, Archie 239
Kerr, Flight Lieutenant Harry 115, 117–18, 123
Kinchela Boys' Home (Kempsey) 5
King, Flight Sergeant Leon 135
Kingsford Smith, Sir Charles 7, 8
  St George, visit to 9–10
Kittyhawks xi, 56, 86, 89, 114–15, 117–18, 120, 125, 131, 162, 274, 294
  Curtiss P-40 61, 90
  Curtiss P-40E 94–5
  Curtiss P-40N 109, 113
  learning to fly 92, 93–8
Korean War 178–9, 231, 236, 287

Laidley 268–9
Lambert, Mick 224
Lang, Harry 271
Lawson, Joe 103
Lennard, Flight Sergeant James 126
Leonard Victor Waters Memorial Park 311
Leyte Island 112
Liberator bombers 168, 185
Lilley, Dr Ian 307–8
Lindbergh, Charles 7
Link trainer 67–8
Llewelyn, Wing Commander Ken 294–5, 308
Lockyer, Flight Sergeant Arnold 185
Lockyer, Private Eric 185
Lolobata 124
Loloda 130

Louise 172
Lowrey, Bert 252–3

MacArthur, General Douglas 61, 87, 111, 124
McEwan, Gladys 202
McGrady, Madeline 23, 30
McIntosh, Ronald (Ron) 16, 25, 30, 43
McIntosh, Ruby (nee Bennett) 25, 43
McIntosh, William 16
Mackellar, Ian 281
McKenzie, Wally 69, 86
McWaters, Fred 16
Main, Henry 281
Malayan Emergency 242
Maluku Islands 115
Manado 141–2, 185
mateship 184, 214–15, 296
  shearers 255, 257
Menzies, Robert 46–7, 62, 83
Middleburg Island 117
Mildura Operational Training Unit 60–1, 63, 66, 69, 86, 90–5
Milne Bay 113
'missing man formation' xii, 302
Mitchell, Len 6–7, 35, 41
Mitchell, Wal 35, 148
Miti 123, 124
Moody, Frank 15
Moody, Mary (Grannie Craigie) 15, 27, 36, 260
moon landing 253
'Moonie Loonies' 192–3, 196
Moree 99–105, 230, 263, 312
Morotai 119, 123–5, 131, 134–40, 143, 150, 160, 166, 185, 252, 277
  entertainment for troops 128–9, 132–4, 153–4, 176
  'Morotai mutiny' 151
  racial tensions 155–6, 158
Morse Code 68, 70
Mundine, Warren 210, 229
Mungindi 232–3
Murri clans 4, 36, 220, 240–1

Nagasaki 173
Narrabri 262–3
Narrandera Flying Training School 73–6, 79, 86, 164
Narromine Operational Training Unit 91–2
Nelson, Flight Lieutenant Arthur Douglas 111
New Britain 109
New Guinea 53, 55, 61, 108
  Australian air operations 109–10, 115–21, 123–7, 129–31, 137–42, 150–1
Nicholls, Pastor Doug 180
Nindigully 3, 5–7, 8, 12, 31, 33, 35, 43, 122, 279, 303
Noemfoor Island 108, 110, 112, 115, 117, 119, 125, 134
Noorama station 231
Nunn, Leading Aircraftman Arnie 137, 208

Oelin 170
Office of the Director of Native Affairs 243–4
Operation Oboe 159, 167–8
Orchard, Kim 284
Orcher, Ruby 217
Oscars 109

Pacific War 53–6, 62–3, 89
Papua New Guinea 53, 61, 110
Papunya 10
Paradise Bay 108
Parry, Flight Sergeant Ron 135
Pathungra Station 249–50, 257
Paul, Flight Lieutenant David Valentine 186–7
Pearl Harbor 47
Pearson, Noel 23, 305–6
Philippines 111, 124, 131, 134, 135, 152, 159, 166
  Japanese invasion 53
pilots *see* fighter pilots
Pistol Packin' Mama 136
Powell, Norman 94–5

Qantas 8, 206
Quinn, Pilot Officer Ted 172–3

Rabaul 61
recruitment trains 51–2
refugees, treatment of 218
Returned and Services League (RSL) 215
Riko Village 170
Rossmore 226, 234–5
Royal Air Force (RAF) 46–7, 62
  aircrew conversion handbook 67

Bomber Command 70, 72, 206
No. 112 Squadron 89
Royal Australian Air Force (RAAF) 46, 52–3, 56, 61, 301–2
75 Squadron 109, 113, 142, 313
76 Squadron 113, 177
77 Squadron 113, 177–9, 311
78 Squadron xii, 108–9, 112, 116, 136, 138, 142–3, 157, 160, 164, 176, 182, 215, 293, 296, 301
78 Wing 109, 112, 124, 126, 131, 134–5, 138, 142, 151
80 Squadron 109, 115, 116, 134–5, 142, 172
82 Squadron 177
86 Squadron 86
American Air Force, and 112, 124–5, 130–1, 152
combat training 85
fitness training 59–60, 68
'Morotai mutiny' 151
New Guinea operations 108–12, 115–21, 123–7, 129–31, 137–42, 150–1
Outback tour (1993) 291, 293
pilot training 72–7, 80–8
postwar 182, 206, 215
racial issues 155–7, 158, 167, 182–7
rating scale 83–4
training bases in Australia 54, 60–1, 73, 79
Royal Australian Navy (RAN) 131

Sabre jets 243
St George xii, 7, 9, 33, 43, 99, 105, 145–6, 201, 229–31, 260
floods (1954) 234–5
RSL club 285, 301, 302
Samarinda 172
Sandakan 169–70, 171
Sandgate 182, 191, 196
Saunders, Geoffrey 268
Saunders, George 147, 202–3
Saunders, Gladys *see* Waters, Gladys (nee Saunders)
Saunders, Harry 180
Saunders, Sergeant Reg 180–1, 184, 218–19, 275, 288
Sciacca, Con 308
Seaver, Ray 281
Seidler, Harry 240
Sepinggan 170–1
shadow shooting 93, 113
shearing 212–14, 222, 231–2, 236–7, 241, 249–57, 264, 308
drinking culture 256–8, 309
'Flying Eight' 254
mateship 255, 257
shearers' strike 237–40, 241
Sims, Dick 278–81
Sims, Jeanette 278–80, 282, 284
Smith, Joe 95–7
Smith, Sergeant Frank 81, 118, 166, 173, 296, 302, 303
Soden, Bill 112, 214
Somers Training School 66–7, 71, 79, 86, 164
South West Pacific Area (SWPA) 53, 61, 107, 109, 124, 155, 177, 185, 191, 287, 313
Soviet Union, entry into war 174
Spitfires 91, 151
Supermarine fighter 61
Stacey, Ida 100
star navigation 11–12
Stedman, Ron 255
Sternes, Jack 7, 9, 33
Stormy Weather 136
Sudlow, Flight Lieutenant Dick 75, 80, 95, 112–15, 118, 125, 129, 137, 150, 152, 157, 160, 173
command team 163–4
Japanese surrender, on 175
Waters, report on 143–4, 168–9, 175

Tabanio 170
Talaud Islands 135
Tarakan 159–60, 165–8, 171, 174–5, 185, 296
entertainment/activities for troops 176–7
Tawi Tawi 166
Taylor, Maria 15
terra nullius 24
Thomas, Edie 149–50
Thompson, 'Bull' 257–8
Thompson, Darcy 192–5, 226, 228, 234
Thompson, Marguerite 192, 226
Thornley, Flight Sergeant Neville 135
Tiger Moths 164, 165, 208, 226, 274, 277
de Havilland DH82 73–4, 76, 80, 81, 94
Tomohon 137, 138, 141, 185

Tondano 142–3
Toomelah Aboriginal reserve 3–5, 7, 13–14, 22–3, 29–30, 36–8, 230
  New Toomelah reserve 204–5, 216, 220
Torres Strait Light Infantry Battalion 184–5
Tothill, Flight Sergeant Cliff 126
Townsville 100, 148
  RAAF Base Townsville's Air Show 294
Trappers Inn 278, 290, 298, 299

Ulm, Charles 8
Upright, Trooper Clive 186
Uranquinty Flying Training School 78–82, 86, 92, 164

Victa Airtourer 280–1
Vietnam War 287
Vogelkop Peninsula 112, 115, 123
Vultee Vengeance dive bomber 61

Walawurru (giant eaglehawk) 10
Walker, Betty 32
Walker, Kath (Oodgeroo Noonuccal) 181, 218, 288
Wallace, George junior 226
Warrambal (Milky Way) 11
Warrego Hotel 299
Wasile pier 135, 138, 142, 143
Watch My Form 136
Waters, Barney 211, 212, 221
Waters, Beatrice 15
Waters, Dianne 231, 234–5, 245–6, 255
Waters, D'Nella Rose 261–2
Waters, Don 3–7, 12, 13, 15–16, 21–2, 44, 100, 145, 211, 230
  death 261
  enlistment 51, 52
  family life 33–6, 38–9, 43, 44–5, 66
  Gladys Saunders, and 198–9, 203
  property ownership 43–4
  segregation/assimilation debate 29–30
Waters, Donald 231, 234, 256, 269, 302
Waters, Florence 5, 7, 31, 40, 44, 278
Waters, Fred 5, 31
Waters, George 4, 31, 36, 39, 40, 106, 216
  death 263
  Moree incident 99–100, 103–5
  storyteller, as 42
Waters, Gladys (nee Saunders) 146–7, 150, 177, 180, 201, 207–8, 229, 234, 241, 243, 246, 297, 312
  Australian War Memorial, gift to 313
  background 201–3
  boxing, and 239–40
  breadwinner, as 266–7
  character 148, 203
  children 219, 227–8, 236–7, 249, 258
  dancing 245–6
  Grace, death of 259–60
  marriage 196–200, 203–6, 209, 222, 226, 247–9, 258, 270, 310
  separation from Len 277–8
  shop in Inala 265
  war service 148–50
  war widow's pension 307, 308–9
Waters, Gladys Julia-Kaye 236
Waters, Grace (nee Bennett) 3–4, 12, 15, 21–2, 25, 43, 66, 105–6, 230, 232
  death 259–60
  discipline and family values 34–5, 44–5, 105
  education of children 27–8, 38–9, 260
  Gladys Saunders, and 146–7, 198–9
  Margie Jones, and 119, 145, 147, 199
Waters, Jim 5, 30, 31, 36, 39, 40, 100, 106, 221, 285
  death 262
  enlistment 45–6, 47, 51–3, 184, 311
  malaria, clinical drug trial 106–7, 262
  Morotai, in 158–9
  postwar life in Australia 216–18
  postwar service (Japan) 179, 217
  Tarakan, on 159–60, 167, 177
Waters, Julia 29
Waters, Kerwin 268
Waters, Kevin 5, 6, 7, 13, 23, 29, 42, 228, 245, 278
  family, memories of 33–6, 147–8
  Narrabri incident 262–3
  rugby league 221
Waters, Kim 302
Waters, Len 'Bones' 22, 81, 282–3, 288, 301
  aircraft spin 96–8
  aircrew, call for 61–4
  alcohol 147, 157–8, 166, 193–4, 204, 257–8, 266, 269, 272, 282, 289–93, 297, 298–9
  awards for military service 196
  Bellevue Hotel incident 194–5

Brisbane, house purchase in 240–1
car accident 261, 266
carpentry 269, 271–2
character 38, 72, 77, 83, 88, 92, 98, 116, 183–4, 198, 212, 213, 222, 229, 251–2, 254, 257, 267, 284–5, 295
childhood 34–5
civilian pilot's licence 207–8, 301
combat training 85, 91–4
compensation 268
dancing 245–6
death 300–1
discharge from military service 196, 276–7, 309
early employment 40–4
education 13–14, 27–8, 31–2, 38–9, 40, 63, 260, 279
emu-egg carving 270–1, 279, 295
enlistment 45–6, 47, 51–3, 56–7
fame xi, 275–6, 288, 294–6, 311–14
first active military posting 108–10, 113
first mission 115
flying, obsession with 7–9, 11, 57, 63–4, 71, 274, 277, 280–1, 291–3, 309, 312
funeral xi–xii, 302–3, 311
gambling 255
Gladys Saunders see Saunders, Gladys
health issues 264–7, 290–2, 308
hit by Japanese 139–40
home on leave 145–8
identity, sense of 284, 306–8
Kamilaroi culture, and 11–12, 71, 113, 238, 270–1
leadership 72, 77, 85, 98, 161–2
Margie Jones 105–6, 119, 145, 199
marriage 196–200, 203–6, 226, 247–9, 258, 270, 310
mechanical ability 13, 59, 64, 85, 157, 208–9
Moree incident 99–100, 103–5, 230, 312
navigation skills 82–3, 85, 92
pilot training 69, 71–7, 80–8, 92–8
postwar employment 205–14, 236–7, 242–4, 265
problem-solving talents 32–3, 64
RAAF graduation 86–7
RAAF re-enlistment application 242–3
RAAF tour (1993) 291, 293
RAAF training 58–61, 66–77, 91–2
return home 179, 182
shearers' strike 237–40, 241
shearing 212–14, 222, 231–2, 236–7, 241, 249–57, 264, 308, 309
singing 245–8
solo flight, first 74–6
songwriter 247–8
sports 176, 221 see also boxing
two worlds, straddling 220, 282, 306–7, 310
Vietnam War, on 287
welfare, views on 288
Waters, Lenise May 219, 226, 234, 262, 275, 302
illness 227–8
marching girl competition 245, 246
Waters, Leonard Victor (nephew) 217
Waters, Marcus 269–70
Waters, Maurice 268–9
Waters, Ranald 5, 35, 209, 221, 262
boxing career 222–6, 239
Waters, Ruby 30
Waters, Thelma 228, 263
Waters, Warrant Officer Peter 135
Wayne, John 149–50
Weambilla 268
Webster, Kevin 254–5
Weldon, Ted 259
West, Brett 311–12
Whalan Station 15–16
Wheatley, John 'Curly' 133
Wightman-Dennison, Florence 16
Williams, Flight Sergeant Teddy 74–6
Wirerai people 205
Wirraways 80, 81–2, 92, 94, 125, 164, 165, 279
Woda Island 142
Wolfe, Althea 32
Wolfe, Jim 32–3, 38, 40, 66
Women's Auxiliary Air Force (WAAF) 79, 105–6, 149
Women's National Emergency Legion 149
Woods, Frank 271
Wraight, Arthur 299
Wraight, Neredah 278, 290, 298–9

Zeros 109